# PowerPoint, Communication, and the Knowledge Society

PowerPoint has become an integral part of academic and professional life across the globe. In this book, Hubert Knoblauch offers the first complete analysis of the PowerPoint presentation as a form of communication. Knoblauch charts the diffusion of PowerPoint and explores its significance as a ubiquitous and influential element of contemporary communication culture. His analysis considers the social and intellectual implications of the genre, focusing on the dynamic relationships among the aural, visual, and physical dimensions of PowerPoint presentations, as well as the diverse institutional contexts in which these presentations take place. Ultimately, Knoblauch argues that the parameters of the Powerpoint genre frame the ways in which information is presented, validated, and absorbed, with ambiguous consequences for the acquisition and transmission of knowledge. This original and timely book is relevant to scholars of communications, sociology, and education.

Hubert Knoblauch is a professor of sociology at the Technical University of Berlin.

LEARNING IN DOING: SOCIAL, COGNITIVE AND
COMPUTATIONAL PERSPECTIVES

SERIES EDITOR EMERITUS
*John Seely Brown, Xerox Palo Alto Research Center*

GENERAL EDITORS
*Christian Heath, Work, Interaction and Technology, The Department of
Management, King's College London*
*Roy Pea, Professor of Education and the Learning Sciences and Director,
Stanford Center for Innovations in Learning, Stanford University*
*Lucy A. Suchman, Centre for Science Studies and Department of Sociology,
Lancaster University, UK*

BOOKS IN THE SERIES

(*Continued after Index*)

# PowerPoint, Communication, and the Knowledge Society

HUBERT KNOBLAUCH
*Technische Universität Berlin*

CAMBRIDGE
UNIVERSITY PRESS

CAMBRIDGE UNIVERSITY PRESS
Cambridge, New York, Melbourne, Madrid, Cape Town,
Singapore, São Paulo, Delhi, Mexico City

Cambridge University Press
32 Avenue of the Americas, New York, NY 10013-2473, USA

www.cambridge.org
Information on this title: www.cambridge.org/9780521197328

First published 2013

Printed in the United States of America

*A catalog record for this publication is available from the British Library.*

*Library of Congress Cataloging in Publication data*
Knoblauch, Hubert.
    PowerPoint, communication, and the knowledge society / Hubert Knoblauch.
        p.   cm. – (Learning in doing)
    Includes bibliographical references and index.
    ISBN 978-0-521-19732-8 (hardback)
    1. Microsoft PowerPoint (Computer file)   2. Presentation graphics
software.   3. Communication.   4. Information society.   I. Title.
    P93.53.M534K66   2012
    302.23′1–dc23            2012017766

ISBN 978-0-521-19732-8 Hardback

If society is conceived of interactions among individuals, the description of the forms of this interaction is the task of the science of society in the strictest and most essential sense.

*Georg Simmel (1896)*

Lectures are silvern, but slides are golden.

*William Henry Young (1896)*

# Contents

# Series Foreword

This series for Cambridge University Press is widely known as an international forum for studies of situated learning and cognition. Innovative contributions are being made by anthropology; by cognitive, developmental, and cultural psychology; by computer science; by education; and by social theory. These contributions are providing the basis for new ways of understanding the social, historical, and contextual nature of learning, thinking, and practice that emerges from human activity. The empirical settings of these research inquiries range from the classroom to the workplace, to the high-technology office, and to learning in the streets and in other communities of practice. The situated nature of learning and remembering through activity is a central fact. It may appear obvious that human minds develop in social situations and extend their sphere of activity and communicative competencies. But cognitive theories of knowledge representation and learning alone have not provided sufficient insight into these relationships. This series was born of the conviction that new exciting interdisciplinary syntheses are under way as scholars and practitioners from diverse fields seek to develop theory and empirical investigations adequate for characterizing the complex relations of social and mental life, and for understanding successful learning wherever it occurs. The series invites contributions that advance our understanding of these seminal issues.

Christian Heath
Roy Pea
Lucy A. Suchman

# Acknowledgments

This book emerged from a series of studies conducted in a research project called "The Performance of Visually Supported Presentations: Genre-Analytic Studies of a Communicative Form Paradigmatic for Knowledge Society," supported by the German Science Foundation (Deutsche Forschungsgemeinschaft). The research team included Melanie Brinkschulte, Felix Degenhardt, Marion Mackert, Anika König, Sabine Petschke, Frederik Pötzsch, Bernt Schnettler, and René Tuma. The explicit plan of the book was to make available the results of the analyses produced by the research team. This book is, therefore, indebted to the work of this research team, the members of whom I am deeply grateful to, and I have tried to make reference to their analyses wherever I draw on them.

Because many people have contributed to the analyses and helped to corroborate their results, I regularly use the pronoun "we" when referring to the subjects of the research. "We" is not meant as a *pluralis majestatis* but, rather, as an acknowledgment of the contribution of the research group to certain findings, findings that have been published in a huge number of publications. The most notable of these is a collected volume published in German (cf. Schnettler and Knoblauch 2007), but the body of subsequent publications also includes some texts in English (cf. Knoblauch 2008).

The data analyzed were for the most part collected between 2004 and 2006, and some up to 2008. Given the rapid technological developments, the fast pace of cultural change, and the time it took to write and rework the book, the findings may be subject to some changes. As far as I can see, these changes are slight and do not alter the major argument of the book.

The longer I was working on the book, the more I realized that my first intention of merely summarizing and translating texts produced during the research project would not suffice. The task of writing the book turned

out to be ever more challenging, particularly since I wanted to address
the question of how the situative performance of Powerpoint presentations are linked to more encompassing societal and cultural changes. As a
result, writing the book demanded much more time than I had expected
and involved many more people than I am able to credit.

My sabbatical in 2010 from the Technical University of Berlin provided me with a fine opportunity to write this book. Furthermore, Cornell
University and its Department of Science and Technology Studies has
been an inspirational place for working on the book, and I am particularly
indebted to Christine Leuenberger and Trevor Pinch for their personal
support during the sabbatical. The Deutsche Forschungsgemeinschaft
supported me in the writing of this book and I am particularly grateful to
Eckehard Kämper and two anonymous referees.

As indicated, the book is, in some sense, the result of the research
endeavors of this research group. It also builds on the work of colleagues
with whom the research project was in contact. Most notably, these include
Henning Lobin, Joachim Knape, and JoAnne Yates. I am indebted to their
research, and I am glad to be able to draw on their results. There are also,
of course, other people who have contributed to the book without having
been part of the research project. Thanks go to Richard Bretschneider,
who was prepared to share his experiences with PowerPoint, as well as to
Benjamin Bossmann, Helmut Esser, and Irmgard Schumann. Lucy Hogan
and Susan Hedahl from the Wesley Theological Seminary have sent me
very valuable information about Powerpoint use in churches. Werner
Rammert, Arnold Windeler, and Sabine Reh kept me informed about what
is going on in the sociology of technology, organizations, and education.
Christian Heath, Paul Luff, Bernt Schnettler, René Tuma, and three anonymous reviewers for Cambridge University Press, who have read proposals
as well as early and later versions of the manuscript, helped to clarify my
thoughts and choice of text and made me revise it for the better – despite
my stubborn resistance to doing so. The facilities of the libraries of the
Technical University of Berlin and of Cornell University have been essential to this study. I am also grateful to Felicitas Heine, Miira Hill, Susann
Klemcke, Isabel Liebener, Christoph Nagel, and Christoph Rechenberg
for their help with texts and technologies, in particular slides and diagrams.
Since the book is concerned with a "visual genre," I should add that I have
tried to use visual evidence only when it is really relevant as evidence and
refers to data that have been subject to analysis. Because of my doubts as to
the "beauty of evidence" and for the sake of brevity I have tried to refrain
from purely illustrative visualizations. Ian Copestake and Jayashree helped

to tame my language and to render the style as easy to understand as my Teutonic English would allow. Needless to say, despite the help, human effort is never without flaws, all of which I am responsible for.

I am dedicating the book to my family, to Barbara, Delia, and Urs, who daily try to convince me more or less successfully that the meaning of life transcends work and science.

# 1    Introduction

## 1. "PowerPoint" and Powerpoint

In April 2010, the journalist Elisabeth Bumiller (2010) published an article in *The New York Times*, entitled "We Have Met the Enemy and He Is PowerPoint."

> Like an insurgency, PowerPoint has crept into the daily lives of military commanders and reached the level of near obsession. The amount of time expended on PowerPoint, the Microsoft presentation program of computer-generated charts, graphs and bullet points, has made it a running joke in the Pentagon and in Iraq and Afghanistan. "PowerPoint makes us stupid...." Commanders say that behind all the PowerPoint jokes are serious concerns that the program stifles discussion, critical thinking and thoughtful decision-making. Not least, it ties up junior officers – referred to as PowerPoint Rangers – in the daily preparation of slides, be it for a Joint Staff meeting in Washington or for a platoon leader's pre-mission combat briefing in a remote pocket of Afghanistan. ... Despite such tales, "death by PowerPoint," the phrase used to describe the numbing sensation that accompanies a 30-slide briefing, seems here to stay. Defense Secretary Robert M. Gates reviews printed-out PowerPoint slides at his morning staff meeting, although he insists on getting them the night before so he can read ahead and cut back the briefing time. ... President Obama was shown PowerPoint slides, mostly maps and charts, in the White House Situation Room during the Afghan strategy review last fall.

The article makes a series of general claims and assumptions that extend beyond the specific military context on which it is focusing. Because they reflect the general knowledge of PowerPoint that forms the background of this study, let me highlight some of these general claims and assumptions. First of all, the article clearly assumes that everyone knows "PowerPoint" and that it does not require any definition or clarification. It seems as if there is a shared general knowledge of what PowerPoint is (although this is quite equivocal). The shared knowledge is related to the major explicit observation: PowerPoint is ubiquitous, at least in the U.S. Army. The general knowledge of PowerPoint seems to be due to its incredibly wide distribution, which extends, in this article, not only to any branch of the army but even to the president. Third, and also explicitly, PowerPoint is evaluated morally – and this evaluation is strikingly poor, as it is blamed for shortcomings, it is deemed "notorious," and it is even called "the devil."

The ubiquity of PowerPoint assumed in the article is, indeed, one of the starting points of this study. When I first considered doing research on PowerPoint around 2002, I was overwhelmed by the speed with which the frequency of PowerPoint use had increased in seminars, in lectures, and at conferences, well before most professors, students, and young teaching personnel would take in their computers and demand that projectors (which until then had been quite rare) be provided. Since then, pupils in schools and even in kindergarten use PowerPoint, and even I have acquired some competence at doing reasonable presentations. As PowerPoint becomes a routine for more and more users and recipients, this routine becomes an issue for the sociologist, who has to ask how and why something became so taken for granted. Why is PowerPoint everywhere?

This question is even more urgent in the face of public debates on this topic that occasionally tend toward strong negative judgments. Quite often the fear is voiced that PowerPoint is responsible for wasting life time and working time or for making us stupid. And, as in the article, the diffusion of PowerPoint is often described as a contamination of hitherto "clean" communication. What used to be rational discourse now becomes distorted or, at least, superficial. As moral judgments are weapons in the social machinery, they are part of the subject matter of sociology. (In Switzerland, the issue even became political when an "Anti PowerPoint Party" was founded by Matthias Poehm, who also initiated an international Anti-PowerPoint movement.) As a sociologist, therefore, I want to ask how and why such a technology as PowerPoint, which seems so "innocent," is the target of so much moral condemnation.

This question is, as we shall see, part of a much larger issue that is linked to the phenomenon itself. Indeed, before we ask the question of how PowerPoint became so taken for granted and why it is perceived as morally contaminated, we have, first, to question what it is we are talking about. What is it that everyone seems to know about? Is what we talk about, the discourse, the same as what we do, the performance of action? This book, however, is not focused only on the knowledge and discourse about PowerPoint and its moral condemnation. Nor is it about the technology of PowerPoint. It is, instead, focused on the way PowerPoint has affected society. PowerPoint is a social phenomenon, and as society is constructed by meaningful social actions, it is also a cultural phenomenon. The book is, therefore, about the ways PowerPoint enters into our many meaningful social actions, both as producers and as recipients of PowerPoint slides and presentations. Therefore the analysis of these meaningful social actions using PowerPoint forms the most pertinent empirical data.

The sociological perspective on the use of PowerPoint in what I call, more precisely, communicative action throws a particular light on PowerPoint that is often ignored. This also becomes apparent in the article quoted. It not only presupposes "PowerPoint" as general knowledge, it also mixes two meanings of the word. On the one hand, PowerPoint refers to the presentation software, which is called "PowerPoint." At this stage one should note that, to the degree that the presentation software owned by Microsoft, "PowerPoint," was diffused throughout society, the trademark of its presentation software also became tantamount to a reference to presentations software in general. People use the word "PowerPoint" even if the presentations they refer to have been made by means of other software, such as Adobe Acrobat, Apple Keynote, Apple Works, Star Point, or Smart Suite, and even many researchers who study "PowerPoint" software and slides do not check whether the slides they analyze are in fact made by means of "PowerPoint." Because "PowerPoint" has become synonymous with all computer supported presentations (in the most diverse languages), throughout the book I will use "powerpoint" as a category of general knowledge referring to any presentation software, and "PowerPoint" only if I am referring specifically to Microsoft's software.

The preference for this different spelling is also due to the second aspect of the meaning of powerpoint, which is assumed to be so much part of the general knowledge. Whereas "PowerPoint" refers to the software including the "slides" produced by it and saved in their format (.ppt, .pptx, or other formats) as well as their transformations into "objects" that can be "passed on" (as the article says, as paper printouts, e-mail attachments, or Internet pages), "powerpoint," on the other hand, refers to something else: the projection of the slides by means of computer software while talking to a live audience in situ. In this second sense, powerpoint is not restricted to an "object" but refers to what I shall call an "event": a communicative action by a presenter, attended by an audience, involving technologies, such as a computer screen, a projector, or a slide, as well as activities performed in relation to both audiences and technologies. This aspect of powerpoint shall be addressed by the notion of "presentation as event." As opposed to many studies on "PowerPoint," this study focuses on the "powerpoint presentation as event" because it includes the software, the technology, and the slides.

The focus on powerpoint as an event means that I am not particularly concerned with studying the software or technology, and all its intricacies, and this is therefore not a study of a technology, of the cognition required for its use, or of its "social uses." As valuable as, for example, science and technology studies are for various parts of this analysis, they are not used here to focus on the technology. Undoubtedly, when looking at powerpoint presentations, technology plays an important role. It seems to me, however, utterly simplistic to equate this "role" with that of an isolated actor and to describe "powerpoint" as if it performed an "action."[1] Although technology "undeniably has effects in the world," these effects are always and immediately part of a meaningful social context. Therefore Pinch and Bijker (1987) are quite right to assume that the meaning of technology needs to be interpreted. I would, however, extend this argument even further: In addition to being interpreted, the "effects" of technology are social inasmuch as they are embedded into meaningful social action. Inasmuch as these actions are at least expressed by these effects, I refer to them as communicative actions. In fact, it will be one of the major empirical tasks to show how the "effect" of technology is tuned into other aspects of communicative action in the case of powerpoint presentations. Because of this embeddedness in communicative action, powerpoint will not be studied as a technology but rather as a form of communication, that is, a communicative genre.

## 2. Communication Culture

The distinction between "PowerPoint" and "powerpoint" has already been proposed earlier in the chapter and runs throughout the book. There are various other conceptual distinctions based on empirical findings that must first be introduced here to prevent misunderstandings as they so often occur in the literature on powerpoint. One of these is the focus on powerpoint as a form of real-life communication in presentations.

Although sociology, the other social sciences, and the humanities have devoted much energy to the analysis of "texts," "discourse," and "communication," attempting to scrutinize events such as the powerpoint presentation is still quite uncommon. Almost all studies on powerpoint and presentations in general seem to assume that the empirical process of communication can be considered like a black box that can be deduced from an analysis of its products, that is, the slides or the participants' "cognition." In opposition to this view, I want to approach powerpoint presentations as a form of communicative action, that is, as communicative genre. That is to say that I want to look at powerpoint as something that is done by embodied actors in time and supported by objects and technologies. Much of the book is devoted to this task, for in observing and analyzing powerpoint presentations as they are bodily and situationally performed in space, time, and social setting, the study pursues the basic goal of any interpretive social science. This goal consists of trying to understand the meaning of social action, which in our context means to understand what a powerpoint presentation is in the course of the social actions performed. The detailed analysis of communicative actions or, as one might phrase it, "doing powerpoint presentations," appears to some to be a futile description of no explanatory value for sociology or of no relevance to "society." However, by using the notion of communicative genre and culture, I want to correct this view, for whatever "powerpoint" may mean to whatever expert (software, information design, rhetorical form, etc.), it is the factual way that people are really using powerpoint that is at stake here. As an empirical analysis of their real communicative action allows for an understanding by the researcher, it warrants the claims of catching the meaning of powerpoint for the actors. Finally, their communicative form facilitates the chance for giving evidence for both, the understanding of the action as well as its meaning for the actors.

The task of an interpretive social science thus consists in identifying the actors' meanings (realized in communicative action). These "first order constructs" (Schutz 1962) are the only valid and legitimate reason for sociology as a science of social reality.[2] Basing the analysis on data representing how powerpoint is "really used" in communicative action – at least "real" in terms of the everyday life we share, as Schutz and Luckmann (1989) call it – warrants social scientific analysis of powerpoint.[3] In doing so it looks beyond preconceptions, at normative expectations, legitimations, or only aspects of the phenomenon.

The focus on the particulars of communicative action is intended to identify empirically the ways that social reality is constructed by way of communicative action, that is, how powerpoint presentations are constructed by the concerted activities of the participants. The analysis does not end with the identification of these methods of "doing powerpoint presentations" but tries to identify general features of these presentations in terms of communicative genre. The notion of communicative genre indicates forms of actions produced and expectations held by actors. Moreover, it constitutes a bridge between the communicative actions in the situation of presentations and the culture of a society constructed by these actions. In this way, the analysis of communicative actions and communicative genres not only serves a descriptive goal, but helps to illuminate how powerpoint presentations contribute to the social construction of society, and how, as a result of their specific forms, they contribute to the social construction of certain aspects of society. (Powerpoint draws in particular on those aspects of society that are referred to as the "information" and "knowledge society," as we shall see.) The analysis of powerpoint presentations as a communicative genre will, therefore, be the basis for the explanation of their ubiquitous role in contemporary society. By explanation I do not mean to identify causal conditions but the ways that those aspects of society that can be described as structures can be traced back to aspects of (communicative) actions. In the empirical sections I try to specify those aspects from which I draw in the concluding sections.

As the meaningful aspects of society often ignored by the focus on structures have been referred to as culture, communicative culture is what is constituted by communicative action (Knoblauch 1995). Correspondingly, as culture is made up of shared meanings, shared objectivations of meanings, and shared patterns of action, communicative culture refers to the communicative action in which objectivated meanings are enacted socially. It is by way of communicative action that we fill our time with others or are oriented to others, even when we are alone. Social life consists of communication, and it is through communicative action that we bestow meaning on it and experience it as meaningful. Communicative action, thus, links social actions via their embodied performance with objectivations, such as objects, signs, and technologies. Communicative culture is constituted by the forms of communicative action, their patterns, and communicative genres. By "communicative culture" I refer to the ways in which we produce and practice communication, in which we talk to friends, to relatives, and to foreigners, and the ways in which we speak, write, and read. Communicative culture, therefore, does not merely consist of signs, technologies, and objects. Thus, powerpoint slides, for example, a medium consisting of signs (letters, diagrams, etc.), technologies (software, electronics, etc.), and objects (monitors, printouts, etc.), do not "just" make sense but are often rendered meaningful in the presentation as event It is the enactment or performance of all these objects, signs, and technologies that renders social life meaningful in action. We know well that the ways we communicate depend on what objects we use for communication: reading books is still a different form of action from reading an Internet homepage, participating in a conversation is a different form of action from talking via a mobile phone, and watching movies is something different from listening to a joke told by a friend. As varied as the different forms of action are, we usually depend on certain forms of action of "genres" guiding our expectations, our courses of action, and our interactive coordination. Communicative genres form the core of our communicative culture acting as the meaningful cosmos constructed by our communicative actions and the things to which they relate.

There is no doubt that powerpoint figures in quite a variety of communicative actions. When tinkering about with a presentation in private, possibly making notes on a piece of paper; when designing single slides on a computer or discussing the order of slides with colleagues, powerpoint forms part of our communicative action. Although they are of some relevance to the presentation of powerpoint, we only refer to them at a few points in this study (for example, when discussing the "rhetoric" of powerpoint as communicative action or the preparatory phase of presentations). As the title makes clear, the powerpoint presentation is the focus of this study, and my theses are mainly related to this phenomenon. My first claim is, therefore, that powerpoint presentations are a communicative genre. This means that they exhibit a certain common form that allows us to recognize and reproduce them. Powerpoint presentation is a temporally and spatially performed communicative genre constituted by this common form of communicative actions. It is this communicative genre to which we orient ourselves when preparing slides on the computer, when giving the presentation, or when watching it. Consequently, this study analyzes powerpoint presentation as a communicative genre built on action, actors, and objects. By detailing the particular and specific features of powerpoint presentations as communicative genre, I try to explain why and to what degree powerpoint has become a ubiquitous and indispensable part of our society and how it affects modern society in general and its different institutional branches – not only the military but also science, business, and other societal subsystems.

Both goals are intrinsically connected since, as we shall see, the immense success of powerpoint in the last two decades is due to features of the communicative genre itself. Or, to put it in other words, the forms of powerpoint presentations as a communicative genre are the reasons for their success. It is not merely by means of the diffusion of technology that powerpoint affects society; nor is it by virtue of organizational transformations that powerpoint became so ubiquitous. Powerpoint became inserted into society as a communicative form, that is, powerpoint presentations, and it is through this form that society – and its communicative culture – was transformed into a "knowledge society" or "information society."

The reference to these two aspects of contemporary society (and societal legitimations) is related to one of the major findings of the analysis: that as a communicative genre, powerpoint presentations are characterized by a triadic structure. This triadic structure consists of objects and technologies, human actors as presenters, and live audiences, in which, as I want to show, these three elements are synchronized, coordinated, and orchestrated in the social situation. Although the presentation is defined by its "liveness," it is in many senses a "hybrid" event depending on prior "organization," preparatory actions, and postprocessing, as well as on objects and technologies. In this sense, powerpoint presentation is a communicative genre that combines technologically mediated communication (i.e., "presentation as document") and local face-to-face communication (i.e., "presentation as event"). Powerpoint is most essentially a mediated genre since both aspects of the genre are mediating and mediated at the same time. The face-to-face presentation is mediated by technologies and institutionalized organizations that enter as mediating structures, that is, as objects, technologies, and social, temporal and spatial orders into the presentation. On the other hand, powerpoint builds on large technological infrastructures, networks, and organizations with more or less standardized codes and a set of available objects such as computers, projectors, and software programs. While all these elements figure in what has come to be called "information," these information technologies and organizations are mediated in that they take the form of social events in which something is communicated. Powerpoint presentations are particularly effective in objectivating these "communicative things" through a range of methods, including visual representations, text, speech, gestures, or technologies. As these "things" are what presentations are about, they are characterized as being the "knowledge" presented, the "knowledge" of presenters, and the knowledge to be gained by the audiences. As knowledge is whatever is communicated by an actor, in powerpoint presentations, "knowledge" is asserted as knowledge by someone, which is simultaneously objectified by information systems available and accessible, in principle, to everyone. Like things, they seem to persist in time and can be referred to and claimed, while they always remain dependent on the situation of communication.

While the situative aspect of presentations shall be called the "presentation as event," "presentation as document" refers to the "information" that can be stored on digital devices and communicated by means of information technologies. Because this communicative genre consists of the situative "exchange of knowledge" or "cognition," the description of the knowledge society constitutes another background for its analysis. From this perspective, the presentation as event is a process in which knowledge is seen to be exchanged between people and organizations. Powerpoint presentation links both: it uses the digital format within the "immediacy" of the situation of face-to-face interaction (which is, thence, simultaneously mediated), and it is a genre that "stores" the information of such presentations and their presenters digitally and allows them to be transferred by means of these technical communication media.

Although powerpoint presentations can build on various predecessors, the merging if the various elements into a communicative genre may be considered as a communicative innovation. Mead and Byers (1968) have coined the notion of "communicative innovation" with respect to the "small conference," a scientific equivalent of a meeting that began in the 1960s. Like powerpoint presentations, small conferences are a type of communicative event, which has its own patterns, forms, and courses of action (analyzed later in detail). They, thus, constitute not only a distinct element in the communicative culture but one that is disseminated with incredible speed into society on an almost global scale. In order to understand and explain this societal relevance, we need to refer to an extensive wider debate that has a bearing on the relevance of this new genre.

## 3. Information and Knowledge Society

The triadic structure of powerpoint as a communicative genre thus refers to and relies on large scale social developments that have been debated widely in sociology as well as in other social sciences: while the notion of information has come to be associated with the informatization of society or "information society," "knowledge" has been considered constitutive of the "knowledge economy" and even the "knowledge society." As powerpoint presentations link information and knowledge, the diffusion of powerpoint presentations can be seen as indicative of a knowledge society and an information society, their differences, and their close connection. Because of their relevance to the structure of powerpoint and the explanation of its success, I want to sketch briefly what is meant by "information society" and "knowledge society." (The reference to a knowledge society in the title of the book is an abbreviation for "information and knowledge society.")

Before doing so, I wish to clarify that these two categories for macrosocietal developments of the last decades should not be considered as the "reasons," "causes," or even "background" factors for the explanation of powerpoint. Instead of being related causally or intentionally to powerpoint, the "knowledge society" and the "information society" should be seen as a result of the very processes of the social construction of reality that yielded the rise of powerpoint. Or, in other words, powerpoint is one product of the social coconstruction of information and knowledge societies, and therefore constitutes a paradigmatic example for its analysis.

The reference to the notion of social construction (Berger and Luckmann 1966) indicates that neither a "knowledge society" nor an "information society" is considered as assured fact or mere ontological reality. Instead, they are more or less reflected descriptions of societies mirrored in and sometimes even initiated by theories about the "information society" and "knowledge society." These theories have been important parts of discourses legitimating the factual social construction of technological infrastructures, public policies, and organization. Governments, cities, and institutions of the most varied kinds (including, of course, technology companies) have for decades invested billions of dollars in order to produce what they considered to be the various aspects of the "information society" and, somewhat later, of the "knowledge society."

As we shall see, the legitimations of both characterizations of society are quite different; whereas the former is built on a technodeterminism, the latter highlights the role of the human actor. As different as the two legitimations are, both have affected major societal actors and have been turned into self-fulfilling prophecies. Indeed, as Hornidge (2007) has shown, the discourse about knowledge society supersedes the discourse about the information society, as aspects of the latter often are implied in the discourses of the former. In this book I cannot reconstruct the whole process of the social construction of the information and knowledge society (for one attempt cf. Knoblauch 2005, chapter IIIB). However, since I want to focus this study on the empirical analysis of a phenomenon that integrates both information technology and knowledge, I shall restrict myself here to a short sketch of the theories of knowledge society and of information society, which allow one to highlight the features relevant to and coproduced by powerpoint.

The notion of the information society refers to theories of society that closely link its recent transformations to information technologies. These technologies include hardware, such as computers, chips, and cables, as well as digital software. From a sociological point of view, the advent of powerpoint occurs in the context of a broader process, which Minc and Nora (1981) called the "computerization of society," or, as it has been designated more succinctly in the French original, informatization ("informatisation"). By "informatization" they refer to the increasing convergence of two disparate technical complexes that had been separated: information and communication technologies (Licklider and Taylor 1968; Webster 1995). This convergence is due to technological innovations in both hardware and software, such as digital information, computer processing, computer networks, digital communication (for example, in the order of their appearance, BTX, compact discs, ISDN,UMTS), programs for calculations, text, and visual processing, for example, powerpoint. The stress on the technical aspects of informatization led to the increasing importance of "information" as the designation for the content of communication by information technology.

The theories of information society assume that informatization has serious impacts on contemporary societies. They claim that information and communication technologies continuously penetrate and determine "private and public life as well as the market spheres, inducing corresponding social, economic and cultural changes" (Kuhlen 1995: XXIII, trans. HK). In the information society everyone "is aware of the importance of information in every aspect of its work, an attitude of mind that makes for the efficient, productive broad utilization of information in every aspect of life" (Dordick and Wang 1993: 22).

The societal relevance of information seems to be twofold. On the one hand, the information society relates to the sheer volume of the communication of information and information exchange. In fact, the measurement of information exchange was one of the earliest methods used to validate the theory of the information society empirically. In the 1960s, Japanese researchers had already started to measure the increase in "information," for example, in terms of the number of phone calls per person and year, the number of newspapers per 100 persons, the number of books published per 1,000 persons, and the number of television sets, phones, radios, and, later, computers per household (Hensel 1990). The result of these studies was quite revealing since they indicated an "information explosion" among those who use these technologies, while later research warned that the asymmetrical access to information technology might lead to an "information gap."

A second way of identifying the societal effects of informatization focused on occupational changes in the social structure. Starting with Machlup (1962/1980), a fourth "informational sector" was added to the three major production sectors: fishing and agriculture, industrial production, and service industry. Porat (1977), whose classification became very influential in public administration, distinguished among four categories of occupations – information producers (scientists, engineers, architects, medical doctors, programmers), information users (judges, administrators, managers), information distributors (journalists, teachers), and information structure professions (printer, cameramen, electricians, etc.) – and occupations specialized in the production, diffusion, and maintenance of information, for example, in education, scientific research, the media, and information technology. According to these two methods, the United States was defined as an information society by 1980, when 45 percent of its workforce was classified as being in the information sector

"Informatization" here refers to the proliferation of digitally based information and communication technologies in the modern "information" society. Informatization is the result of technological inventions and diffusions, economic competition, and monopolization, as well as massive political policies and interventions on the local, national, and international levels. As an "information society" is characterized by a technical infrastructure, it is related to new patterns of social action, new forms of institutional power, and social inequality addressed by prior research.[4] Yet, despite the alleged precision of such numbers, the very notion of information was and is still insufficiently defined, as are the means of measuring information (Dordick and Wang 1993). First, the "rate of information" depends on more or less arbitrary definitions, such as the equation of one minute of music with the information of 120 words in a lecture. Second, the various kinds of classifications of information in the organized work of different professions have never been empirically verified (Nass 1988). Third, the notion of "information" lacks any clear definition.[5] As varied as the notions of information may be, they seem at least to include any knowledge mediated by means of or inscribed in information communication technologies.[6]

Despite the lack of a clear definition of information and despite the fact that its heyday has passed, "information society" is by no means an irrelevant or even outdated concept. The processes described by this notion refer to massive transformations of societies that occurred around the 1960s in the West and Japan and increasingly elsewhere, leading to the construction (in a literal sense) of material infrastructures for various information technologies and their dissemination into various spheres of society (education, science, art, etc.). As mentioned, the concept of information society has been much used as a means of legitimation for actions seized on by governments, intergovernmental organizations (the United Nations [UN], and European Union [EU]), as well as other governance structures; nevertheless, in cooperation with companies producing hardware and software they have succeeded very efficiently in the "informatization" of society. This informatization has been described by Castells as a structural transformation into a "network society." He argues that "the technological and organisational ability to separate the production process in different locations was based on the construction of information and communication technologies linkages" (Castells 1996: 386). Sproull and Kiesler (1995) have also underlined the relevance of information and communication technologies, such as computer networks or satellite telecommunication, for the transformation of the organization of work.

As stressed previously, the information society is not just a "macrosocial phenomenon" but a process realized in communicative action and expressed in a communicative culture. Thus, with respect to various forms of information technologies, Heath and Luff (2000) have shown how work activities are affected by the use of these technologies. By means of technologies activities are distributed spatially, and they require new forms of interactive coordination and organization. Powerpoint is, as I want to show, another example of this transformation of communication. Informatization, in this sense, refers to the increasing use of information technologies in the process of communication and, consequently, the transformation of genres and the generation of new genres. One particular consequential feature of informatization is related to the vast technological infrastructures created in this process. These infrastructures affect communication in a way that has been labeled under the notion of mediatization (Krotz 2001; Couldry 2008; Lundby 2009). "Mediatization" refers to the effects of the technological mediation of communication on social action and social structure. It includes the informatization or digitalization of already existing media, resulting in a convergence of media, the technical networking of technologies and services, the sophistication of communication, and the increasing artificial intelligence of objects. The notion of mediatization appears to be very useful for the analysis of powerpoint presentation if one does not misunderstand it as relating only to the "mediated" level of action and communication "beyond" and separate from face-to-face interaction.

Mediatization also means the immersion of mediating technologies, such as computers, projectors, and wireless and other communication devices, into situations of copresent actors. It implies situations of interaction that are distributed and, simultaneously, "contextualized" by the materiality of the technology. By analogy with Gumperz's (1981) use of contextualization in the meaning of the rules of the situative use of linguistic and paralinguistic signs that bestows their specific situative meaning, I would like to call contextualization the rules of the situative use of any object, technology, or sign. A mobile phone not only allows one to communicate with someone absent, it also contextualizes this communication in a specific situation by providing it with objectivations, that is, the materiality to be perceived in the situation. By means of communication technologies, mediatization not only transcends space (and time), it creates contexts of communication by inserting media into local contexts.

Another feature of communication that is affected by informatization technologies lies, undoubtedly, in the potential for creating and consuming visualizations. The omnipresent monitors, screens, and other visual displays support the process of visualization, and it has also been discussed with respect to the informatization of society. Friedhoff (1991), for example, has characterized visualization as the most decisive effect of the informatization of society. In addition to new digital technologies, the notion of visualization allows the transformation of linguistic codes into visual codes. Moreover, it allows for the generation of new visual conventions. Instead of seeing things "live," some authors fear that the reality of things is increasingly dependent on its visual representations, on the simulations of reality or on "mediated vision" (Walker and Chaplin 1997). The visualization of information is, apparently, also an essential feature of powerpoint presentation. In fact, powerpoint is considered to be one of the most effective means by which visualization is accomplished, and it, therefore, has been blamed for mixing information and edutainment into what (Postman 1993) called "infotainment." Instead of considering visualizations in isolation as designs for information or as one "modality" of signs that correlates with other modalities, I shall take visualization as being contextualized in a complex process of mediated and local communicative actions. Visualizations are one among many different constitutive aspects of the communicative genre of powerpoint presentations. Their relevance can be seen in the fact that they figure both in the presentation as document and in the presentation as an event. It is this two-sided character of visualizations that allows them to be linked not only to (encoded) information but also to "knowledge" (and, in a more psychological sense, "cognition"). Knowledge or the knowledge society is, therefore, the second major theoretical reference in the analysis of the social relevance of powerpoint.

As with information, "knowledge" has also been used to describe a process that affects society in general on a global level, that is, a knowledge society. Knowledge has been identified as one of the major resources of contemporary economies, it is a major dimension for the structure of social inequality in contemporary societies and, therefore, one of the major topics for the social engineering of contemporary society on every political, administrative, and organizational level of any form of governance (ranging from families to districts and counties to national and, above all, intergovernmental institutions. Although knowledge in a more general sense of any socially mediated meaning orienting action has been the subject of a specific field of sociology (Knoblauch 2005), "knowledge" (in quotation marks) here is referred to as that which is considered legitimate knowledge by the various instances of governance and their related institutions of knowledge accreditation or acknowledgment. Since science figures as the major institution not only for the production but also for the accreditation of knowledge, "knowledge" is often equated with and reduced to scientifically approved knowledge. Let me briefly sketch the notion of the knowledge society before clarifying how it figures as both constituting and being constituted by powerpoint.

There is no doubt that, in general, knowledge and its socially organized transmission are crucial features of any society. In many societies, the relevance of knowledge is accounted for by the investment in institutions of primary, secondary, sometimes even tertiary and lifelong education. The two latter forms are, indeed, already among the features of the modern knowledge society, for in the last decades, the importance of knowledge has increased to such a degree that it has been said to define contemporary society, which, therefore, has been labeled the "knowledge society." Following the model of modern society already established by Comte in the nineteenth century, the "knowledge society" has continuously been referred to in terms of (positive) scientific knowledge. Thus, in 1966 Lane defined the "knowledgeable society" by what one would best call "scientifically based objective and instrumental knowledge." A knowledgeable society is one in which members routinely follow scientific standards, in which a considerable amount of resources are devoted to research, and in which it serves organizations and their purposes. In a slightly different vein, in 1973 Daniel Bell declared "knowledge" to be the decisive resource of the post-industrial society to come, using "information" and "knowledge" almost interchangeably.

As much as Bell recognized the economic importance of knowledge (which he used synonymously with "information") and the social structural significance of "knowledge workers", the reference to science remained manifest even in those cases in which somewhat more general definitions were attempted. Thus, Stehr (1994) considers knowledge almost in the fashion of the sociology of knowledge as that which guides action and is linked to the subject of action. However, in his analysis of the contemporary "knowledge society" he follows the much narrower notion of knowledge. It is

> the advancement of science into more and more social spheres which characterizes knowledge society. Everyday action becomes more scientific, politics turns into the politics of knowledge and economy into the knowledge economy. Science and technology are remaking our basic social institutions, for example, in such areas as work, education, physical reproduction, culture, the economy, and the political system. (Stehr 1994: 9)

This equation of "knowledge" and "scientific knowledge" is one of the assumptions most commonly shared among theorists and proponents of the knowledge society, and it will have consequences for the explanation of powerpoint presentations: its knowledge is seen as basically determined and defined by scientific knowledge; even the economy, they claim, is subjected to scientific knowledge, for "knowledge" has been recognized as the most important source of wealth not only by business but also by national governments and international organizations that have recognized it as a major resource for the societies of nations and the world (UNESCO 2005).

The equating of knowledge with scientific knowledge is of particular importance in the case of powerpoint presentations. Although this communicative genre is designed to "present" knowledge (and to fix it as information), its relation to scientific forms of knowledge communication is less obvious regarding other forms of communication, notably from business and computing. Against this background, the legitimation of the "knowledge society" and its social reality are crucial issues for this study.

The "knowledge society" has become part of a global discourse, and, as with the "information society" somewhat earlier, its global acceptance has resulted in its implementation by a range of national and international political programs (Knoblauch 2005). In these programs, the orientation toward a notion of knowledge that, in principle, refers to science is maintained. Thus, science and scientific processes of knowledge production and acknowledgment remain the most legitimate institutions in deciding what may be considered as valid knowledge. However, the dominance of science is not unequivocal. Because of its acceptance as an economic resource, "knowledge" has also become one of the most accepted "resources" for economic organizations and, in the neoliberal extension of market principles to other organisations (public administrations, churches, and universities), for organizations in other institutional fields, such as politics, religion, and science. Although the notion of knowledge here remains vague, it is important to keep in mind that it commonly differs from information in its relation to subjects.[7] Knowledge may be referred to as "know-how," "know what," and even "implicit knowledge" of acquiring, producing, managing, and selling services and objects. In this area, knowledge is not merely a private matter but an organizational asset, "a form of collective intelligence beyond that of the individual" (Isaacs 1993: 28), so that whole organizations turn into "learning organizations" (Kim 1993).

From the perspective of the sociology of knowledge, "knowledge" is, in both cases, reduced to what may be more precisely called "legitimate" knowledge. For in the "knowledge society" and "knowledge organization," knowledge is not "just there" but subject to processes of negotiation, acceptance, canonization, and transmission by more or less institutionalized teaching and learning processes. It is exactly at this juncture that powerpoint plays a prominent role. The powerpoint presentation is, in a nutshell, the communicative form of knowledge. It is by the very form of the communicative actions performed in powerpoint presentations that something that can be treated as "knowledge" is constructed. As knowledge is in principle intangible, it depends on being objectivated by communication, that is, as word, sentence, or diagram. The knowledge society depends even more on processes by which "knowledge" can be objectivated, fixed, and made transferable, without allowing it to be expropriated. Powerpoint presentations are the very form for this objectivation and fixation, and, while they allow it to be ascribed to the presenters (and their teams), they also enable it to be transferred in the informational infrastructure of organization, networks, or the World Wide Web.

Certainly, powerpoint is by no means the only form in which "knowledge" is being constructed. There is a range of other forms characterizing the communicative culture of knowledge societies. In addition, powerpoint presentations are not a new form ab ovo. Rather, they take up earlier forms and turn them into a communicative genre, characterized by the ambiguity of "knowledge" as being scientific and economically useful at the same time.

The relation between knowledge and subjects is typically institutionalized in various forms of learning. Powerpoint presentations, however, are not restricted to learning institutions. Because of their ubiquity, they are part of almost any other institutional sphere in contemporary society, such as the military, politics, or religion. Powerpoint presentation as a communicative form of knowledge cannot be reduced to "learning" situations; nor can it be grasped in terms of mere "cognition," as one of the most prominent theories on powerpoint assumes. Instead, powerpoint is a form of knowledge communication by means of information technologies.

Given the restriction of theories of the knowledge society to (legitimate) knowledge, one must add the relevance of communication. In fact, one of the explanations for the ubiquity of powerpoint presentations consists in the thesis that the growing importance of knowledge is linked to organizational changes expressed in the increase in joint ventures, strategic cooperation, project cooperation, and networking; a highly flexible workforce; and an informal division of labor, labor relations based on trust, and participative decision making.

As can be seen, neither the information society nor the knowledge society explains the ubiquity of powerpoint. Rather, powerpoint constitutes one of the ways in which both "knowledge" and "information" are being constructed as features of modern society. The powerpoint presentation, I want to argue, is the phenomenon where the societal dimensions of information technologies, that is, the "information society" and "knowledge society," converge, or, to say it in less reifying, constructivist terms, powerpoint presentations result from the socially constructed technical infrastructure of information transmission and its social dimensions: that is, the information society and the socially constructed relevance of knowledge, knowledge organization, and the knowledge society.

The duality of information and knowledge is expressed in the basic duality of powerpoint itself. For powerpoint is, on the one hand, a digital and informational document; on the other hand, it is an event contextualizing this "information" in a specific situation by presenting the knowledge of a particular person. Being dependent on computers, software (not only for presentation), and projectors, powerpoint presentations are definitely related to information technologies.

In this sense, the presentation as document is regarded as "information" that can be stored on digital devices and communicated by means of information technologies. Because this communicative genre consists of the situative "exchange of knowledge" or "cognition," the description of the "knowledge society" constitutes another background for its analysis. From this perspective, the presentation as event is a process in which knowledge is seen to be exchanged between persons and organizations.

Powerpoint presentations link both: they use the digital format within the "immediacy" of the situation of face-to-face interaction (which is, thence, simultaneously mediated), and they constitute a genre that "stores" the information of such presentations and their presenters digitally and allows their transfer by means of these technical communication media. By mediating between both these aspects, the success of powerpoint, then, contributes to the social construction of both the "knowledge society" and the "information society."

This is not just a general remark. Rather, both aspects are, in a way, imprinted into powerpoint itself. For, on the one hand, PowerPoint as a software program creating *presentations as documents* is based on information technologies, and since their production as well as their distribution can draw on Internet resources, they are part of large networks of information technologies, such as intranets and the Internet, "a society whose social structure is made around networks activated by microelectronics-based, digitally processed information and communication technology" (Castells 2009: 24). On the other hand, it is one of the features of powerpoint presentations as a mediated communicative genre that it is not only built on virtual documents and digital data but refers to an "event" in real time and among real people interacting – *powerpoint presentation as event*. Powerpoint presentations as an event integrate technology, audiences, and presenters. Although in essence a form of communicative action, as a performance and as a product it is ascribed and ascribable to authors and considered to be their "knowledge," thus contributing to the social construction of the knowledge society.

At this point, one may, of course, ponder the question of whether the two sides could not be considered as the two opposite poles "technology" and "actors," which form the axis on which the debates in the sociology of technology, science and technology studies, or "actor network theory" revolve. Although I shall touch upon this issue at various points, I want to pursue another question that is of equal importance to social theory. How are "local" events related to the society as a whole? Or, to formulate it differently, how can the global success of powerpoint be explained?

In order to answer this question, I shall not start from the assumption shared by most that powerpoint is mainly a presentation software or a "digital document," that is, information technology, software, and a visualization of information. From the sociological point sketched earlier, powerpoint is part of communicative actions to such a degree that it evolved into a communicative genre coordinating the actions of a huge amount of people. Therefore, the question is not why one has to consider the presentation as a communicative genre and not as a technology; rather, I want to reverse the question: why is it that actors need to perform the communicative genre despite the fact that the "information" is available and accessible easily by means of the technical infrastructure? Furthermore, why is this communicative genre so successful? On the basis of the analysis of video data on the performance of powerpoint presentations as communicative genre I want to argue that, in a manner of speaking, it is the very deficiency of "information," that is, presentation as digital document, that necessitates the presentation as an event. Action, interaction, and embodied performance allow one, as it were, to "heal" and "repair" what many see as the deficiency of presentations as documents and information in general. In order to avoid the normative associations of "healing" and "repair," I prefer to say that information is "contextualized" by means of action, interaction, and performance. The action of presenting slides to an audience by a speaker – its performance – bestows meanings and thus situationally creates knowledge not inscribed or encoded in the documents. Performance as the embodied form of communication in time, rather, adds corporeality and sociality, and with it time, space, and new meaning to the information.

Performances of communicative actions in the presentations are, of course, not independent of presentations as data, the software, the technology. This not only holds for the relevance of events for documents but also the other way around: information technology provides a material context for "information" in the presentation event and allows its mediation, as digital document, to other contexts and situations. By contextualizing "information," presentations allow the audience to relate to someone who is presenting and, thereby, representing it. This way, they contribute to the social construction of knowledge – what is presented can be acknowledged and legitimated as the "knowledge" of someone (in different roles, e.g., as "author" or as "performer"). The legitimation of knowledge is no abstract process; it is rather embedded in the event of a presentation, since it is prepared and performed by the speaker (or presenter) with the technology before an audience who take the presenter and speaker to represent the knowledge. This knowledge is then communicated by means of the presentation as digital information to other contexts, for example, downloaded, attached, or integrated into the Internet or "information management systems."

The thesis of this book is that powerpoint presentations are a communicative genre contributing to the construction of the knowledge society. The powerpoint presentation is, as it were, one piece of furniture in the interior architecture of the knowledge society. Previously I have tried to make clear that the "knowledge society" is not an objective entity built on the positive knowledge of science but, rather, a social construction by means of the communicative forms that are considered as legitimate "knowledge." As an institutionalized form of the communication of "knowledge," powerpoint follows a twisted path. Although science is considered the major legitimatory institution for knowledge and the origin of its forms, powerpoint presentations seem to be neither originally nor necessarily derived from the sciences or humanities. Thus, knowledge takes on a less scientific form than theorists of the knowledge society assume. The knowledge society is, however, not a mere ideological illusion produced by a neoliberal extension of economic forms of communication into other spheres of society and built on the exploitation of nature and those who are globally not part of the knowledge class. By "knowledge society" I mean, rather, a society that depends on the construction of what is indisputably considered to be knowledge. As I stress that knowledge cannot be observed other than in some form of communication, knowledge societies depend on the institutionalization of such forms of communication, which are considered as "entailing," "representing," or indicating "knowledge." Powerpoint presentations, I claim, are such a form of communication, and, therefore, they contribute to the continuing belief in the knowledge society – on the basis of technologies and structures that are provided by the "information society" (which is itself a concept that was used as a self-fulfilling prophecy: its proclamation and anticipation in the 1960s led to its very construction in the decades that followed).

As part of this thesis, I agree with Yates and Orlikowski (2008: 83), who claim that the presentation genre emerged and disseminated in response to the recurrent requirement to share complex information with multiple people in face-to-face interaction. In addition, I want to show that its particular character as a communicative genre is due to the fact that the coordination of face-to-face interaction is immersed in a technical structure of the information society that provides it with stability and standards. On this ground I want to contradict the claim made by Yates and Orlikowski (2008) that the informational products and their materializations as slides, files, printouts, and so on, are "derivative" of the event These products are, rather, mediatizations between contextualized situations mostly by means of digitalization and the informational infrastructure. In a somewhat simplified way, one could say that the duality of powerpoint as event and powerpoint as document bridges the gap between the technologically based information society and the new organizational forms of the "knowledge society" (or, using even more basic categories, between technology and acting subject). In being a "document," the powerpoint presentation constructs, on the one hand, more or less decontextualized "information" to be transferred anywhere anytime. In immersing the "digital document" in a situated event, the presentation allows for the contextualization of the decontextualized situative features of information and relates it to subjects as producers and recipients. Since this happens in communication, knowledge is, first of all, a form of communicative action that depends on competent actors and information technology. It is the institutionalization of communicative forms and the global diffusion of the technology that result in a new communicative form of knowledge contributing to the social construction of the knowledge society.

## 4. Structure of the Book

The book is based on the study of a range of empirical aspects of powerpoint presentations, and it also draws on a variety of different data and methods (see Appendix II). As mentioned in the Acknowledgments, the different aspects have been analyzed by research groups, so that, at times, I am summarizing the results produced by members of the research groups in which I was participating, and sometimes those for which I have been the principal investigator. In order to account for the range of data and methods, the book cannot follow the inductive strategy of the research process. Although it results from empirical analysis, it organizes the results in a way that follows and supports the general argument sketched earlier and elaborated in the Conclusion.

The next chapter offers a short history that focuses on the invention of the PowerPoint software and on the background of neighboring inventions, such as projectors. Although historical in nature, the chapter will not try to reconstruct powerpoint sociologically as a process of technical innovation. Rather, it will try to indicate the duality of the technical innovation that is so crucial to the thesis here: Powerpoint is not only a new digital document format to be considered as technology; it was accompanied by another "communicative" invention: namely, the powerpoint presentation, which provided one of the major contexts of use for the digital product. The historical overview underlines the distinction between these two aspects of the powerpoint presentation, the presentation as document. on the one hand, and the presentation as an event, on the other.

The rapid dissemination of the software as well as, somewhat later, the event gave rise to a number of studies that have been dispersed all over the social sciences and beyond and have not so far been adequately summarized.

After the history of PowerPoint, I want to continue this chapter by giving a rough overview of these studies and try to identify the major tendencies. If one looks at these studies, there are a huge number that take a more or less explicit normative and critical stance toward powerpoint already mirrored in the newspaper article quoted at the beginning of this chapter. The most visible and prominent example of these normative critical views is that expressed by Edward Tufte, whose arguments I want to sketch briefly. As he takes a cognitivist stance on the visualization of information, I shall then turn to another set of empirical studies that try to focus on powerpoint more as a process in which "information" is communicated, highlighting its "effects" and "efficiency." The final approach addresses powerpoint as an event and attempts to define it as a genre.

The sketch on genre builds a nice bridge to presenting the concept of the communicative genre that provides the backbone of the empirical part of the book. As the social sciences often suffer from the lack of clarity of those categories on which their analyses are based, I have deemed it necessary to lay out at least rudimentarily the set of basic categories (action, communicative action, communicative genre, knowledge) on which the analysis builds. Following this path, I propose the notion of "communicative genre" in order to get hold of the specific communicative aspects of powerpoint presentations. Based on the notion of communicative action, communicative genres like this can be considered the "institutions" of communicative actions and the kernels of communication culture. Chapter 3, therefore, outlines the notion of communicative action and communicative genres and delineates the three levels of analyzing communicative genre. The distinctions among the three levels should not be misread as a kind of ontology. They instead allow the data to be sorted out and to provide an order for the analysis. In this way, the distinctions among the three levels, internal, situational, and external, bestow a structure on the subsequent empirical chapters.

Chapter 4 is the first empirical chapter using data on the presentations as event. Following the analytical structure of communicative genres, it focuses, first, on the internal level. It starts by looking at the action part of the powerpoint presentation and the products of what is being produced before the event. Powerpoint presentations are part of an action project and are reminiscent of rhetorical action, that is, communicative actions strategically prepared by actors. The analysis then turns its attention to scrutinizing the products of their actions, the "slides", which also have to be prepared in advance. In some sense, particularly in the case when written manuscripts are used in the presentation, this obviously holds true for the speech or talk produced "live." Although some may focus on the analysis of the "information" encoded into the slides, the analysis then turns to what regularly happens to the slides in the presentation: they are framed by speech. Because this is what happens empirically, speech and slides shall not be analyzed in isolation. Rather, the analysis of speech poses the question as to how it is related to the slides. I want to frame this question in another way by asking how the two modes, the visual and the spoken, are synchronized and coordinated in time, on the local level of slides and their elements, as well as on the level of the macrostructure of the whole presentation.

Already the analysis of speech and slides demonstrates that meaning is not just "information" encoded in the visual and linguistic signs but that it depends on the local and situative interplay between both on the "intermediate level" of analysis. This interplay happens in the situation in which the presentation is performed. The importance of this situative performance becomes very obvious if we extend our analysis to other aspects of the communicative action. One important example is the use of the body in, for example, pointing. It is no surprise that pointing is the most emblematic gesture for powerpoint presentations. In Chapter 5, I shall, therefore, focus on the relation between the visual and the spoken with respect to body, time, and space. As will be shown, pointing plays an important role in that it succeeds in performing knowledge and even in creating meaning that cannot be detected from the slides. As pointing is connected to the body, the whole body, and even the body formation, the relation between human bodies and between human bodies and other objects in space is brought into play. In fact, the body is shown to connect the triangular structure of the presenter, the technology and its projected item, and the audience like a pivot. This triadic structure or triangle forms the core of the powerpoint presentation as a communicative genre. Having outlined this structure, I turn from the activities of the presenter and his or her body to an analysis of the role of the audience in the presentation, and, finally, to the role of technologies, such as computer, projector, and "slide." While the audience is being analyzed with respect to the ways it "acts" in the presentation and contributes to the interactive character of the presentation so often ignored by its critics, the role of technology is studied by focusing particularly on technical failures. Technical failures not only demonstrate the dependence of human interaction on the technology, they also show that technology frames the genre so that changes in technology lead to variations and transformations of the genre.

Next to computers, projectors, and pointers, presentations depend on a number of other objects. The setting of the powerpoint presentation constitutes the starting point for the analysis on the external level, which is constitutive of the communicative genre powerpoint presentation. Settings serve to frame the presentations and provide them with a spatial context. As the temporal order of presentations, they are part of an organization of presentation that transcends the situation of the presentation as a form of face-to-face interaction. Note that the elements transcending the situation are part of the communicative genre. This holds for objects contextualized in the situation, such as chairs and lecterns. It also holds for the technological infrastructure, ranging from computers, projectors, and informational networks that function as mediators to other situations It is also true for the meeting that serves as a major link between the situational order of the presentation and its external level, particularly organizations. Powerpoint presentations in meetings are one of the ways in which organizations account for the increased role of "knowledge" – how they produce and manage what they consider to be "knowledge." By processing "knowledge" through information technology (as "knowledge management" or "information management"), they rely on technology that is provided by the "information society". In order to explain the success and ubiquity of presentations in general and powerpoint presentations and their current ubiquity in particular, both are considered in a historical perspective as the institutionalization of meetings and the diffusion of technology.

Chapter 6 sums up the analytical results of the empirical chapters in order to answer the questions posed at the beginning: Why are powerpoint presentations ubiquitous? Why are they morally contended? How are they related to the knowledge society? Originating in the fusion of information technology and meetings, powerpoint is a communicative innovation, a new genre of communication. As a communicative genre, powerpoint is specifically characterized by the triadic structure of technology, audience, and presenter. It is this very structure that is the reason for its communicative innovation and explains its success and ubiquity: technology mediates the presentation to the extensively constructed informational infrastructure, which, again, contextualizes the presentation. Particularly formal organizations provide a "place" in situations of interaction as well as spaces, times, and personnel in order to contextualize meetings. Since technologically standardized "information" is deficient with respect to specific situations of communication, it requires its contextualization in situative performances in which it can be ascribed to an author as knowledge. In this way, powerpoint presentations contribute to the communicative culture of the knowledge society.

# 2    On the History of PowerPoint

This book is not particularly about *the* presentation software called "PowerPoint" as opposed to other softwares. It is about presentations as events in which presentation software is used, most often yet not exclusively PowerPoint. Therefore, the goal of the analysis is not to compare PowerPoint to other software and its capacity to create presentations as documents. It is about powerpoint because the name of this software has become synonymous for both: any software for presentations as well as the presentation as event. Since the rise of the presentation as an event has been tightly linked to the success of this software, we need to have a closer look at how it developed.[1]

By looking at the history of PowerPoint, I do not want to focus on the social construction of this technology, as, for example, suggested by Pinch and Bijker (1987). It is quite clear that the software has been subject to different interpretations in the course of its development. In fact, as we shall see, the question as to what problem is solved by powerpoint seems only to become clear with the dissemination of projectors after 2000. (I will touch upon this topic when turning to the diffusion of powerpoint.) As stated in the beginning, however, it is not the technology that is my focus, because technology is not just a subject of interpretation; nor is it just linked to actions that make "use" of it, like an actor somehow related to the human agent performing his or her communicative acts. Rather, powerpoint as a technology is part of the communicative genre in the same way as the letters and paper (or monitors) form part of a novel, and moving pictures and screen or monitors form parts of a film. Yet, powerpoint will not be reduced here to a "medium" of action (as in the presentation as document view). Offered here is a different approach. Rather than a study of technology that indirectly grasps the phenomenon under study through narrative reconstructions and interviews that are "about" or a result of their own ethnographic reconstruction of narratives "on" the technology, the technology shall be analyzed "in action," as Heath and Luff (2000) formulate it so aptly.[2]

The theoretical focus on action or (as I think is analytically more precise) communicative action also has methodological support in that I believe that the analysis of actual use in real life situations provides an empirically much more powerful basis for determining the "meaning" or the "interpretation" of a technology or its role as an "actor." Therefore, this short history of PowerPoint mainly serves as a background for the analysis of the communicative forms of its use, particularly since it aims to demonstrate that this communicative innovation was related to the technological development and to show how this was achieved. In this sense, the reconstruction of the technological development only provides a kind of prehistory of the communicative form (of which it, of course, is a part) reconstructed, therefore, by an archaeology of communication linked to the invention of the PowerPoint software.

## 1. The Archaeology of PowerPoint

The history of PowerPoint could be written from various angles: that is, as the history of the software program, of the company that developed it, or the technologies required for presentations with powerpoint. There is, indeed, a long history of such technologies. The *laterna magica*, for example, was already in use in a way comparable to presentations as an aspect of lectures in the seventeenth century (Peters 2007), and various later technologies, such as the episcope or the opaque projector, could be elaborated in this context. PowerPoint, however, is initially a projection technology as a means to produce "slides" (a notion to be used rather metaphorically in this context). In order to focus on the specific contribution of PowerPoint and to avoid excessive historical review, I am going to focus on the technologies most specific to PowerPoint – slides, projectors and software – and try to trace their invention.

The major forerunners of PowerPoint are the 35-mm slide, used with a slide projector, and the overhead projector, using transparencies or foils. The slide projector (a refinement of the magical lantern) and the overhead projector gained popularity from the 1950s. The overhead projector was invented by James Earl Bancroft, who received a patent in 1947.[3] Since Bancroft had been working for the American Bowling and Billiard Corporation, the "projector," as he called his invention, had the purpose of projecting the scores of bowling matches.

This invention relates ... to projectors ... in which a true image ... of an object is situated in front of an observer and is formed on a screen situated in the field of vision of this observer, so that he or she can see both the object and the image without shifting his position and merely by shifting his gaze. (Pias 2009: 19, trans. HK)

Pias (2009), who has reconstructed the history of the overhead projector, observes that the overhead caused a fundamental change in the order of seeing that also has consequences for any presentation: overhead projections transform anything that is written privately into something public, observable to both the presenter and an audience. The public nature of what is projected is also a feature Bancroft had in mind when he imagined the use of his invention in other contexts, that is, "in connection with lectures, speeches, educational work, sales promotional work, etc." (Pias 2009: 19, trans. HK).

The success of the overhead was linked to the development of transparent slides by the American company 3M. One has to recall that copying was still in its infancy when overhead projection started. The effect of visual inversion that occurs in copying posed a peculiar problem to developers. The "transparency" developed by 3M constituted an early solution to this problem since it allowed the user just to turn the copy over so that the inversion could be reversed. From the start, transparencies were sold in large numbers: the U.S. Strategic Air Command already required 20,000 slides a month in the 1940s. At that time, the Federal Aid to Education program of the U.S. Government triggered a heated debate on overhead technology in the classroom; it also boosted sales of overhead projectors to a very high level.

The other major medium prior to PowerPoint yet relevant to its design were slides. A "slide" refers to photographic copies of documents predominantly in a 35-mm frame. The format of these slides goes back to the invention of special cameras in the 1920s, before their widespread use began in the 1950s, and it was further fostered in the 1960s when Eastman Kodak introduced the "Carousel" projectors featuring round trays, which later became very common in business meeting rooms. Slides were also very popular in schools and universities as well as in private settings.

Despite their popularity, the 35-mm slides slowly lost ground to transparencies, for the slides were much more expensive, needed professional graphics, and were more difficult to use. The diffusion of transparencies was boosted massively by the introduction of lower-cost portable projectors, invented by 3M in the 1970s. In addition, copying technology improved rapidly, until copy machines allowed any paper document to be copied onto transparencies. The growing popularity of the overhead is also reflected numerically. In 1965, 100,000 overhead copiers were sold in the United States. Though in 1975, a little more than 50,000 went on sale, decreasing costs and increasing portability made the number of sales rise again, to 120,000 in 1985. By the mid-1980s there was an overhead projector in more than 90 percent of U.S. classrooms (Austin, Rudkin, and Gaskins 1986: 17). As Parker (2001: 79) remarked, "Now anything on a sheet of paper could be transferred to an overhead slide." According to Austin, Rudkin, and Gaskins, (1986) who were credited with inventing PowerPoint, the market for both slides and transparencies was worth $3.5 billion in 1984, $5 billion in 1985, and an estimated $10 billion in 1988. They (1986: 29) guessed that annually more than 1.1 billion presentation slides had been produced in 1985, of which only 12 percent were 35-mm slides and only 1% were overhead transparencies produced on a computer. The rest would have been copied overhead transparencies.

In order to understand the success of PowerPoint, another emergent technology for presentations at this time has to be mentioned. In 1984, a new liquid crystal display (LCD) projector had been constructed by the New York inventor Gene Dolgoff. Based on liquid crystals, the projector aimed to allow presentations even in bright light. Although its time was still to come (as was true of other projection technologies), and although it was still unreliable and very expensive, this invention had an impact on PowerPoint from its very beginning. Already in 1986 Gaskins had envisaged that the LCD projector would replace the overhead projector and that the personal computer would be connected to it via a cable. Even at that early stage he suggested that "before devices are introduced" (Austin, Rudkin, and Gaskins 1986: 29), software should be provided for highlighting, fades, transitions, and cycling color. In 1988, Dolgoff founded the world's first LCD projector company, and in 1989 he was awarded the first contract with the U.S. Defense Department, which later allowed him to define the standards in this business.

## 2. The Double Invention of PowerPoint

The invention of PowerPoint itself goes back to the cryptographer Whitfield Diffie of Bell Northern Research at Mountain View, California, a company that made its living from database products and programs for the Macintosh computer. In order to facilitate the preparation of a presentation with 35-mm slides, Diffie wrote a program that allowed the use of graphics that could be printed out on a laser printer. The program contained a storyboard that sketched the content of the slides, which could then be used as templates for the graphic designers in his company. He soon expanded it in such a way that a page contained a number of frames with commentary around them. Parker (2001: 79) considers this the invention of the "slide show on paper." He did not photocopy the slides but sent them to other designers for improvement and later used the improved slides as a kind of script for lectures.

Although the program still had problems of often yielding results that were not intended, Robert Gaskins, who also worked for Bell Northern Research, was inspired by this solution. Gaskins is described by Parker (2001: 80) as a former Berkeley Ph.D. student, "who had a family background in industrial photographic supplies and grew up around overhead projectors and inks and gels." As opposed to Diffie, he had experiences in business and, thence, could imagine the use of such a program in that context:

> Based on my experience traveling around the world for this project and receiving hundreds of presentations from people who used overheads and slides and flipcharts (a few made on computers, most not), I began to think about the possibility of a new application to make presentations using the then undelivered future graphical personal computers such as Macintosh and Windows – the idea which would later be the basis for PowerPoint. (Gaskins 2009, n.p.)

Although Diffie established the ground for PowerPoint by inventing the technology, he later credited Gaskins with the invention. "Bob was the one who had the vision to understand how important it was to the world, and I didn't" (Parker 2001: 80). Gaskins never did claim to have made the technical invention. His contribution lay rather in his ability to imagine a use for Diffie's technical solution, to market it successfully, and, as we shall see, to link it to a "communicative invention," the presentation as an event. It is important to note here that the ambivalence between the information technology of the software and the event is clearly mirrored in this double invention.

The basic idea of PowerPoint was to integrate the graphics into the slide; doing so, as explained in a business plan from 1984, "allows the content-originator to control the presentation"; moreover, Gaskins wanted the presenter to create the presentation and "to get rid of the intermediaries – graphic designers" (Parker 2001: 81). Thus, PowerPoint was to be conceived of as a "personal presentation tool, designed for use by the content-originator directly, and not for use by the corporate communications partner" (Austin, Rudkin, and Gaskins 1986: 36).

Gaskins then attempted to generate money in order to promulgate this idea and market it. It was during his search for investors that the name "PowerPoint" was born, as is recalled in a now-legendary story: after a trip to get financial support for their project, Gaskins and his colleagues were "sitting in an airplane window seat watching the tarmac scroll by under the plane as it approached the runway for takeoff and the trip home. Now in some airports there is a specific point on the runway where the plane is supposed to stop and bring their engines up to full power. This point is usually painted in the runway, with the label Power Point. The name seemed perfect for the product they were producing" (Bajaj 2008).

Gaskins's successful pitch for this idea allowed him to leave Bell Northern Research and to found a new Silicon Valley firm, Forethought, of which he owned a "sizeable share." Together with the software developer Dennis Austin he began to work on a program called Presenter. "Presenter is a program designed primarily for producing overhead slides (in color and in black and white), and can be used also for producing 35 mm slides and video presentations" (Austin, Rudkin, and Gaskins 1986: 2). Based on a floppy disc, Presenter was programmed on a Macintosh and allowed to produce black and white text and graphic pages that a photocopier could turn into foils. The slide as part of a presentation therefore constituted the physical metaphor that they were trying to transfer to the computer (Austin, Rudkin, and Gaskins 1986: 12ff.). Drawing on a study on the effects and uses of overhead transparencies by the University of Pennsylvania, Austin, Rudkin and Gaskins (1986: 12ff.) concluded that the two media also represent two different uses and two market segments of quite different size. While adapting the metaphor of the professional (35-mm) slide, it was the mass market of overhead transparencies that Gaskins was targeting. One can only guess that the notion of the slide persisted because it was associated with the more professional setting than the transparencies.

After Forethought had been moved from Mountain View to Sunnyvale, California, Gaskins and Dennis Austin, who was mainly responsible for the programming, shipped what was now called "PowerPoint 1.0" in April 1987. Although the market for such a program was still small, Microsoft acquired Gaskins's Forethought for $14 million in August 1987. Forethought was turned into the Microsoft "Graphics Business Unit", led by Gaskins, a unit that was not located on the Main Campus of Microsoft and is also said to have differed in many respects from Microsoft's organizational culture.

The Graphics Business Unit team remained in the Silicon Valley, where it moved, in 1988, first, to Menlo Park; then to a former Apple building in Cupertino; and, finally, in 2000, to a campus with other Microsoft Bay Area companies (such as Hotmail and Web TV) in Mountain View, California.

PowerPoint 1.0 (PPT 1.0) was still very much a Macintosh product in that it was designed for the Apple Laser Printer, which allowed the production of professional foils for overheads. In 1988, PowerPoint 2.0 was published. The program could now perform spell checking and was facilitated to create color schemes. In 1988, there were PowerPoint 2.0 versions in English (American and British), French, French Canadian, Swedish, German, Italian, and Dutch. Sales then totaled $4,536,915 of MS PPT 1.01 and 2.0. This means that in eleven months of 1988 about twenty-three thousand five hundred units were sold worldwide, with roughly one-tenth in the United States.

Although the slides included graphics from the outset, these graphics had not been produced by the software but by external companies specialized in graphic design. Even the menu of PowerPoint 2.0 still contained the command "send to Genigraphics", referring to a company that specialized in graphic design. The data were sent by modem to the photographic studio of a local or regional office of Genigraphics, which sent it back via snailmail a day later. Genigraphics had been the company from which Gaskins had already ordered the first graphics on Presenter. Indeed, in the 1970s, the National Aeronautics and Space Administration (NASA) had been cooperating with Genigraphics, which produced thousands of diagrams for the training of astronauts. At this point in time, the production of diagrams was very much specialized – one hour's work on graphics was worth $240. Genigraphics alone possessed of twenty-four production sites in all major U.S. cities with professional designers who produced diagrams for almost every Fortune 500 company in the 1980s and for the U.S. government (Microsoft Memo 1988: 7). This changed with the PowerPoint 2.0 version for Windows 3.0, designed for "self-made slides", including Microsoft Graph. This version was shipped onto the international market in 1990, and at this point, PowerPoint still had a lot of competition from other companies, such as Aldus Persuasion (for Apple Macintosh), most of which also were based on Microsoft disk operating system (DOS), such as Harvard Graphics and Lotus Freelance.

The success of PowerPoint went hand in hand with the increasing standardization within Office: Microsoft tried to combine and integrate PowerPoint, Excel, and Word, meaning that they used the same menus and codes so that every application looked the same. It is this integration into

Office and the corresponding standardization "that would eventually make PowerPoint invincible," as (Parker 2001: 82) wrote. The graphics were also contributing to its success. Though originally based on an accidental collection of transparencies (*PC Magazine* 2007), the "indent marker" that turned every bullet list into a paragraph had already been part of the specifications of "Presenter" (Austin, Rudkin, and Gaskins 1986).

Later clip art was added. Originally it has been created by Cathleen Belleville, a graphic designer who had worked for PowerPoint from 1989 to 1995. She had modeled her stick figures on a former college roommate and had never expected these "Screen Beans" (as she called them) to become modern business icons (Parker 2001: 82). The same may be said about the AutoContent Wizard, which was part of the earlier versions of PowerPoint. The version of 2004 offered a huge range of visual elements, such as 24 layout templates, 110 slide background options, 67 variants for slide transitions, and 228 clip art files addressing the most diverse types of events – a number increasing in later versions of the program. Later versions also allowed the insertion of other kinds of data, such as tables, photographs, or films.

The success of PowerPoint was immense. The first three types of PowerPoint (1.0, 2.0, 3.0) were shipped in more than twelve national languages. From autumn 1992, with the publication of PowerPoint 3.0 for Macintosh (PowerPoint 3.0 for Windows was produced in May 1992), PowerPoint had an additional function that allowed the user to present the slides by way of a video outlet (in addition to printing or sending). By 1992 their market share was 63 percent of presentation graphics software sales on Windows and Mac with sales of more than one million copies in 1992 – the year Gaskins left PowerPoint. In that year, revenues grew to more than $100 million. By 1993, PowerPoint became the most profitable unit of Microsoft. PowerPoint 4.0 was already fully integrated into Windows. Shipped in August 1995, Windows 95 and Office 95 consolidated the success of PowerPoint (version 7.0), for not only was the program now well integrated into Microsoft,[4] it also enjoyed the enormous success of Windows as one of its standard programs, so that it now became *the* standard presentation program. From 1997 it included animated slide transitions, automatic layouts, clip art files, and the infamous AutoContent Wizard (which, originally considered as a joke by the designers, was to become one of the most characteristic features of PowerPoint) (Yates and Orlikowski 2008). By 2001, PowerPoint dominated the market at 95 percent. In 2003, the revenues for Microsoft accounted for $1 billion. "By then," Gaskins writes, "PowerPoint was being used by over 500 million people worldwide, with over 30 million PowerPoint presentations made every day" (Gaskins 2009, n.p.).

The success of PowerPoint was not only detrimental to other presentation software programs; the success of the "self-made" slides also impacted on the graphics industry. Genigraphics, which had produced the graphics for Forethought, was so severely affected that the company was on the verge of bankruptcy in 1994. Ironically, the company was acquired by a manufacturer of LCD projectors. Overheads were also affected, as the symbolic "Overhead Festival for Forgotten Media," which took place in Copenhagen in 2005 (www.overheads.org), demonstrates.

## 3. Presentation as Digital Document and Presentation as Event

The success of PowerPoint in the 1990s was mainly related and restricted to PowerPoint *presentation as documents*. PowerPoint presentation as event did not take off so early. As Richard Bretschneider, the program director of PowerPoint since 1993, stresses, "For the first few years I was on the team, we targeted large television style monitors, because projectors were very expensive and not very reliable" (Bajaj 2008: 1). The fact that the company had projectors in their conference room no earlier than 2003 also indicates the lack of relevance this notion of presentation had to PowerPoint. Indeed even in 2010, the company still preserved the notion of the presentation as document. From the perspective of Microsoft's Richard Bretschneider, one of the essential ideas behind this invention was that it provided an overall form: "that all the different slides were created as one document – as a presentation."[5] The intention behind the release of the 2007 version of PowerPoint was, as Bretschneider said, in order for the program to create pitch books, which had become important in financial companies to evaluate other companies and businesses. User studies at Microsoft PowerPoint remained equally preoccupied with the documents when addressing other users' application of the program and their interests, such as the creation of menus on PowerPoint by restaurants, sales advertisements by households, or hymns by churches (*PC Magazine* 2007).

Although the view of presentations as documents produced by the computer software program is quite plausible for the designers of computer software, one should not forget that before its invention PowerPoint (alias "Presenter") had also been designed for other purposes. The fact that the inventors chose the name "Presenter" (which was changed to "PowerPoint" because of a trademark problem) shows that the idea was not restricted to "slides" as documents. Even if some contend that Gaskins was strongly oriented toward the slide as a "physical object," it is important to note that he also envisioned the presentation as an event. Already in 1986, he specified the idea of a slide show by means of Presenter as follows: "Although most presentations are printed for final display, Presenter allows you to use the computer as a 'projector' if you like. The images are shown one at a time on a computer's screen, without tools, menu bar, or other windows. The show can be presented manually, pressing the mouse button or some key(s) to change slides" (Austin, Rudkin, and Gaskins 1986: 4). Thus Gaskins foresaw that "the much cheaper video projectors and programs such as presenter should give rise to an entirely new phenomenon – presentations with the informality of overhead transparencies, delivered in lighted business meetings, but using video generated directly from diskettes instead of actual overhead foils" (Austin, Rudkin, and Gaskins 1986: 22). The presentations he had in mind were definitely based in the social context of business meetings: when in 1986 Gaskins shared his speculations about the market, he wrote that "only 1 business meeting out of 40 makes use of visuals of any kind" that may be produced by computers and, increasingly, personal computers (1986: 13).[6] Thus the presentation as event was defined as a specific target for the use of PowerPoint.

Gaskins did not content himself with this vision but realized it early in a spectacular form. I would like to remind the reader that the function of PowerPoint 3.0. to present the slides by way of the video outlet (a function, as mentioned earlier, that Gaskins had already insisted on early) was only a technical option when it was released in 1992. Nevertheless, it was in this year that Gaskins gave this technical function a usable form, as the "world's first laptop PowerPoint presentation" took place on February 25 in the Regina Hotel in the center of Paris. Gaskins recounts:

> With a laptop actually under my arm, I entered at the back of a ballroom filled with hundreds of Microsoft people from the European, Middle Eastern, and African subsidiaries. I walked through the audience carrying the laptop, up to the podium at the front; there I opened the laptop, and plugged in a video cable on the lectern. I began delivering a presentation to introduce PowerPoint 3.0. for Windows, using PowerPoint running on the laptop feeding video out to a projector the size of a refrigerator which put the "video slides" onto a huge screen behind me. No one had ever seen PowerPoint running on a portable computer before, let alone being used to produce a real time video show in color with animated builds and transitions.... The audience, all Microsoft people who talked to customers

frequently, grasped immediately what the future would bring for their own presentations; there was a deafening applause. (Gaskins 2009, n.p.)

Although one may doubt that this product demonstration was the very first exhibiting the communicative patterns of powerpoint presentations,[7] the vital role of this particular presentation was that Gaskins had succeeded in turning the vision he had had years before into reality. Moreover, the seeming technical ease with which it was conducted was very convincing to the audience. As Gaskins frankly concedes, this ease was "staged" in a rather laborious way. First, the computer hardware resembling a laptop barely existed. No such equipment was to be found in Europe, so everything that was needed to improvise these technologies had to be flown in from the United States. Secondly, there was no readymade equipment comparable to a projector to be used. Specifically for this presentation, a unique machine, which took the form of a massive video projector the size of a refrigerator, was built, The technicians spent the whole day before the presentation linking this machine to the video projector, and Gaskins was very aware of the importance of the performance: "Testing and tweaking went on far into the night, but on Tuesday morning, I could 'casually' carry my laptop up to the front, plug in the video cable, and start my PowerPoint. The demo went off without a hitch" (Gaskins 2009, n.p.). The ease of this presentation must have been a sensation, for, as he added, "when we demonstrated at trade shows, we were mobbed" (Parker 2001: 81).

Although there are again doubts whether this was the first computer-supported presentation using a projector, to the extent that it must be considered an invention, the event as performed and described by Gaskins certainly exhibits most of the features of what we here call a powerpoint presentation.[8] Thus, next to the technical invention of the software that allows the production of the "presentation as document," powerpoint also implies a second invention, which, somewhat later, involves a presenter, a computer, and something projecting what the presenter has produced by means of the software onto a surface visible to a live audience.

As indicated earlier, PowerPoint has gone on to see a tremendously fast diffusion. It has become so common that the software became part of general knowledge and a practice shared by an increasingly large part of the professionally active populations in contemporary societies. With its rapid diffusion, powerpoint moved from being a technology providing designs for presentations into a technology that was itself linked to the very form of presentation. This is expressed in the fact that "PowerPoint" not only became synonymous for the various types of software used in presentations, it also became the specifying feature for the genre of presentation, namely, the "powerpoint presentation," which is the declared subject of our study. As we shall see, powerpoint presentation as communicative genre is not only linked to the software technology and the hardware developments of projectors, but also relates to the growing importance of the meeting, a characteristic of the transformation of organizations within the last few decades. In addition, it builds on the already existing form of presentation developed prior to the use of powerpoint. Since I am not concerned so much with the specific diffusion of the technology as with the communicative genre, both aspects will be treated in later chapters. In this way we can see how they are related to and constitutive of the communicative genre of powerpoint presentation. Therefore, we have, first, to identify the features of this genre and clarify the ways in which to analyze a communicative genre like powerpoint presentations. It is only on this basis that we can, second, try to understand how the communicative fused with the presentation and the meeting into a communicative genre that has become so paradigmatic for communicating knowledge. In order to acknowledge the specific perspective of this analysis, it is necessary to locate it within the social scientific research on powerpoint (and PowerPoint).

## 4. PowerPoint Is Evil – Discourse and Studies on Powerpoint

Only a few years after the technology was available, PowerPoint became a ubiquitous phenomenon. One could say that PowerPoint turned into a familiar phenomenon both for an increasing number of people and as part of the (mostly professional) aspect of their everyday lives. While the pattern of its diffusion and ubiquity will be sketched later, at this point it is important to outline the discussion around powerpoint. In fact, the rapid and dynamic dissemination of PowerPoint was reflected by an increasing number of publications on powerpoint in the public as well as, somewhat later, empirical studies undertaken by professionals and social scientists. PowerPoint became a topic in public discourse and, thereby, part of the general stock of knowledge, as exemplified by the article quoted in the Introduction. Two features of this knowledge need to be stressed. First (as shall be elaborated in more detail later), although public discourse typically refers to PowerPoint and underlines its features as software, the debate was not triggered by the technology already available in the early 1990s, but by the diffusion of powerpoint as presentations, which started to become widespread in the late 1990s and became commonplace after the year 2000.

Second, as will be seen in the third section of Chapter 6, the rapid diffusion of powerpoint in new institutional areas outside business stirred a great deal of criticism and even resentment of both powerpoint and, even more often, the software PowerPoint.

Reflecting the global distribution of powerpoint, public discourse on the topic found resonance at an international level, and despite the diversity of that discourse, there are a number of positions that recur and specific authors who represent them. One example is Edward Tufte, whose theses criticizing powerpoint have had broad global resonance. After briefly sketching the public debate, therefore, the essential arguments put forward by Tufte will be reviewed. His "cognitivist" approach takes the perspective of information design and focuses particularly on the presentation as document. His focus on the document, that is, the digital product, is shared by a number of other authors who address powerpoint from a technical point of view. Typically, they also share views as to how powerpoint works, which are based on a model of communication implicit in Tufte's writings (without necessarily sharing his moralizing standpoint toward PowerPoint). This is an information cognition model, according to which information is "in" the document and can be transmitted to the recipient as "cognition." Consequently, analysis within this framework focuses on the analysis of the "document" and its technical, visual, or linguistic features (or their "multimodal interplay").

With respect to the question of how powerpoint forms part of a communication process, we can identify a second approach, represented by another group of studies. These studies typically investigate the "effects" and "efficiency" of powerpoint with respect to the audience. By implicitly following the sender-recipient model of communication, they look at the information encoded in the slides (i.e., certain items from the curricula of school or university teaching) as input and compare it to their output (i.e., "knowledge," which is tested, for example, through exams). Methodologically, they rely on questionnaires submitted by viewers of presentations. Note that in both kinds of studies, the information cognition and the sender-receiver studies, powerpoint presentations are never addressed alone. Whereas the information cognition approach focuses on the technical representations, mostly the slides, the sender-recipient model studies consider the presentation as event like a black box. Moreover and unfortunately, while the first branch of studies is often highly normative, sometimes even polemic, the results of studies from the second branch are, as we shall see, sometimes contradictory and in general inconclusive. After presenting an overview of these studies, we then turn to a third type of study, which empirically addresses powerpoint presentations as events, or, in one of the most prominent approaches, as a genre and thus provides a bridge for sketching the concept of communicative genre in the chapter that follows.

## 5. Tufte and the Public Discourse on Powerpoint

Powerpoint has stirred an immense public discussion with innumerable articles in newspapers and on the Internet as well as in other media. Even when conducting presentations with powerpoint, discussions about the value of powerpoint may arise among participants. On various occasions, I have myself witnessed that the sheer fact of whether someone had used powerpoint, or not, would provoke an argument for the positive or negative evaluation of the presentation (in either direction). The debate about powerpoint is not restricted to the public sphere of the lay audience but extends to various professional fields, such as science, business, and politics. If we consider the public discourse on powerpoint, which is accessible also to nonprofessionals in the mass media, we find a heated debate over the value of "PowerPoint" presentations, although it is not always clear what notion of presentation is referred to in this debate – to presentation software in general, to the special Microsoft software, to presentations as events, or to presentations as documents. It is difficult to say when the public debate started, but it seems plausible to locate this beginning somewhere around the year 2001. Richard Bretschneider, who was then working for PowerPoint, claims that it was one of the famous "Dilbert" comic strips that made the critiquing of powerpoint popular.[9] Also in 2001, an article by Ian Parker that internationally is one of the most often cited in this context, was published in the *New Yorker*. On the basis of various interviews, his article not only provided one of the first historical "narratives" about powerpoint but established the public tone for debate by quite unequivocally opposing PowerPoint: "But PowerPoint also has a private, interior influence. It edits ideas" (Parker 2001: 77). Keller expressed this point in the following way (2003: 1): "PowerPoint squeezes ideas into preconceived format, organizing and condensing not only your material but – inevitably, it seems – your way of thinking about and looking at that material." In fact, most of the public discourse is dominated by harsh critique, indicated by Keller's rhetorical question "Is PowerPoint the Devil?" – and answered affirmatively: "PowerPoint has a dark side [because] a complicated, nuanced issue invariably is reduced to headings and bullets. And if that doesn't stultify your thinking about the subject, it may have that effect on your audience – which is at the mercy of your presentation" (Keller 2003: 2). This critique sometimes becomes explicitly normative, as, for example, when Simons (2005) demands its prohibition: "Ban it now."

The harsh critique is not very new. The public discourse on power-point often takes up well-known topoi of cultural and media criticism that have been used in the past, as with, for example, the overhead projector (Pias 2009). Thus, Keller (2003: 5) compares PowerPoint to a drug since "its astonishing popularity, the way it has spread exponentially through the culture, seems analogous, in a way, to drugs. Think of it as a techno-logical cocaine – so effortless to embrace initially, so difficult to relinquish after that." Nunberg (1999) makes PowerPoint responsible for the decay of public lecturing and a "communicative pauperisation," and the editor of one of the major intellectual weeklies in Germany, *Die ZEIT*, predicts the "intellectual decline of the occident being processed by PowerPoint" (Joffe 2007, trans. HK).

The public critique of PowerPoint is often explicitly hostile. Nonetheless, there are also a few proponents for PowerPoint. Leaving aside the authors of how-to books (to which I will turn later), authors such as Kjeldsen (2006: 9) argue that PowerPoint bullets are merely a checklist for key points to help presenters give presentations, while Gabriel even goes so far as to claim that it has positive potential: "PowerPoint, instead of destroying old skills of arguing, theorizing, and communicating, can generate new learn-ing opportunities entailing discovery, criticism and plurivocality" (Gabriel 2008: 256).

The fact that proponents of powerpoint act as defenders by building on the arguments against PowerPoint is certainly linked to the somewhat unique position of the most cited critic on PowerPoint, the computer sci-entist Edward Tufte. The public as well as the academic criticism of power-point can be best exemplified with respect to Tufte, as he is not referred to only in the public discourse. Because of his reputation in the field of infor-mation visualization, he is also a voice respected by academics and even by experts in the field of presentation software (including, as I was told, some members of the staff of PowerPoint who attended his lectures attacking PowerPoint and who grudgingly accepted his critique). As Grady (2006: 222) states, "He has achieved an almost guru-like status among design-ers working in advertising, public relations, and a wide array of occupa-tions and industries concerned with the analysis and display of data and information."

Tufte's arguments have been particularly effective because of his undoubted academic achievements in information visualization and have had immense international resonance in the public media. One of his most quoted arguments concerns his involvement in the U.S. board that investigated the *Columbia* shuttle disaster after its disintegration in early 2003. Tufte claimed that an overloaded and misleading powerpoint slide, supposed to indicate gaps in the safety system, was one of the reasons for this catastrophe. The slide, he argued, contained a disorderly list of bullet points, and it was the intensely hierarchical bullet list, Tufte concluded, that led people to ignore the danger.[10]

Tufte formulates his critique on the basis of a cognitivist approach to design.[11] In the cognitivist perspective, slides are said to increase the sensory stimulation of messages. Cognition research, particularly in cognitive psychology, assumes a positive relation between arousal and learning, in that emotionally arousing materials enhance learning motivation (Weiner and Alkin 1992). Information processing is crucial, leading to debates about the different channels of processing, that is, the auditive channel processing sound and a visual channel processing images. As Pavio (1990) argues, the combination of verbal and visual information may enhance learning so that PowerPoint may contribute to that. On the other hand, Lang (2000) claims that both channels have limited processing capacity, which may result in the problem of cognitive overload. The role of cognitive psychology for PowerPoint is expressed in such elements as the infamous "rule of seven," which proposes that a presenter never use more than about seven items on one slide, an instruction that, according to Tufte, goes back to the information psychologist Miller and his paper the "Magical Number Seven" (G. A. Miller 1956).

In his famous booklet "The Cognitive Style of PowerPoint" (Tufte 2003), later reworked as "The Cognitive Style of PowerPoint: Pitching out Corrupts Within" (Tufte 2006), Tufte hardly touches on conceptual questions relating to cognitive theory, communication, or even his core notion, cognitive style.[12] His critique is, instead, based on an empirical analysis of some two thousand PowerPoint slides, which he compared with thirty-two control samples (presentations not produced in powerpoint). The critique raises a large number of issues, which can be summarized succinctly into three arguments: First, the technicalities of the program PowerPoint appear to be deficient; second, these restrictions lead to the deficient "cognitive style" of the information; affecting, third, the presenter, the audience, and their cognition.

The shortcomings of powerpoint are due to the technicalities that determine human cognition. As a software program, PowerPoint, for Tufte, exhibits various shortcomings. Leaving aside the "low spatial resolution" (which allows only a few elements to be clearly identified on the slide), the program favors a deeply hierarchical single path structure. By this he refers to the bullet list and the possibility of hierarchical subordination. Worsening these weaknesses is what he coined PowerPoint "phluff," that is, the standardized graphic elements, and "chartjunk," that is, diagrams and tables that, he argues, are unable to match the complexity necessary for most statistical tables. Therefore, PowerPoint only allows for a low rate of "information", that is, cognitive underload, since nearly

> all PowerPoint slides that accompany talks have much lower rates of information transmission than the talk itself ... the PowerPoint slides *typically show 40 words, which is about 8 seconds of silent reading material.* The example slides in PP textbooks are particularly disturbing: in 29 books, which should use first-rate examples, the median number of words per slide is 15, worthy of billboards, about 3 or 4 seconds of silent reading material. (Tufte 2003: 169 original emphasis)

This is opposed to speech, which proceeds at a pace of 100 to 160 words per minute, and reading, which is even "three times faster than a presenter can talk" (2003: 184). As a consequence, "the PP slide format has probably the worst signal/noise ration of any known method of communication on paper or computer screen" (2003: 22).

The deficiencies of the program are, second, not punctual; instead, they result in what Tufte calls the "cognitive style" of PowerPoint. Although avoiding a definition of the notion of "cognitive style," he identifies various consequences. The use of PowerPoint leads to rapid temporal sequencing of thin information rather than focused spatial analysis; it tends toward a foreshortening of evidence and thought, and finally to a breaking up of narratives and data into slides and minimal fragments.

Oversimplification, foreshortening, and fragmentation are features of the cognitive style of the information that affects, third, presenters, audiences, and their cognitions: "The cognitive style harms the quality of thought for the producers and the consumers of presentations" (Tufte 2003: 158). In addition, it affects their social relations, "since the pushy PP style tends to set up a dominance relationship between presenter and audience, as the speaker makes power points with hierarchical bullets to passive followers" (ibid.). In sum, the cognitive style affects presenters, audiences, their cognition, and communication of information: "The core ideas of teaching – explanation, reasoning, finding things out, questioning, content, evidence, credible authority not patronizing authoritarianism – are contrary to the cognitive style of PowerPoint" (2003: 161), so that "no thoughtful exchange of information, a mutual interplay between speaker and audience" occurs (Tufte 2003: 158).

In his critique, Tufte makes no pretense of making clear evaluations, since an "evidence presentation" is "a moral as well as an intellectual activity" (2003: 9). Therefore, he does not recoil from such an apologetic statement as "PowerPoint is evil. Power corrupts. PowerPoint corrupts absolutely" (Tufte 2003). This evaluative stance has influenced the public discourse and even PowerPoint's supporters; it is also shared by a branch of academic criticism within a Marxist and a Foucauldian theoretical frame that has focused on powerpoint presentations. Thus, Kaplan reproaches the program's reification, for PowerPoint is not only used to objectify or naturalize knowledge so that it becomes a fact (Kaplan 2010). For Kellner (2006) this reification is linked to the commodification of previously non-colonized sectors of social life and the extension of bureaucratic controls into the realm of leisure, desire, and everyday life. In his dissertation, Pece adds a Foucaultian twist to this critique: PowerPoint supports a form of control, authority, discipline, and administration and, thus, "becomes part of a greater system of control and influence within our decision making halls of government. It encourages theater over substance, simple ideas of complex discourse, and acts as a useful device for those furthering a one-sided agenda" (Pece 2005: 3). Even if Tufte does not refer to the Marxist or Foucaultian positions, his critique shares some of their anti-capitalist resentment of powerpoint with its "smirky commercialism that turns information into a sales pitch and presenters into marketers" (Tufte 2003: 161). The resentment is extended to the producers, the monopoly of Microsoft, for to "describe a software house is to describe the PP cognitive style: a big bureaucracy engaged in computer programming … and marketing" (Tufte 2003: 161).

Although not explicated by him, one can deduce that Tufte accepts the cognitivist model of communication as information. The individual seems to be coined by the information that is inscribed in the object in various forms. The information that can become cognition is considered as encoded in the slides or the "presentation as documents." This model resembles the informational model of communication, for example, of Licklider and Taylor: "A communications engineer thinks of communicating as transferring information from one point to another in codes and signals" (Licklider and Taylor 1968: 21). According to this model, the "cognitive style" imprinted into the information design determines what is communicated by the participants and, consequentially, their cognitions. Although he is focusing on presentations as documents, Tufte extends this view to his idea of how the communication process in the "presentation as event" really works: "Beginning with a title slide, the presenter unveils and reads aloud the single line on the slide, then reveals the next line, reads that aloud, on and on, as the stupefied audience impatiently awaits the end of the talk" (2003: 160). As we will see, the assumption that presentations only consist of the repetition of the slide is empirically untenable. Moreover, as Yates and Orlikowski (2008: 77) stress, Tufte "conflates the use of graphics in written documents such as articles and newspapers with the use of graphics as visual aids in oral presentation"; this is not only an empirical shortcoming: he also fails "to distinguish between fundamentally different genres."

## 6. The Inconclusiveness of Studies on Powerpoint

Whereas the study by Tufte became commonplace in public discourse, there are a huge number of more or less social scientific studies that are not so frequently cited. The majority of these studies follow a model of communication similar to Tufte's, yet they treat the presentation as mass media communication. Assuming that the presenter can be compared to a sender who intends to transfer information, the audience of such presentations is considered to be like a receiver. While the information cognition approach then focuses on the products and the information inscribed, the sender-receiver model focuses on the recipients of communication. Since these studies typically follow standardized quantitative methods using questionnaires, they also prefer studying recipients in standardized institutional settings, mostly schools and colleges. On these grounds, such studies (which are mostly undertaken in the context of learning and education) focus instead on the "acceptance," the "evaluation," and the "efficiency" or "learning outcomes" achieved through powerpoint as compared to other technologies.[13]

   Such studies are so numerous that one must refer to secondary analysis. With respect to the evaluation and the reaction of students to slides, Levasseur and Sawyer (2006), for example, conducted an extensive review of the social scientific literature on powerpoint in the classroom.[14] This secondary analysis finds that many students report preferring computer-generated slides to other presentation methods, as they help to improve the organization of classes: "Virtually all of these studies have shown that students respond quite positively to the use of computer-generated slides in the classroom" (Levasseur and Sawyer 2006: 107). In another secondary analysis of studies on the effects of PowerPoint conducted by Szabo und Hastings

(2000: 186), the conclusion is slightly different: "Generally, it appears that Power Point lectures ... mainly add to the entertainment rather than the education of the students."

The inconclusive, partly contradictory evidence is true of various aspects, as the same ambiguity is found with respect to the "effect" of powerpoint. With regard to "learning outcomes" in schools and universities, Bartsch, Cobern, Kristi (2003) report that the use of powerpoint produces better learning results than use of overheads, although they qualify this evaluation by saying that the use of "expanded PowerPoint" is less successful than use of "basic PowerPoint." The study by Blokzijl and Andeweg (2005) concludes that students learn more from presentations with powerpoint than from regular lectures to the extent that slides contain more text. Schultz (1996/1997), studying the use of powerpoint in business seminars, also finds a "significantly improved level of performance" that leads to better understanding. Whereas Lowry (1999) supports the view that powerpoint leads to improvement in learning, Rankin and Hoaas (2001), on the other hand, in their study find that there are no changes with respect to learning effects among students of economics. Comparing psychology undergraduates taught using classic methods and powerpoint, Szabo and Hastings found no significant difference in academic achievement between the groups using different media, although they concede that a "PowerPoint lecture may benefit recall (or perhaps recognition) from memory" (Szabo and Hastings 2000: 187). In a study on the use of PowerPoint among 143 students in teacher education, Ahmed (1998) shows that students taught with PowerPoint did not score much better when compared with students taught with overheads. These studies seem to indicate a general positive evaluation of powerpoint by students, which is, however, not necessarily based on the greater achievements derived from the technology but by the fact that "students prefer a medium that does not generally produce more learning" (Levasseur and Sawyer 2006: 116). Blokzijl and Naeff (2004: 73ff.), on the other hand, find that although 56 percent of their respondents prefer PowerPoint to overheads, "properties typical of PowerPoint are mainly mentioned as annoyances."[15]

As the evaluations differ, results from comparisons of courses with and without slides also remain quite inconclusive so that different studies arrive at different conclusions. The same holds for the question of whether more extended uses of graphics would change learning behavior. Thus, Simons in his study of 3M study groups checked to what degree an audience would recall, comprehend, or recognize certain elements of the presentation ("learning effectiveness"), to see whether they would prefer something presented in one format more than another (emotionality), and how the audience evaluates each presentation format (Simons 2000). As most studies show, he finds that adding more graphic elements does not result in more effective learning.

As numerous as these studies are, their results are obviously quite inconclusive. Even studies using the same methodology often arrive at opposite results. The overall picture can be summarized in the words of Levasseur and Sawyer: "Put simply, the majority of studies comparing computer-generated slide-based instruction against other instructional methods have failed to find significant differences in learning outcomes" (Levasseur and Sawyer 2006: 116).

## 7. Presentation as Event and Genre

Although some studies of the kind sketched previously suffer from methodological shortcomings, one may in general doubt whether the model of communication presupposed by them does any justice to the phenomenon under consideration. Most of the previous studies follow a transmission model of communication. Powerpoint presentations are seen as documents that provide (more or less efficient) "information" by way of the "presentations as documents" to people and their cognition. Whereas they either ignore or neglect presentation as event or treat it as an inaccessible black box, another type of study tries instead to address exactly these aspects of powerpoint presentations. One may call such approaches ethnographic in general, since they look at the very performance of presentations in situ. Thus, Stark (2008), for example, looks at the "demonstration" of powerpoint presentations in political settings, and Lobin (2009) analyzes the linguistic aspects of powerpoint presentations while considering the performance as well as the preparation and the publication of the presentation. In a similar vein, Yates and Orlikowski (2008) have studied powerpoint presentation somewhat ethnograpically through the study of the role of presentations within organizations. As such they are particularly important to this study since they analyze powerpoint presentations as a "genre." Furthermore, Schnettler and Knoblauch (2007) have proposed an approach that seeks to integrate linguistic, communicative, and sociological aspects by analyzing powerpoint presentations as a communicative genre.

Before I elaborate the latter approach, let me first turn to the study by Yates, Orlikowski, and their team. Basing their analysis on the genre theory of Miller (1984) and Bazerman (1995), Yates and Orlikowski (1994) combine it with the structuration theory of Anthony Giddens. Following his idea whereby the "duality of structures" describes social actions that constitute structures that, again, affect these actions, Yates and Orlikowski consider genres as structures resulting from actions. Genres are a socially recognized type of communicative action that yields and exhibits a distinctive and useful organizing structure that serves again to guide actions. Genres are not dependent on the actors' motives but are to be defined by the content, the participants, the form, the time, and the place of actions by which they are produced.

Drawing on ethnographic studies of the use of powerpoint in different organizations, these categories of genre analysis are applied by Yates and Orlikowski to powerpoint presentations with respect to several dimensions. To name the most important dimensions, genres, first, are defined by a concise content, and by a certain order of introduction, body, and conclusion. Second, they involve certain kinds of participants, such as colleagues inside an organizational unit or across organizational units, or clients to whom presentations are made. Third, they may take different forms, for example, the "pitch preez," in which a company presents its services to potential clients. In their empirical study of the use of powerpoint in business organizations, Yates and Orlikowski found that powerpoint as a genre is used in different places and supports different purposes. As part of their project, Brooks (2004) studied a large systems engineering firm in which powerpoint presentations formed part of either "technical talks," "get acquainted talks," pitches, or "project and program reviews."

Yates and Orlikowski stress the equivocality of "powerpoint" in that they not only consider powerpoint as events but as documents. Yet, instead of the dual distinction proposed here, they distinguish the presentation as event (the "original") from a range of what they call "corollary genres", that is, "genres that are enacted alongside the original, and that ultimately may evolve into separate genres" (Yates and Orlikowski 2008: 73). In the same way that, for example, the letter has evolved in some organizational environments into the organizational "memo,"[16] powerpoint presentations are also transformed into Web-based slide shows, printed "decks," distributed in person or by mail, or data files in various formats, such as "pdf" or "ppt," which can be attached to e-mails. Being defined as a "corollary genre," the presentation as (digital) document differs from the presentation as an event. As part of an event, these documents become part of a social context in which not only an audience is "co-present in the same physical space to the presenter" (Yates and Orlikowski 2008: 75); in addition, the presentation as an event is defined by the copresence of the digital document as part of this situation. Both corollary genres and events, are, however, subject to change. Thus, as Yates and Orlikowski observe, "older" genres of organizational communication are substituted by these power-point "corallory genres": instead of a written report, a powerpoint deck is produced; instead of a briefing text, a set of presentation slides is sent; instead of a plan, a presentation is produced; and even a "deck" or stack of paper printouts of slides is often treated as the final deliverable document to clients in many business organizations.

The distinction between the presentation as an event and its "corollary genres" is also treated by Lobin (2009), who underlines that the presentation is prepared as a projected action by an actor or a set of cooperating actors and then set on stage, while the document produced is subject to a "publication process" (Lobin 2009: 186). In the publication process, digital documents, printouts, or files that can be distributed like any media are produced. In fact, the digital document is not necessarily bound to a certain materiality or medium: it can be, for example, shown on a screen, printed out on paper, or projected onto a wall. It is a visualized sign encoded into an information processing system. As varied as the document may be, it is characterized by a medium that fixes the signs, be it in print on paper or electronically in the computer and on the screen.

Despite the fact that these studies contribute to our knowledge of powerpoint presentations, their deficiency lies in that they typically focus on the structures of signs encoded into documents. In fact, one of the most fruitful applications of Yates and Orlikowski's "genre theory" consists in the attempts, mostly by information scientists, to transform the structure of the presentation as an "event" into a technical design (cf. Antunes, Costa, and Pino 2006). This transformation means that the event itself is considered as a product that can be made available to users as a "social medium." As much as such a transformation contributes to the creation of "social media," the transformation of, for example, a life presentation into a video conference presentation by means of special meeting software follows patterns that are typically different from the event on which they draw. Although the social media are a good example of the role of informatization and knowledge exchange in contemporary society, in this book I want to focus on the presentation as event, which certainly entails the presentation as document. Since the technological mediation of communication by information systems is already a feature of powerpoint presentations, their specificity can, I argue, only be identified if one appreciates their communicative character.

By recognizing the genre features of powerpoint presentations identified by Yates and Orlikowski, my own analysis tries to draw on the notion of communicative genre. As we shall see, the notion of communicative genre gives a richer impression of what the genre is about. It also allows the integration into the analysis of the most varied aspects of powerpoint – from linguistic to visual, organizational, and technological (particularly the ones presented in Schnettler and Knoblauch 2007). Finally, the notion of communicative genre allows the vast gap to be bridged between studies on the most detailed forms of communicative action constituting powerpoint presentations, on the one hand, and the general cultural significance and societal effects of this communicative genre, on the other hand. Because of the foundational importance of the notion of communicative genre and its onvious differences from the notion of genre used by other researchers, it is important to define it clearly and to delineate the way it contributes to the structure of the subsequent empirical argument.

# 3 Communicative Action, Culture, and the Analysis of Communicative Genres

As Yates and Orlikowski (1992) have demonstrated, the notion of genre is advantageous when analyzing powerpoint presentations, as it allows the presentation to be addressed as both document as well as event. Furthermore, it takes into consideration that presentation as a structure is built on, and constituted by, social actions, and it acknowledges the ways in which they contribute to the organizations in which they are performed. As mentioned, however, it seems to me that the powerpoint presentation is better and more specifically addressed as a "communicative genre," rather than a "genre," and there are three decisive reasons for this preference. First, whereas the notion of "genre" is often used to refer to the product of social actions, "communicative genres," additionally, stress the temporality, spatiality, and corporeality of the actions performed. Thus, they refer to the "text," that is, a document, as well as to the actions in the situation in which the document is being used, produced, transformed, and interpreted. On these grounds, they draw on data that represent these features, such as visual and audiovisual records of the actions. Second, while there are huge differences with respect to the analysis of genres ranging from very detailed linguistic and visual analysis of slides (Bazerman 1995) to the ethnographic description of organizations (Brooks 2004), the refined methodology of analyzing communicative genres allows the integration of various different data and data sorts into one overarching concept. Third, whereas this notion of genre builds on Giddens's (1984) view of them as "structures" resulting from "social actions,"[1] the notion of communicative genre addresses the specific *communicative aspects* of action defining genres, such as the visual quality of the slides, the bodily behavior of presenters, or the spatial structure of meetings. Obviously, these aspects are often ignored in analyses focusing on "social action." Powerpoint presentations are not just social action plus a presentation format (which can be turned into a program); rather, communication bestows a communicative form on action. It is in and by this form that meaning is produced. As such it is a certain form of communicative action that is characteristic of powerpoint presentations. Because the visual slides, the use of technology, and the interaction between presenter and audience are essential to the powerpoint presentation as document and as event, it is more adequately addressed as a communicative genre.

The notion of communicative genre that was proposed by Luckmann in 1985 and further developed by Günthner and Knoblauch (1995) is very tightly linked to the notion of communicative action. For those interested in the theoretical question of how action, technology, objects, and the body are intertwined, it is certainly necessary to make a short theoretical detour.[2]

## 1. Communicative Actions and Genres

Although the notion of communicative action was coined by Habermas, I want to make use of it in a way that accounts for that definition's shortcomings. As is well known, Habermas (1981) identified three ideal-types of social action. Nonsocial actions orienting to changes in the (common) world are "instrumental" or "teleological" actions. Social action, on the other hand, is oriented to someone else. This orientation is expressed in the form of a sign, so that social action can be coordinated by the use of signs. Language as a system of signs contributes in a particularly important way to social action since it implies three different kinds of validity (or truth) claims. In this sense, communicative action means that actors are oriented to other actors (social claim on norms), attempting to refer to something (objective claim on propositions) and to express themselves (subjective claim on truthfulness). In communicative action, all these claims are made simultaneously, even if one or the other may prevail. If a communicative action is challenged, actors are supposed to give reasons for their claims in such a way that, ideally, the various claims are met. There is a third type of action if actors use language but pursue instrumental goals, which Habermas calls "strategic action." When acting strategically, we communicate without trying to arrive at a common understanding but only to pursue our egoistic goal. Whereas strategic action is only a mixed type, Habermas's distinction between instrumental and communicative action is the basis for his infamous "doctrine of the two empires": the life world, on the one hand, constituted by communicative action, and the social system, constituted by instrumental and strategic action.

Although Habermas was to recognize the relevance of communicative action, his concept suffers from two major shortcomings. First, he considers language to be the major feature of communicative action – and the one that is most characteristic of it. From the philosophy of language and the logocentric tradition of philosophy in general, he inherited the method of looking at speech as if it were only reading written text so that his notion of communicative action suffers not only from a language bias but also from a (almost Protestant) text-centeredness. For Habermas, it is basically language that defines by its form and structure what claim is made. Thus language entails the "power of the better argument" and, ultimately, communicative rationality. However, as a result of this emphasis, Habermas neglects not only the bodily forms of communication other than voice and alphabetic texts, but also visualized forms of written codes, such as diagrams, charts, or pictures (e.g., in the case of legal or scientific evidence). Second, his notion of communicative action draws an artificial distinction between social and communicative actions and teleological or instrumental actions. The problems of this distinction become particularly pertinent in the distinction between the "socio-cultural life world," constituted by communicative action and guided by "communicative rationality," and the "system," constituted by strategic and teleological action, which is guided by instrumental rationality. As plausible as the analytical distinction between the action types may be, it leads to a strange view of the world as separated into two realms.

These shortcomings, I want to argue, are overcome if we do not reduce the notion of communicative action to language or to signs at all but extend it to any objectivation, a notion adapted from Berger and Luckmann (1966). For even if we reduce communicative action to language, one cannot ignore the fact stressed by Saussure that any meaning (*signifié*) requires a material carrier (*significant*), be it a letter written by hand, a sound spoken by mouth, or a technical device or a visual representation on a computer screen. Since any communicative action implies, presupposes, and depends upon the production of this material carrier, it must also always be an instrumental action, or, as Schutz and Luckmann (1994) call it, a kind of "work."

Objectivations certainly must not be restricted to linguistic signs. Icons, tattoos, tastes (such as the taste for wine or certain food), or tactile patterns (as, for example, forms of communication with and between the deaf-blind) can also be considered objectifications and can even be codified into sign-systems or related to linguistic systematizations. It would, however, be misleading to determine their meaning within systems or structures only, as even the use of language can be shown to be dependent on its performance in action (Hymes 1974). Thus as much as objectivations are characterized by their material character (*significant*), their meaning is not built with respect to the structure but results from their use in actions.

The notion of objectivation covers this aspect, too. It refers to objects "produced" by actions as well as to the "production" of objectivations or the process of objectivation and, thus, links structure and process. This link is not established mysteriously; the major reason for the objectivity of communicative action lies in the fact that it is performed by the body. Be it through the articulation of a sound, the writing of a letter, the pressing of a button, or even a glimpse, it is the body that links any action to the world. It is because of the embodied character of communicative action that instrumentality is always part and parcel of communicative action – be it in speaking or in e-mail communication. As a consequence, the analysis of instrumentality of action necessarily ignores other aspects of communicative action. As embodied, communicative action, therefore, it is always an action performed in time, which is to say that actions cannot be reduced to "choices of meaning" – as rational or irrational as they may be.

Acts of work-producing objectivations depend on the body, and therefore the body plays a decisive role for communicative action. It is by means of the body that meaning can become "socially visible." Bodies allow the experience of what I do not only by myself but also by coactors whose communicative action, again, can be experienced by me. The temporality of bodily working and its experience (and interpretation) are well covered by the notion of performance (Baumann and Briggs 1990).

The fact that the body (and the objectivations affected by it) can be experienced by me and others (and by me as others) results from the process of intersubjectivity: that is, I see you seeing me or it (cf. Schutz 1974). The body, thence, is the gateway for what Schutz and Luckmann (1989) call "common environment," that is, what we take to be accessible to me and to others. There is no doubt that notions as to what can be perceived by me and by others vary massively according to particular worldviews, so that some people may encounter dead ancestors, angels, or the Holy Spirits whereas others might reduce the world to what is positively to be described, for example, by "protocol statements." The assumptions made by the worldview are included in the "meaning" of action, and it is because of their decisive relevance that we cannot reduce communicative action to overt "behavior." Only inasmuch as the meaning is transmitted socially (again by communicative action) is it referred to by the notion of "knowledge." Knowledge also includes the question, Who is to be considered as subject experiencing the environment "like me"?

When referring to the performance of the body, one should remind the adult reader of the intricate processes by which we learn to "use" our body. Whether it be writing using the alphabet, speaking a language, or even walking upright, all this "behavior" needs to be learned over very long time phases. Learning to do certain things is certainly a good example of what we call action (be it induced by others, i.e., teachers, or induced by one's own "will"). The notion of action refers to the process in which we reflexively turn to "do something" (even if both what we want and the will to realize it are dependent on knowledge, power, or institutionalized discipline). The example of bodily conduct (e.g., gestures) also indicates that actions need not remain subject to our reflections. They can become part of a "habitus," an embodied knowledge that is realized in "practice."

As the performance of powerpoint is also guided by embodied knowledge, habitualized in other forms of interaction, it is important to mention that "practice" does not refer to "unconscious" action. Rather, it is based on habitualized activities of embodied consciousness that have been analyzed phenomenologically in some detail in terms of typification, sedimentation, routinization, and habitualization: When speaking, pointing, or writing on a computer keyboard, for example, we dispose of a huge range of such habitualized actions, which – and this is the point – need not be reflected upon further. Since we know well that the slightest problem may cast a doubt on these habits and can make us reflect, rethink the actions, or even reconstruct their (right) course, it seems utterly misleading to refer to these habits as "unconscious," and infinitely preferable to refer to them as habitualized. Because of the importance of such habitualized processes, it would appear useful to refer only to these habitualized aspects of communicative action as "practices" or, to be more specific, "communicative practices."

As communicative action, habitualization is, however, not only a subjective process. Insofar as it involves the body as a primary medium of sociality, the body provides the basic forms of communication. Note that this bodily communication is always two-sided and reflexive, for the body is an object in the common environment allowing for objectivations in various modalities (visual, acoustic, etc.) while experiencing the common environment as well as the body's own objectivations in various sensational forms, be they visual, acoustic, olfactory, or others.

As a form of social action, communicative action implies other bodies. Therefore, one of the major tasks of communicative action consists in the coordination of bodily performances: the sequential structure of conversational interaction is one example of the coordination of bodily conduct, that is, oral speech, which has been intensively studied through conversation analysis (Sacks, Schegloff, and Jefferson 1974). As the study of the interaction order in the tradition of Goffman (1981a) has made clear, other forms of bodily interaction also involve intricate forms of bodily coordination, as for example, pedestrians crossing an inner city road.

It is not only bodies that are coordinated. Communicative action also serves to synchronize the action's motives. One example is the inversion of the "in-order-to motive" into a "because motive," as analyzed by Schutz (1962): the question asked by someone "in order to" get an answer by the other is switched and becomes the reason for the other to answer "because" he or she has been asked. One can note here that the synchronization does not mean that actors have the same motives (or that they do have them reflexively): the person playing poker may only pretend to have good reasons to raise the ante. Both the coordination and synchronization of communicative action rely, of course, on certain objectivations. These need not be signs following the rules fixed by syntactic and semantic structures. As Katz (1999), for example, demonstrates, cars and their movements when driven by people may be acting communicatively: how someone passes another car may not only arouse emotions but also cause someone else sequentially to make a move against the overtaker. (Emotions, here, result from the difference between the meaning of driving in the sequential order and the meaning of the various sequences to the actors performing them.)

The fact that drivers conceive of their cars very often in terms of their own body image (and apply this conception when moving the car) indicates that communicative actions not only imply the construction of the meaning of objects. As communicative actions affect the common environment, they also contribute to the construction of reality inasmuch as they quite literally produce objectivations, be they momentary or lasting. Since all objectivations serve to coordinate and synchronize actors, communicative actions tend to harmonize both conduct and motives. The act of pointing, as it occurs in powerpoint presentations, will be an important example of this.

In order to highlight the objectivated character of social action, one is reminded of Weber's argument that nonbehavior may become socially relevant, too (Weber 1980). In fact, the one who does not answer my question does indeed act – in this case impolitely. If one, however, takes a close look at the examples of "pure" action, one realizes that this "nonbehavior" is, in fact, always part of a more or less institutionalized pattern of communicative interaction: one acts who does not respond to a prior question, opening the institutionalized expectation of a question-answer sequence (Goffman 1981a); also the policeman acts who does not intervene in a crime (given the institutionalized duties of his role), and the same applies to the person who does not take steps to rescue a drowning person shouting for help (given an institutionalized ethics of solidarity or charity).

Actors tend to develop certain expectations as to when or how they need to act at a certain point in time. Therefore, communicative actions are obviously subject to institutionalization. Since communicative actions include objectivations, this means that institutions exhibit certain forms with respect to both objects as well as objectivations, that is, communicative forms, patterns, and genres. Much has been said about the communicative meaning of cultural objects, signs, performative patterns, forms of talk, and communicative genres. Whatever their meaning may be, the notion of communicative action underlines that it is essentially dependent on the embodied performance of action in space and time. It is in this sense that they can be considered as institutionalizations of communicative actions. This not only holds for objects and signs but also for technologies. Technologies can be seen as institutionalized inasmuch as they stabilize certain steps of action with relation to objects and bestow on them a certain expected form (Rammert 2006), ranging from the use of a hammer (which bestows the "sense" on the hammer), to complex sociotechnical systems (as, for example, in airplanes) in which actors need to read the signs (designed by the system's engineers) in order to seize on the next action. Because technologies are objectivations imparted in actions, communicative actions can be mediated: they can be encoded in sign systems (such as the alphabet), represented by "media" or technologies of objectivations (paper, chalk, blackboard, television screen), and performed by technologies of transmission (telephone, television networks, Internet).

Although these objects, signs, and technologies already imply institutions, Berger and Luckmann (1966) have hinted at an additional aspect of institutions. On the basis of intersubjectivity and communicative action, certain typical forms of objectivation are established wherever similar problems of coordination and synchronization occur. The process of institutionalization is linked to a process in which sequences of action are habitualized. In phenomenological terms one would say that polythetic action steps, each of which had been very conscious and reflexive originally, are fused into a monothetic grasp so that we can execute these actions "automatically." (This occurs most often if forms of actions are handed over to third parties, such as apprentices, pupils, or children and become what Weber calls "traditional action.") Also communicative actions are performed routinely in such a way that actors do not need to think about the ways they act. The ritual of greeting can be seen as a well-known example of how routinely executed sequences of action can be projected, coordinated, and synchronized en bloc. Another example would be cooperation at work (Heath, Luff, and Knoblauch 2000) including technologies. One could call this kind of habitualization "black boxing," as Latour (2008) suggests, yet this notion not only overlooks the fact that any "black box" is an objectivation that carries meaning in action; it also ignores, as Pinch and Bijker (1987), for example, demonstrate, that even simple technologies such as bicycles are subject to massive interpretation that exceeds whatever may be "instrumental."

Communicative genres are institutions of communicative action. That is to say that they are patterns of action that are typically expected and performed in certain situations. While the fact that they are typically expected allows actors and observers to identify them by their recurrence (a feature we can exploit methodologically), their relevance for certain situations indicates that they are seen to solve certain problems of communicative action. Once established, such solutions can be "handed over" to other actors who are facing the same problems (or at least believe they are). As communicative actions are objectivations, these solutions are also objectivated. Mediated by the materiality and temporality of communicative actions, they take on certain forms depending on the kinds of bodily actions performed and objects used and formed. It is not these objectivations that we consider to be generic; rather, communicative genre refers to the forms in which these objectivations are produced, enacted, and interpreted.

Since institutionalization fuses actions and their meanings to more or less extended black boxes, communicative genres may become subject to all kinds of reinterpretations. Berger and Luckmann (1966) call it legitimation – a notion that was prominently taken up by neoinstitutionalism in a somewhat isolated manner (DiMaggio and Powell 1983). Legitimations are the ways in which institutions are rendered meaningful particularly to those who have not participated in their construction. They are not stable but continuously subject to a communicative process of canonization and negotiation and conflict. Following Keller (2003), one could refer to this process as a discourse. The discourse of PowerPoint sketched previously provides a good example of legitimations. For the question of whether the genre allows one to "transmit information" or whether it fails to do so is a discourse on powerpoint that tries to make sense of the genre to and within certain institutional spheres, such as business, education, or science. In a sense, the how-to books, to which we will turn later, can also be seen as legitimations. In this case, they make sense of the genre on the level of the individual actor. Although legitimations are, therefore, an issue for any study of communicative genres, the focus of this analysis is not on the discourse of powerpoint (or even "PowerPoint") and their stereotypes; instead, I focus on the very process that discourse refers to, that is, the powerpoint presentation as a communicative genre.

On the most basic level communicative genres, such as sayings, narratives, greetings, conversion stories, jokes, or tall stories, are forms of social action and interaction sequences produced by and oriented toward the actors (Günthner and Knoblauch 1995). Thus, powerpoint slides produced by presenters that are shown to an audience are expressions of actions. Communicative genres may vary significantly with respect to the degree to which they are fixed and formal. Some communicative genres are only vaguely structured, such as a small-talk conversation, an argument among adult members of a family, or teaching among friends (Knoblauch 1990; Luckmann and Keppler 1991). On the other hand, teaching in schools, an academic dissertation, disputation, a sermon, or even the "moral sermon" of a state president (Luckmann 2003) is a strictly organized communicative event. Whereas the former may only be routinized practices that are "tacit knowledge," the latter are fully developed institutions to which special knowledge, experts, and more or less elaborate symbolic legitimation are devoted. Powerpoint presentations obviously belong to the latter category.

Communicative genres may also vary with respect to the materiality of objectivations. Whereas some communicative genres are mainly based on bodily conduct and performance (e.g., boxing matches), others are characterized by sound (a dance), language (a poem), or visual representations (a painting, a powerpoint slide). Genres also vary with respect to the mediality and the kind of mediatization, the technology used, and the range of actors involved. Thus, a meeting by video differs significantly from a live meeting, which, again, exhibits a difference from a religious service. Finally, communicative genres also vary with respect to temporality. Speech genres may range from the performance of a proverb to an epos, visual genres from the contemplation of a photograph to an exhibition, and so forth. Given this huge array of variation, it is helpful to draw distinctions among three levels for analyzing communicative genre.

## 2. The Three Levels of Genre Analysis and Communication Culture

As institutions, genres are total social phenomena. In order to analyze communicative genres methodically and provide empirical evidence for them, it has proved useful to distinguish among three different levels for the analysis of communicative genres (Knoblauch and Luckmann 2004). In order to prevent misunderstanding, I should stress that the distinction among these three levels does not presuppose ontological features of communicative genres. That is to say, the communicative genres are not divided into three parts; instead, the levels represent different analytical perspectives on the kinds or types of communicative actions described as genres. Their relevance lies not in their ontology but in their usefulness in identifying recurrences of aspects of communication and typicality of action. The distinction into three levels follows two basic principles: on the one hand, they are determined by the theory of communicative action in general, which divides action, interaction, and institution; on the other hand, they are guided by the "materiality" of communication and the ways and means by which we produce and use empirical data, that is, "data sorts." Thus, while action products or how-to books are used to infer the intentions of actors giving presentations, audiovisual recordings are the kind of data taken to represent the situative communicative interaction. In order to analyze the situations and their context, I draw on interviews and statistical data.[3] Nevertheless, one should be aware that these distinctions are not intrinsic to the phenomena under study and are often overruled by the intimate cohesion of the features divided analytically.

The major reason for applying these three levels to the data is that they provide an order for the analysis with respect to both (a) the empirical data as well as (b) the theoretical framework. This becomes quite clear in the course of the analysis of powerpoint, as the order of the subsequent chapters is structured according to the three levels: following this methodological sketch, I shall first analyze the "internal level," before I turn to the intermediate, and, finally, to the external level of communicative genre of powerpoint presentations. Therefore, it may be helpful to delineate briefly the features of, and differences among, these three levels.

The *internal level* of the analysis of communicative genres relates to the products of communicative actions as (and as if) they were objectivated by the actors. In a similar way to nonstructuralist rhetoric, literary criticism, or media studies, it refers to those aspects of genres as products of actions that can be analyzed either by looking at the (typical) intentions of actors producing them or by analyzing the objects they intentionally produce in their actions, such as the words they speak, the texts they write, or the diagrams they draw. For this reason, the analysis on this level follows the methods of conventional "genre" analysis as used in theology, literary criticism, rhetoric, film studies, or, as in the case of the powerpoint slides analyzed later, information design and linguistics. Considering genres as forms of communicative action, there is a specific focus on knowledge that guides actors, as, for example, the categories, designations, and names for communicative forms ("fairy tales," "riddles," "jokes," "western movies," or, in certain milieus, "conversation stories"). These categories are of even more importance if they are part of ethnotheories produced by practitioners in order to teach, orient, and guide actors. With respect to powerpoint, for example, we find a huge array of advice and consultancy, ranging from videos to books and seminars. For this study, advice books have been considered in order to reconstruct the typical action orientation ascribed to, and presupposed in, actors who are preparing powerpoint presentations.

The internal level of genre analysis also includes the structure of the products. With respect to powerpoint, the products are mainly the texts and the slides produced. As with other written texts, such as love letters, religious psalms, or technical instructions, slides for powerpoint presentations also often take on certain patterns, which can be analyzed in terms of, for example, visual codes, linguistic registers, speech styles, or rhetorical figures. In complex communicative genres, such as sermons, lectures, or television shows, "minor forms" are entailed, such as idioms, formulas, proverbs. Moreover, their content can be characterized as being guided by certain "motifs" ("happy family," "winter landscape," "flying coach"), "figures" (e.g., witches, detectives, cowboys), topoi ("road movie," "learning organization," "subsistence") and "macrostructures" (narrative, argumentative structures, beginning, middle, ending). To give an example, in his analysis of oral conversion stories, Ulmer (1988) showed that they take on a similar form in many different settings. Their specific feature consists of a certain temporal structure of the events narrated: the biographical narrative of the conversation story is divided into a preconversion phase, presented in an increasingly negative way; a paralinguistically prominent conversion experience; and a postconversion phase presented in positive terms. Features of other communication genres include, in the case of oral texts, the lexicon, but also prosody, voice quality, or linguistic variety. The analytical repertoire is even more extended if we include visual and audiovisual forms, such as photographs, films, and television. Thus, Keppler (1985) has shown how television news is constricted by a specific mixture of verbal and pictorial elements, including "on" and "off" text, color, and highlighting, and how these elements are used to constitute media formats, such as comments, or media figures, such as "eyewitnesses" or "experts." Taken together and considering their specific form of reception (watching TV, reading, walking through a museum) and production, these forms and their reception constitute particular "media genres," such as the photographic portrait, the news, the criminal story, or the western (again with their subgenres) (Crane 1992).

Whereas analysis on the internal level focuses on social actions and their objectivations, on the *intermediate level of analysis* we look at interaction in situ and objectivations *in actu*, that is, the performance of communicative actions in social situations.[4] While the notion of communication stressed the sociality, temporality, and materiality of action, the additional notion of performance helps to underline that communication cannot be reduced to, for example, an abstract "selection of information" (cf. Luhmann 1984) but is performed, that is, realized and enacted by a body in time and space.[5] With respect to the analysis of powerpoint, the distinction between the internal and intermediate levels turns out to be of the utmost importance since it parallels the distinction between the presentation as digital document and the presentation as event. In a sense, the intermediate level corresponds to what Goffman (1981b) calls the "interaction order," for it is here that we account for social interaction: the performance of actions is not only oriented to and designed for someone else, as we assume on the internal level; we also look for the intersubjective coordination and synchronization of actions, that is, for interaction in social situations of mutual perception. Interactive coordination is fixed particularly in "rituals" (Goffman 1967) and "forms," (Goffman 1981a) such as openings, tag questions, and closings (Goffman 1981a; Jefferson 1973; Sacks, Schegloff, and Jefferson 1974; Schegloff 1968). In fact, the systematics of turn taking in conversation (Sacks, Schegloff, and Jefferson 1974) provides an impressive example of a reflexive order created in the performance of communicative action. Interactions also include rituals, such as the opening of a conversation or the initiation of its closure. The closing of powerpoint presentations by a special slide is such a ritual element as to deserve special attention in the analysis that follows.[6]

As mentioned, the notion of performance underlines the role of the body in communication. It is because of the body that actions become part of social life, and it is also the body that allows the experience and perception of the social world via the senses. It is, finally, also by way of the embodied nature of communicative action that objects, media, and technologies become, so to say, necessarily and logically part of the social world. This observation is not only of theoretical importance but also empirically conspicuous. As we shall see, the presenter's body in particular constitutes an important communication device. The body not only synchronizes slides and speech, it also locates "the presentation as document," including technology and objects, in a spatial setting of social actors. Thus, the presenter's body functions as a pivot connecting the major elements of this genre by interacting with the audience and with the technology (such as computers, projectors, or paper manuscripts). The presenter's body; slides, that is, the visual image projected by the technology; and audience constitute the basic triangular structure that, I claim, is constitutive of the powerpoint presentation as a genre.

On this level, analysis focuses on situated interaction, such as, for example, the ongoing speech and bodily performance of a presenter, using powerpoint technology in front of a live audience. In the next step, I want to include other objects, such as the materialities and forms constituting the setting of the presentation. At this point, studies and methods in the field of the "ethnography of communication" or "ethnography of speaking" founded by Hymes (1974) are of particular interest.[7] Although the ethnography of speaking has mostly focused on language and speech in social situations, that is, "speech events," it provides a useful tool for the analysis of the context of communicative action, such as "setting," "participants," "goals," and "purposes" (1974). Extending the notion of speech events to communication, the category "event" proves useful for the analysis of the shop conference, the medical consultation, or the sales show (Heath 1986; Knoblauch 1987; Ten Have 1989). It also figures importantly in the analysis of communicative genres and particularly of powerpoint presentations.

The notion of "event" refers to the situated aspects of communicative genres characterized, first, by a certain focus of attention, by a certain material form and setting, a temporal structure, and some kind of social organization transcending situational interaction. Thus, the powerpoint presentation as a genre can be part of different kinds of events, like a church service, a departmental meeting, or a conference. The "meeting" is the most common kind of event featuring powerpoint presentations. According to Schwartzman (1989: 7), meetings involve "three or more people who agree to assemble for a purpose ostensibly related to the functioning of an organization or group." As a special form of event, meetings are situations of communication in which certain kinds of actions are performed: "It is in these forms, and only in these forms, that individuals are able to transact, negotiate, strategize, and attempt to realize their specific aims" (Schwartzman 1989: 37).

Though they have a situative character, meetings constitute one important link to the *external level of genre analysis*. As Schwartzman (1989: 38) observes, the meeting, for example, exhibits a "loose connection between action and organizational system." In being prepared, organized, and subject to reports, reconstruction, and postprocessing, meetings, as events in general, transcend the situation and relate to or mediate what is often considered as "social structure." This external level is of some importance for powerpoint presentations, for it is due to this external level that they figure as part of a quite different range of meetings, such as committee meetings, board meetings, and staff meetings. Also supported by the mediatization of technologies, powerpoint presentations are connected to other situations in formal organization or communication networks: as "files" in information management systems, as "documents" to be read, as "products" of work, and so on. By the ways in which they recruit the audience, by the kinds of actions performed or the tasks pursued, and by the forms of presentations given, they also contribute to the very structures they seem to presuppose, that is, formal organizations and communicative networks. This double character is what one, drawing on a notion by Goffman, can call the institutional reflexivity of communicative genre. They are related to social structures, which they contextualize in situations. This institutional reflexivity of communicative genres is particularly important in the case of powerpoint presentations. Albeit organizations and organized communication are a necessary condition for this genre, providing objects, technologies, audiences, and presenters, they also serve as a context of temporally and spatially neighboring situations and allow contextualization of the presentation in a specific situation. As a communicative genre, powerpoint presentations bestow a certain form on what is happening in the situations, organizations, and communication networks.

The external level hints at the observation that communicative genres are not just situational performances; their institutional character becomes observable already through the sheer recurrence of the generic forms. It is also observable if one follows the traces of the genre in space, in time, and in terms of people, that is, the ways by which they transcend the situation and are, reflexively, contextualized in the situation. As the traces transcending the situation are communicative (signs, objects, and technologies), they form part of the communicative culture of society. Society is typically analyzed in a way that strips it of its communicative constitution so that it appears as a mere grid, a social structure. Action is considered as following norms or conveying meanings (ignoring the process in which meaning is objectivated and exchanged), organizations as decision apparatuses (without looking at the processes that produce these decisions in time). In this sense, powerpoint presentations can be said to be part of, relate to, and result in the "social structure," such as organizations, functional subsystems, or sociotechnical infrastructures. That is to say, some genres, such as the church service, the scientific lecture, or the sales pitch, are "located" in and simultaneously produced by certain organizations, social milieus, or sociotechnical systems (Rammert 2006; Pinch 2008). The same holds for the love letter, the telegram, the homepage, the chat or twitter, which are dependent on quite demanding institutional and sociotechnical arrangements.

Therefore, the analysis of communicative genres looks at how, where, and when communicative actions take on certain forms, the description of the forms indicating the social problems they serve to solve. The distinctions among these three levels help to identify these forms and to focus on the kind of form preferred. In some cases, such as church services, communicative genres may include a huge variety of forms, for instance, prayers or sermons, rituals, a general order, and often even a certain social network providing the milieu for the recruitment of participants. In other cases communicative genres can be built on only a few aspects routinely objectivated in the same form, as in the case of the e-mail exchanged in a huge information network or the letter based on an institutionalized postal infrastructure.

In general, communicative genres are the more or less fixed forms coordinating and synchronizing actions. As such, they constitute the stable core of the communication culture. Of course, the communication culture also includes the fluid negotiations of meanings, symbols, and values, as Keyton (2005) argues. Communicative genres are, however, the "institutions" within this culture of communication.

Communicative genres are, obviously, total social phenomena that are constructed by communicative action, their routinized practices, and objectivations in settings that already impart preconstructed objects, technologies, and social structures. As with any analysis, genre analysis also in a way "dissects" the total social phenomena at various levels. Such "analytical" dissection of social phenomena has been criticized for failing to grasp hermeneutically the holistic meaning to actors. Therefore, I should make it very clear that the hermeneutical goal of understanding the social phenomena (Soeffner 1997) is a basic procedure for the treatment of all data used in this study. The reason for the distinctions among the three levels of genre lies in the very fact that any kind of analysis differs with and depends (mutually) on the kind of data used. I refer to these differences as data sorts (Knoblauch and Tuma 2011). Data sorts designate the differences in the ways data are produced in action (and habitualized practice), how they are processed, and how they are interpreted (made understandable) and analyzed (in terms of the research question). These differences demand different forms of evidence and different kinds of warrant. Particularly on the basis of the huge amount of very diverse data sorts available to this project, it is essential to emphasize that, for example, the comparative analysis of slides as products created by actors needs to be different from the comparative analysis of slides as part of the performance of powerpoint presentation. While what I shall call the synchronization of text and slides, for example, is based on visual representation of slides and the transcribed text used, the interaction between presenters using slides and audience depends on video recordings and video analysis. To give a final example, while the more than two hundred presentations as events recorded on video can be compared regarding their qualitative similarities and differences, the number of meetings, projectors or presentation programs sold needs to be interpreted as an indication of the external level, such as organizational, technological, and sociostructural aspects of the genre.

The analysis of the data on various levels that accounts for different data sorts allows, on the one hand, systematic empirical evidence to be provided for my findings and arguments. This empirical evidence seems particularly important in the face of the harsh debate surrounding PowerPoint and the lack of relevant empirical jusifications. The integration of the empirical analysis into the holistic notion of communicative genre, on the other hand, provides the foundation for theoretical generalizations of these empirical findings. As the general theoretical framework has already been introduced, the focus now turns to the empirical evidence, which is presented step by step and level by level. The Conclusion will then summarize the findings at each level and integrate them into the general theoretical framework, which has been selected as a result of the empirical analysis. The levels of analysis, the major data sorts as well as the analytical categories and findings are summarized in Diagram 1.

Diagram 1: *Levels of Genre Analysis, Data Sort, and Analytical Categories*

| Level of analysis of communicative genre | Data sort used to analyze | Analytical category (examples) | Analytical finding (elaborated below) |
|---|---|---|---|
| **Internal level** | Slides, Manuscript, Speech (rhetorical) | Action Strategy Speech style Macrostructure | Text-visual code Presentation styles Paralleling Ratification Synchronization Duplication |
| **Intermediate/ situative level** | Audiovisual recordings (Video Analysis) | Turn Sequences Performance Participation framework Body formation | coordination orchestration of slides "creative pointing" Triadic Structure Asymmetric production format "knowledge" |
| **External level** | Photographs, ethnographic observation, interviews, statistical data | Setting Spatial order Institutional Spheres | Structural Diffusion Standardization Institutionalization |

# 4    The Internal Level: Slides, Speech, and Synchronization

## 1. Rhetoric of Visual Presentation

If we look for ways to analyze powerpoint presentations as a form of communicative action, the first field to start with is rhetoric. In emphasizing the linguistic aspects of communication, rhetoric considers oratory as a form of social action by which the actor pursues a certain goal, that is, to entertain (*delectare*), to transmit knowledge (*docere*), or to incite an action (*movere*) with respect to an audience. Traditionally this goal is pursued by language, but the emphasis in classical rhetoric on language is overtaken by various recent rhetorical approaches. With respect to powerpoint, Kjeldsen (2006), for example, opts for "media rhetoracy," that is, a rhetorics aware of the technical potential of the media. Media rhetoracy "represents the ability to create and communicate" statements by using tools such as powerpoint (Kjeldsen 2006: 12). Also Engleberg and Daly (2005) consider "presentation speaking" as the most encompassing form of "public speaking," and Liebert (2005) suggests integrating powerpoint presentations into a "rhetorics of presentations". He admits, however, that the analysis of visual presentations in academic rhetoric is still in its infancy, and for this reason, we cannot refer to rhetorical studies of presentations. Instead, we find a huge number of practical guide books, how-to books, instructional texts on powerpoint presentations, as well as seminars and courses on the topic. These advice books cannot be considered as systematic empirical studies, yet they serve several purposes that are relevant for the analysis of powerpoint presentations as a communicative genre. Advice books regularly describe how presentations should be rather than how they really are. For this reason they cannot be considered descriptive data of the performance of presentations; yet, they represent normative orientations toward presentations and, thus, a kind of "ethnotheory" of the genre, that is, knowledge on the genre.

Second, in providing the actor with a normative view on how powerpoint presentations should be held, one can assume that their norms influence the actions of those readers who learn from these books (and the seminars guided by them). Since the advice is distributed widely by various media (including seminars), they represent typical knowledge and ethnotheories about powerpoint presentations. Third and most importantly, advice books usually also describe the preparation of presentations. Thus, they look not only at the "presentation as event," which is the focus of this study, but also at the actions performed before and after presentations.

Although I shall address this transsituative horizon of presentations as link to the external level, I should emphasize that the preparation and processing of presentations are topics in their own right. They could be studied by, for example, the participant observation of actions by which slides are designed at the computer as a workplace study (Heath, Luff, and Knoblauch 2000) or by the ethnographic reconstruction of the division of labor involved in producing, improving, and postprocessing powerpoint slides in organizations. Here I shall turn to another data sort, for in order to sketch the typical actors' orientation toward powerpoint, I can draw on two studies of how-to books, by Mackert and Degenhardt (2007) and by Lobin (2009).

How-to books on presentations (including powerpoint) constitute a distinct subgenre of rhetorical advice books. This subgenre treats powerpoint presentations like other rhetorical forms of speech and oratory. Powerpoint presentations are seen as a form of visually supported oratory by means of which an actor pursues strategic goals. Presentations, in this sense, are seen as projected, prepared, and performed by an individual who is the origin, the author, and the presenter of the presentation. The presentation is seen as an instrument, a medium, and a genre by means of which the actor pursues his or her goals, which are, as Engleberg and Daly (2005) specify, "informational" and "persuasive." This kind of orientation of action, which could, following Habermas, be called "strategical," becomes explicit in the academic translation by Knape of the practical goal. For Knape (2007: 53) the crucial question of the rhetoric of powerpoint is, "What are the felicity conditions of a form of communicative action oriented toward efficiency and success?"[1]

This perspective of strategic communicative action is shared by the more practical advice books. Howell and Bormann (1988: 10), for example, argue that presentations are mainly about motivation, and the presenter a "change agent" who either "maximizes options," "establishes directions," or "limits options to one." Thus by recommending the advantages of the object it has been arguing for, the "three triangle outline" suggests that any presentation terminates in a "call for action." The importance of the motivation to action is also supported by the producers of PowerPoint. As a representative of PowerPoint stresses in an interview, "If you're presenting to a group, then you're there to motivate them in the same manner. If you aren't, then get off the stage and just send a memo. Everyone will be happier." As in any rhetorical (and communicative) action, the goals are to affect the audience, expressed, for example, in the WIIFY-formula by the renowned presentation adviser Jerry Weissman: the goal of identifying "what's in it for you" should be the major consideration of any presenter.[2]

The rhetorical perspective on presentations emphasizes the fact that speech is planned and prepared in advance. In addition, it refers to certain linguistic forms or rhetorical forms of speech. As with most rhetorical forms, they are considered to be prepared before their performance, produced in advance as texts, memorized and possibly also rehearsed as talks. In order to highlight this preparatory feature of the event, Lobin suggests comparing presentations to the "mis-en-scène," or staging, or, as Fischer-Lichte calls it, "the process of planning, rehearsing and fixing strategies … according to which the materiality of a performance shall be realized."[3] As part of the staging, how-to books give strategic advice and suggest concrete action steps to be taken and communicative features of the genre to be applied. These criteria for the content follow classical rhetoric for public speeches, such as "Purpose, Audience, Credibility, Logistics, Content, Organization, Performance" (Engleberg and Daly 2005: 10 f.).

Since advice books present something like a praxeology of powerpoint presentations, it may be useful to consider the steps recommended by them in more detail. The communicative action of powerpoint presentations is subdivided into several different temporally consecutive steps. The presentation follows a temporal trajectory starting with a preparatory phase. According to the advice books, the preparatory phase demands the analysis of the situation by the presenter-to-be. The presenter-to-be should start with the definition of his or her goal, search for arguments, determine the structure, look for apt verbal and visual design, think about available technical means, and so on. He or she should consider social as well as temporal and spatial aspects (audience, room, time available, etc.) of his or her planned presentation. As part of this phase (and in accordance with the classical rhetorical *inventio*), the ideas for the speech are to be collected so that the presenter is able to formulate the goal and the topic of the presentation. At this point, advice books suggest making spatial and technical arrangements and taking care of the "subjective factor" (stage fright). As the *dispositio* in classical rhetoric, these ideas should, in the second step, be put in an order so that the structure of the presentation may be determined. (Often they follow the Aristotelian order of "introduction"; "main part," including various arguments; and "conclusion.") The rhetorical *memoria* can be covered by a printout of the presentation, a powerpoint storyboard, or a deck.

The performance of the presentation is also an issue covered by advice books (corresponding to the classical rhetorical *actio*). With respect to performance, the speaker should consider her or his decorum and appearance and acknowledge her or his rhetorical virtues (clarity, objectivity, comprehensibility, etc.). Particular stress is laid on what often is called "nonverbal" actions and their "harmony" with the verbal actions, the audience, the visualizations, and the technology. They also address other aspects of presentations, such as "forms of audience address" concerning the ways of coping with questions from the audience and with discussions. The last phase refers to those actions by which the presentation is assessed (i.e., feedback questionnaires) or is processed as data files or transformed into data banks.

The decisive difference between the presentation and other forms of rhetorical oratory is mostly seen in the use of visual devices and the use of certain technologies. Advice books on powerpoint presentations account explicitly for the role of visual media and forms in various ways. Whereas this part is still marginal in older advice books, which stress the role of speech and text, more recent books increasingly acknowledge the importance of visual elements, and some advisers, advice books, or specialized Internet pages even prioritize visual elements.[4] By "visual elements" they refer to font, size, and colors of types; the ratio between text and visual elements; and the meaningful use of graphic elements, such as pictograms, charts, diagrams, tables of various kinds, organograms, icons, symbols, and combinations of these elements. Advice is also given concerning the question of how to design the individual slides. A specific feature of practical advice books is general rules of thumb, such as the rule of three, the rule of seven, or "seven deadly sins of overhead foils."[5] These elements are sometimes related to an explicit notion of "visual rhetoric." In advice books, this notion is hardly ever explained but mostly legitimated by commonplaces, such as a Chinese proverb ("A picture tells more than a thousand words") that is quoted in almost every second advice book analyzed by Mackert and Degenhardt (2007). By means of these visual elements, presentations are labeled as "designs for your ideas," that is, as "information" in Tufte's sense. As visual displays they are also considered to be persuasive since they are part of an actor's strategic action plan and conceived of in terms of "efficiency." The role of visuals is described quite variously as "supporting statements," "guiding attention," or "triggering" actions" visually.

## 2. Slides, Text, and Speech

As the literature on the linguistic patterns of rhetorical forms is vast and elaborate, it seems more important to turn to the visual aspects, which seem to constitute the *differentia specifica* of presentations. Slides are the principal result of preparatory actions of presentations and the most specific and enduring objectivation or "product" (as "document") of power-point presentations. Here they are of importance because they enter into and form part of powerpoint presentations. Although the empirical analysis will focus on powerpoint presentations as events, they always importantly include slides. Since there are no detailed workplace studies of how slides are created or how they are "read" and discussed in other contexts than presentations, outside presentations, I have to rely on the product itself, that is, the slides. It seems necessary, therefore, to have a closer look at the slides.

Before scrutinizing the slides themselves, it is necessary to emphasize that it is the slides that are taken to represent, for example, by the advice books, the new "visual" aspect of presentations. Powerpoint presentations are defined as computer supported visual presentations of digitalized documents. The notion of slides refers colloquially to these documents (sometimes also called "foils" or, as a series of slides, "decks"). "Slide" is, however, a somewhat misleading metaphor. As mentioned, the notion of a slide is clearly derived from the use of the 35-mm projector. Whereas these slides used to be tangible carriers consisting of material frames including the negative of the image to be projected, "slides" in powerpoint presentations take on a somewhat different quality. Although they are objectivated visually in the presentation, they are not linked to one specific material carrier or "medium." Slides can be watched on a computer screen, on printed paper, on canvas, on a television monitor, or elsewhere. Essentially they depend on some informational hardware (a computer, a USB stick, or a server) and software (Presenter, PowerPoint, etc.). To the actors, the metaphor of the slide is helpful because the slide is, from their point of view, not really palpable. It is fixed on data storage devices in bits and bytes that are not directly accessible to human experience. Since they only become accessible and represented by the digital document produced via information technologies, "information" in this sense is constitutive of and built into any presentation as event. It is in this sense that I refer to a presentation as a "document" (which is part of information technology). The link between slide and information society becomes even more salient if one takes into account that the visual aspects are regularly produced either by the presentation program, inserted by drawing on visual data on the Internet, or by transfer of data produced by other technologies that allow digital transmission (video and photo cameras as well as the respective software).

In accordance with current language use, I shall refer to slides as individually framed visual units depicted and to be perceived usually in a square format. The various carriers I shall refer to as "screens." If elements of one slide are projected or subdivided, so that they become visible one after another (i.e., if single items of a bullet list are sequentially animated), they are referred to as "builds" (Yates and Orlikowski 2008: 83). A series of slides will be called "presentations as documents," and their permanent representation on paper or similar material as "decks."

While slides are often studied without respect to the context of their use, I want to focus here on slides that have been part of presentations as event. In doing so, I draw on Pötzsch's (2007) study of 653 slides used in fifty-eight real presentations as events in diverse contexts, such as science and education, administration and business. Pötzsch's analysis serves (a) to provide a means of orientation regarding the empirical forms and types of slides used in the kind of presentations we are analyzing and, thereby, (b) to provide the ground for the analysis of the other modalities of communication, such as words, body formation, and situational contexts.

When analyzing powerpoint slides as documents, some might expect an attempt to reconstruct the "grammar of the visual" (Kress and Leeuwen 1996), focusing on visual design features. However, when looking at these slides, one immediately realizes that they are hardly ever visual but that written text constitutes an essential element of their design. Even if there are some types of slides that avoid words, the majority include text and words. In fact, the importance of words is quite clear, for the graphical display of words may even be said to be one of the core features attracting many users and actors. If one wants to identify the visual elements used on powerpoint slides, the distinction between text and nontext visual design is basic.[6] As varied as the visual and linguistic forms may be, Pötzsch demonstrates in his study that such slides exhibit a number of typical features, which are summarized in Diagram 2.[7]

Although PowerPoint has been designed as a graphic program including a lot of visual elements, the majority of the slides analyzed consist of text only. Following Pötzsch, we can distinguish four subtypes of these

| Text Slides | Text-picture Slides | Visual Slides | | | | |
|---|---|---|---|---|---|---|
| Lists & Bullets | Ornamental Text-pictures (Ornamental, Metaphorical) | Photographs and Films | | | | |
| Plain Text | Illustrative Text Picture (film) Combinations | Diagrammatic Elements | | | | |
| | Emblematic Illustrations / Representative Illustrations | Tables | Dia-grams | Organ igrams | Chrono-logies | Topo-graphies |
| | | Visual Text Combination | | | | |
| Graphically Designed Text | | Collages of Pictorial Elements Pictures / Videos / Films | | | | |

Diagram 2: Types of slides.

*textual slides.* The most important text format is constituted by *lists* and *bullet points.* Lists and bullet points refer to vertically and horizontally ordered sets of paragraphs, often indicated by the use of dashes, hyphens, squares, arrows, and similar graphical signs. In the sample collected, the bullet lists are by far the largest subtype (164 slides); they are also present in other text oriented slides (231 slides), as well as in most other types of slides. The units of lists and bullet points range from one word to fragments of sentences and long strings of sentences to lists of all these elements. As opposed to Tufte's (2003) finding that powerpoint slides typically exhibit too many hierarchical levels,[8] the slides in our data corpus had few, most often only one level of subordination. Also the infamous "rule of seven" mentioned earlier appears to be rarely applied.

A second type of text dominated slide type consists of *plain text* without bullet points. Because it is less commonly used (40 slides) than bullet point type slides, it also differs from them in that it is rarely combined with a slide title. Although it simply represents texts in different fonts, one must stress again that text always exhibits graphical elements: words are,

introduction & overview

Background: interdisciplinary research project
«coorporation and safety in socio-technical systems»

1. Video-analysis of practice

2. Practice of video-analysis

3. Videobased interviews

10th December 2004          Cornelius Schubert, TU Berlin                    1

Slide 1:  Ornamental slide.

for example, arranged in tabular order, or they may form a circle or a triangle. An even more complex graphical design characterizes the third type,
that is, bullet lists arranged in different spatial orders on the slide, that is,
in two parallel lists.

Since the software offers a range of such elements (e.g., for graphic
highlighting), the transition from text to *text-picture slides* is smooth.
Closest to text slides are those using visual elements as ornaments to the
texts. These visual elements are mostly derived from clipart, digital copies
of comics, photographs, and so on. Although this type is less frequent in the
corpus with some 100 slides, we should distinguish two subtypes here: one
type uses the graphic elements as an ornament decorating the texts but not
adding substantially to it, whereas the other type (represented in Slide 1)
adds at least some meaning through metaphorical visualization (beauty as
visualized by a flower).

In the first type, the graphic icons only resemble what is mentioned
in the text (for example, coins for "money"), whereas in the other ornamental type the topic is represented visually, as in this slide, where the
field ("video") is represented symbolically by the picture of a video cam-
era (which has been obtained by a graphic download from the Internet).
Yet, both these cases of "ornamental text-pictures" differ significantly from
an "illustrative text-picture combination," in which the visual part takes a
more "leading" role. Illustrative text-picture combinations are also used to
comment on or exemplify the text. Pötzsch (2007) suggests distinguishing

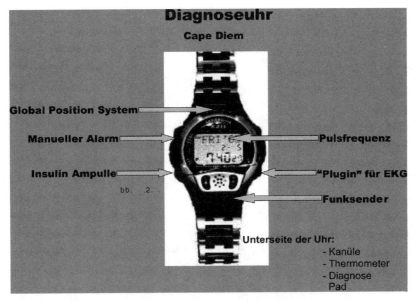

Slide 2: Representative illustrative type. Reproduced with permission from Bio-future presentation, Frau Prof. Frauke Melchior.

between two subtypes: on the one hand, emblematic illustrations are found in slides where the text is combined with a symbol, a logo, or pictures that have a clear denotative function as representing an institution, a group, or another social entity.

These types are different from representative illustrations, that is, slides, on which the visual elements are a part of, or identical with, the meaning of the written words, as in Slide 2. Although one would assume that this type is very frequent, there were only 27 slides of this type.

The last and most popular type is constituted by *visual slides*. Visual slides are characterized by dominant visual elements and text that plays only a minor role as designation, label, or legend. Given the variety of visual elements, visual slides appear much more diverse than text slides. Nonetheless, we can identify various typical diagrammatic elements, characterized by geometrical and rhythmic structures of the space of slides. Organigrams, chronologies, or topographies, easily produced by the software, are subtypes of visual slides (92 cases in the corpus). Other frequent visual elements supported by the software are various diagrammatic forms and shapes (such as pie charts and bar graphs). In recent updates of the software, a number of new diagrammatical elements have been added, and

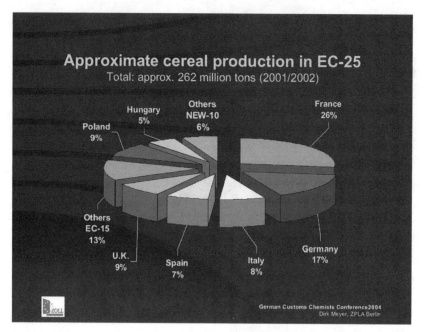

Slide 3: Diagram type. Reproduced with permission from Zoll, German Customs Chemist Conference 2004, Dr. Uwe Schlick, ZPLA Berlin.

a number of elements used in the presentations analyzed are from sources other than the presentation software.

In addition to the type of slides in which certain visual elements dominate and provide a clear reference, another type of slide (with 63 cases in the sample) combines the dominating visual element with textual elements in the manner of a collage. These collages may take the form of posters, as presented in (mostly) scientific presentations, displaying several phases, parts, methods, findings, steps.

The "purest" visualized forms are the photograph and (including sound) the video or film. However, most of the visual slides involving photographs and video (27 cases) do not make use of the software's layout management. Visuals are sometimes presented within the frame of the slide but most often as a slide show or a video film only. By using pictures and presentations this way, the powerpoint presentation assumes the features of other genres, such as the slide show or cinema show.

In addition to these visual forms, presentations may employ acoustic media. Whereas sound files are mostly restricted to certain audiences (professionals specialized in music, linguists), acoustic effects are also frequently used. In Chapter 5, Section 5, we shall encounter a presentation in

## Roughness Effects on Hairy Pad Attachment

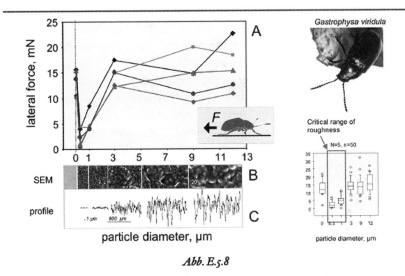

*Abb. E.5.8*

Slide 4: Collage of visual elements. Reproduced with permission from Bio-future presentation, Frau Prof. Frauke Melchior.

which the sound of a mechanical typewriter is used. Also the famous presentation by the U.S. general and secretary of state Colin Powell, in which he convinced the U.S. government to wage a second war on Iraq in 2003, included a "ching ching" sound effect from the television series *Law and Order*, borrowed lines from the mafia soap *Sopranos*, and featured the voice of the movie character Austin Powers (shouting, "Oh yes, baby").

### 3. Multimodality and the Synchronization of Speech and Slides

The role of the text in the slide as well as film and acoustic data indicates that the slide cannot only be considered as visual. Tufte framed his critique of PowerPoint as part of the problem of visual evidence. Therefore, it seems necessary to discuss this issue in terms of the visual turn and the question of the visualization of information and knowledge (Pötzsch 2007). Though "the world told is a different world than the world shown," as Kress (2003: 1) rightly stresses, it should have become evident that the "worlds shown on the slides" are often only "words shown." That is to say, text plays a crucial role in the slides in powerpoint presentations. Despite the importance of the graphical elements, the analysis of powerpoint presentation should, therefore, not aim at a grammar of the visual, as Kress and van Leeuwen (1996) proposed. Neither do I intend to go into more detail with respect to the relationship between written text and graphics, which has been called "multimodal" by Bateman (2008), because the slides studied here (as with most slides) are not just designed as visual objects including written text; all of them form part of a presentation. As such, they are accompanied by speech, a modality I want to analyze on the "internal level". The "multimodal" character of powerpoint presentations encompasses talk, text, graphics, visuals, and sometimes even sound and video. Lobin (2009: 67) defines powerpoint presentation, therefore, in terms of multimodality as a "textually organized form of communication consisting essentially of a spoken text by a speaker (the speech), texts, diagrams, pictures etc., projected by some software, and the activities of the speaker at the desk or eventually on a stage." Indeed, three modalities are essential to the analysis of presentations on the internal level: (a) they are characterized by a (rather formal) speech or (rather informal) talk; (b) they encompass visual elements (which again may be words or other types of signs); and (c) they are enacted in what we call performance. These modalities can be objectified in quite different media (speech can become a text, often on paper; the slide can be part of a deck published on the Internet, and the performance can even be recorded on video and published as a podcast). The event called a presentation is characterized by all of these modalities being enacted simultaneously.

When focusing on the interplay between speech and slides in the following chapter, the analysis on the internal level partly follows the logic of multimodality. According to Kress, a mode is "a socially shaped and culturally given semiotic resource for making meaning. Image, writing, layout, music, gesture, speech, moving, image, soundtrack and 3D objects are examples of modes used in representation and communication" (Kress 2010: 79). Within the frame of the analysis of communicative genres, it is essential to stress that the relation between speech and slides is constructed by two different data sorts, that is, slides and audio recorded speech. When studying the interrelation between both "modes," one should keep in mind that the differences have been separated artificially by the technical means available and the practices of the researchers collecting the data. In this way, they serve as a resource for describing the features produced by the actors; however, they do not suffice to define the communicative genre but only the "internal level". The focus on "speech," therefore, is a reduction of a more holistic form of communication, such as the speech, bodily conduct, and audience interaction, which will be analyzed later. At this internal level this focus will allow a demonstration of the fact that powerpoint presentations do not just build on the "information" encoded in the slides but, rather, that speech contributes to, and can be shown to be, constructing their meaning in interacting with the slide.

Speech and talk – the former referring to the more formal, the latter to the less formal forms of oral communication by the presenter – either follow a prepared text or are produced in situ. Although one can, following Lobin (2009), distinguish between the visual "projection event" and the "speech event," they are closely interrelated. Since this interrelation is produced in time and inasmuch as it is produced by the presenter as speaker, I want to refer to it as synchronization.[9] Presenters synchronize what is seen on the slide with what they say in their oral communication. More generally, synchronization is the temporal coordination of visual and oral communication, and as will become clear later, this "multimodal" synchronization forms part of a more complex and holistic process of orchestration, which includes, in addition to the presenter, the participation of audiences and technologies. Before turning to the kinds of synchronization in presentations, some remarks on oral communication and the language of presentations as events are in order.

## 4. Speech and Talk

As with text on slides, the texts of speeches or talks are characterized by a certain lexicon. The lexicon is defined by the kind of words and special expressions typically used on the slides and in the speech. Generally, the lexicon has a knowledge function in relating to the speaker; it denotes something the speaker is supposed to know. It also relates to an order of knowledge since it is supposed to represent something. Finally, the words of the lexicon are addressing someone. The functions of the language are discernible by the special repertoire, expressed by expert language. In this sense, the lexicon is also emblematic, representing a social order of knowledge assumed to be shared by a social group and their common interest. This may include loanwords, linguistic adaptations, or certain discipline-specific metaphorical usages. Thus, scientific lectures use a lexicon derived from the disciplinary background of the speaker or the assumed background of the speaker (Techmeier 1998: 907). One should not consider the lexicon a trivial thing for it not only is a code in which knowledge is framed, but also relates to an often institutional order of knowledge: that is, different lexical items represent different institutional spheres, such as in business presentations, presentations in church, or academic presentations. In the lexicon of sciences clear differences appear with respect to, for example, the humanities. This also holds for business, as Schoeneborn's study shows with respect to powerpoint slide texts in an international company. According to Schoeneborn (2008: 143 ff.), the slides stored as part of the knowledge management system of the company he studied contained various typical lexical items, such as truisms, and tautologies, such as "integration takes time" and "flexibility needs discipline." Other forms are recommendations for action ("keep key project members within the project," "be realistic and practical," "communicate developments early and frequently to ensure involvement") and, finally, success factor items with headwords such as "positive working culture," "easy internal communication," "championship from the top."

The boundaries between the lexical registers and their transformation or shifts (e.g., that the latter lexical items may nowadays also be found in scientific organizations) are of some sociological interest but cannot be pursued here. Also the differences in the grammatical and prosodical styles of oral communication in powerpoint presentation can only be mentioned. Thus, the formal correctness of grammatical constructions and their intonations varies enormously. When reading written manuscripts, the style is typically defined by shorter tone units and the narrowness of intonations, whereas the conversational style of presenters not using manuscripts in addition to the slides exhibits longer tone units and a more varied range of intonation. Presentations based on written texts use formal registers that are explicit, and often their syntax is quite elaborated. Oral presentations without manuscripts, on the other hand, exhibit features such as anacoluths, deictical elements, parenthesis, and phonetic reductions of word endings. This style has the largest intonational range, and well-versed listeners are still able to distinguish different institutional intonational styles, such as a "sermon style" in churches from a sales pitch or an intellectual academic style. If one looked for more encompassing ways to define this style, one might follow Biber and Finegan (1994) and distinguish various styles, such as the "frozen style," "formal," "consultative," "casual," and "intimate." Whereas the presentation based on written texts is well characterized by the formality of style, speech not based on written text typically can also exhibit an elaborated speech style that safeguards the text's coherence. Many presentations, however, are characterized by an informal register, building on implicit meanings, parataxis, and deixis.

The majority of powerpoint presentations, however, seem to oscillate between two kinds of styles: the rather formal "speech" oriented toward the manuscript type (plus slides) and the rather informal "talk" (plus slides) oriented toward the casual "fresh" talk (Goffman 1981a). They often include elements of both, switching between rather formal, text-oriented parts and rather informal fresh parts. Most presentations, therefore, can be characterized as showing *colloquial formality*. Even if the slides suggest a formal lexicon, they are often orally "translated" into an informal lexicon, and even if there is a formal manuscript, this is often accompanied by fresh talk. The informality of the oral formulations is compensated for by the written style of the words on slides.

## 5. Linguistic Deixis, Paralleling, and Communicative Things

As stressed previously, speech can only artificially be separated from the presentation as event. It is in the social event that actors synchronize speech and slides in ways that shall be analyzed here.[10] The notion of synchronization highlights that oral communication is not only added to the presentation of the slides in a way that each mode determines meaning on its own. Rather, it is one of the generic features of presentations as events that speech and slides are tuned in simultaneously and situationally, so that we can consider their temporal coordination, that is, synchronization, as an essential resource for their meaning.

The most obvious way to synchronize speech and slides as well as speakers and audiences is, of course, through linguistic or discursive deixis. As Brinkschulte (2007, 2008) has shown, powerpoint presentations exhibit a number of linguistic deictic procedures by which the spoken language can be related to the slides. In her study of deixis, on which I rely here, anaphora, reflective pronouns or what she calls "topicalizations of the verb," are among the most common linguistic devices by which deixis is performed.

According to linguistic theory, the deictic function of linguistic forms depends on the *origo*, that is, the "here-now-I" system of subjective orientation (Bühler 1982/1934: 149). However, since what "right here" or "there" means in such a situation is not only dependent on the speaking subject but also on the addressee for which the utterance is designed, deixis also presupposes some kind of intersubjectivity that takes into account that the speaker is a person who is relating to someone else.[11] For this reason, Hanks (1990) has suggested a "sociocentric" view of deixis. A very clear case in question is the *demonstratio ad oculos*, that is, the deictic reference to a photograph slide, as exemplified in Fragment 1 in a presentation which included the Slides 5 and 6 and Fragment 1.[12]

Slide 5: Chapel.

Slide 6: Statue.

## Fragment 1

1    [slide (5)]

2  S:    Here you can see Jüterbog, the monastery. This year, in the second half
        *Hier sehen sie Jüterburg das Mönchenkloster. Dieses Klosterwird in diesem*

3    from this year the cloister will be newly reopened as a cultural centre and
        *Jahr in der zweiten Jahreshälfte als Kulturzentrum neueröffnet und wird*

4    an exhibition will be shown there.
        *dort eine Ausstellung präsentieren.*

5    [slide (6)]

6    therefore here Luther...[1] =
        *Deswegen hier Luther...*

The speaker shows a picture of a building and refers to it by the deictic spatial adverb "here." Note that "here" simultaneously relates to a location shown on the picture and to the slide showing the picture. In addition, the speaker assumes the sociality of the deixis by referring to the second-person pronoun "you." As with most deictical references, they are used in a plain representational sense as a *demonstratio ad oculos*. Not only is the reference to the visual part of the slide, but this is taken to represent what is referred to linguistically. Speech not only turns slides into grammatical objects, it also fosters the objectivation of slides and the impression of "realness." The *demonstratio ad oculos*, however, does not work on the basis of the visual only; it is not what Lobin (2009: 64) calls monologic. Rather, visualization in powerpoint presentations depends on the synchronization with speech (or other modes of the presenters actions, such as pointing or body movements, to which we will turn later). The objects shown on the picture (be they photographs, diagrams, or words) are taken to represent what is being said (except in contexts in which this representation has become a topic in itself, as in artistic or visual studies). This way, the *demonstratio ad oculos* duplicates the meaning.

Let us consider another example of duplication by the *demonstratio ad oculos*. After having explained a series of types of rice listed in a table on the slide, of which the last type is "broken rice," the presenter in this fragment turns to the next slide (Brinkschulte 2008: 24f.).

It is not only that the slide includes a list item called "broken rice" followed by the picture: the picture is also linked with a legend that again is "broken rice"; in addition, this is repeated by the spoken words "broken rice." It is not that the thing is real, but the reference to the picture is taken as the reference to the thing called broken rice. Again, the picture is taken

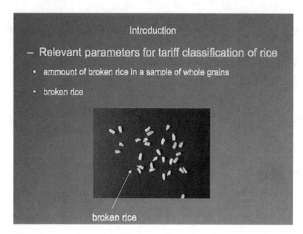

Slide 7: "Broken rice."[18] Reproduced with permission from Zoll, German Customs Chemist Conference 2004, Dr. Uwe Schlick, ZPLA Berlin.

## Fragment 2

1  S:  And  now  by  way  of  conclusion  now  there  is  the  broken  rice  just  mentioned
    *Und zum Schluss jetzt noch eben den eben schon erwähnten Bruchreis*

as representing the real thing as part of the real world – without any qualification. Therefore, an announcement like "I have the evidence" takes on a very distinct meaning in these contexts for what one may better call the duplication of representation, where by duplication I mean that the visual level of signs or words and the spoken level are reinforcing each another.

If one realizes that duplication is a means of relating speech and slides by using similar elements in different codes (spoken words, letters, visual representations), duplication can be identified as a case of a more general type. As there often are even three modes of relating visual slides and language (written words, spoken word, visual representations), the duplication as the explicit repetition of the "same" elements in speech and on slides can be considered to be one case of *paralleling*. Paralleling does not just refer to the duplication of certain aspects. Consider, as an example, Fragment 3 from a presentation in the context of urban planning:

In line 1, the speaker starts with a new slide and a new topic: "pathways of development" (in urban planning). He interrupts his grammatical construction in line 3 and restarts with the same formulation (rhetorically in the form of a *zeugma*) with a new sentence, a question (4). This question is formulated as alternative: paths that are either "promising" (line 5) or "petering out" (line 6). Although the speaker neither uses any deictic reference nor points to the slide with his finger, the reference to Slide 8 is implicitly clear if one looks at its visual structure.

## Fragment 3

1    S:    (clearing the throat) then there are diverse < clearing the throat, (3,0)>
       *S:*    *dann gibt es verschiedene*

2          path of development, that is also erm sociologically
          *Entwicklungspfade, das ist auch äh unter soziologischen*

3          of course a quite interesting-
          *Gesichtspunkten natürlich n interessantes-*

4          erm a quite interesting question which pathways of development
          *äh ne sehr intressante Frage welche Entwicklungspfade*

5          of pioneers prove to be promising
          *von Pionieren sind eigentlich erfolgsversprechend*

6          and which ones peter out
          *und welche (-) verlaufen im Sand.(1,7)*

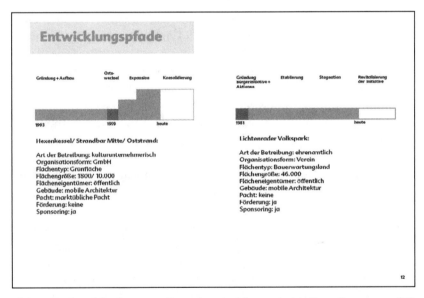

Slide 8: Paths of development. Reproduced with permission from Overmeyer, IRS Erkner.

The apologies for the fact that parts of the text on the slide cannot be identified by the reader would already have been due in the event of the performance in which this slide has been shown. For the members of the audience could not read the text on the slide when it was shown (since it was so small) – with the exception of the title. As most experts on information design would consider this slide to be a disaster, one can argue that the recognition of the words on the slide is not essential for the presentation. Or, to put it in another way: the presenter shows that it is not the words, unreadable because of their small size, that are relevant to the presentation. Rather, it is the graphic structure that is of relevance here because it is the thing most visible and referred to (as we shall see). Whatever may be taken from the slide, it illustrates a duality, and it is also a dual structure the speaker produces in his speech by the alternative between "promising" and "petering out." The dual alternative in speech, thus, is paralleled by the dual alternative on the slides.

At this point it is important to emphasize that, even if most parts of the slide cannot be read, its title can be identified on this reproduction, which is "Pathways of Development" ("Entwicklungspfade"). It is this title that is duplicated in the sentence formulated by the presenter as the subject of what is divided up into the two alternatives. Since the title of the slide and the subject of the sentence are duplicated, the wording serves as a *recognition marker* to the audience and possibly to the speaker himself (who made a short pause after clicking the slide) and referred to the alternative paralleled.

It may be helpful to remind the reader of Tufte's and other critics' assumptions discussed previously that the slide constitutes the core of the presentation. In this case, however, the slide is rendered meaningful by the accompanying speech. The phenomenon of paralleling demonstrates that it is the synchronization of spoken text with certain visual elements of the slide that is basic for an understanding of the meaning of the presentation. As opposed to the normative views held by many advisory books, which condemn "redundancy" of visual and speech text, the "redundant" paralleling is very frequent for good reasons: in this way speakers can not only indicate what they refer to on the slide but also extend whatever is said and still relate it to the slide.

Paralleling can take the forms of contrasts and bullet lists ("first," second," "then," "then"). Also, lists, graphically marked by bullets are among the most common forms to be recognized both visually and verbally by the speech (often, the parallels between the speech and the slides are facilitated by the texts on the slide). The most obvious means of paralleling is, of course, quoting or reading the slide. Note that in this way, there is not only a temporal synchronization of speech and slide; since speech relates to the spatial order of visual elements (including text) on the slide, the spatial dimension of the presentation is obviously made relevant. Since this spatial dimension is particularly important to the performance, I shall focus on it later. Here, it suffices to say that the spatial order of text and visuals is paralleled temporally by reading. Another way of paralleling is through reformulations: speakers repeat a sentence or a clause and transform their grammatical structure, turning, for example, substantives on the slide into verbs in the speech ("management of work" on the slide may be transformed into "and you manage the work" in talk). Paraphrases may leave the order of a number of words and parts of sentences and embed them in new constructions. An essential instrument for the establishment of parallels is the use of at least some recognition markers. Recognition markers are oral and written linguistic elements that can be perceived as identical in the speech and on the slides. (In some cases unequivocal visualizations may also do.)

Presenters typically do not just use one form of paralleling or follow only one pattern of synchronization. In most of the cases analyzed they mix the different forms of synchronization, as Brinkschulte (2008: 8) shows. Take, as an example, a presentation on inflammatory bowel disease, which extends over a number of slides.

The major strategy of paralleling consists of the recurrent use of certain elements on slides and in speeches. Here, these elements are lexical, as in the use of certain words. Also syntactical constructions and parallelisms are used as paralleling recognition markers. By means of the recognition markers, the use of the fragmented slide text can be understood as citing and thereby localizing something on the slide; fragmented texts may also be transformed into syntactically formed sentences, so that even various fragmented items may be paralleled by syntactically correct sentences. "Great Britain" is rephrased as "England," and items on the slide are expanded in a more or less clear way. Recognition markers also serve as additional speech acts: utterances made in paralleling may be summarized, commented on, and formulated in such a way that speakers explain the meaning of what is shown on the slides (Heritage and Watson 1979). Finally, some items are only part of the visual presentation ("geographical trends"); others are only part of the speech.

Paralleling differs in some significant sense from deixis. "Deictic reference is a communicative practice based on a figure-ground structure joining a socially defined indexical ground, emergent in the process of interaction, and a referential focus articulated through culturally constrained schematic knowledge" (Hanks 1990: 314). Like deixis, paralleling requires schematic typificatory knowledge (of visual forms, of written and spoken words, of contrasts, etc.). However, the relation between the slide and spoken words need not be established by special linguistic deictic devices. Paralleling does not need any deictic lexical items at all, neither

| Slide (text) | Speech |
|---|---|
| | |
| "geographical trends" | - |
| Mainly NorthAmerica | "and interestingly these diseases are to be found mainly in North America" |
| NorthWestern Europe | in NorthWestern Europe |
| Especially in Scandinavia and Great Britain | especially in Scandinavia and England |
| North-South Gradient | there is also a North-South Gradient ("Gefälle") |
| - | there are few chronic inflammatory bowel diseases |
| - | patients with inflammatory bowel diseases in Southern Europe |

Diagram 3: Text on slide and in speech.
The words on the left-hand side represent the topics mentioned explicitly on the slides; the topics in the right column are expressed in oral communication.

a "finger" nor any other extra means for "pointing," "showing," or "referring." It seems already to point "to something," an "epistemic thing," as one may call it, through its cross-modal self-reference. This capacity to "objectify" items of presentations into things is well known from science studies (Rheinsberger 1997).

As opposed to Rheinsberger's notion of "epistemic things," the construction of such objects, however, is not restricted to science. Moreover, since the construction of these "things" that are "in" the presentation is put into effect by communicative means, they are best called *communicative things*. Communicative things are not just "topics" we talk about. They are what one can refer to as the "knowledge" that is ascribed to the presenter, offered in the presentation, and objectified in its digital form. As part of the presentation their "thinglike" character can be seen in the fact that communicative objects are being referred to at various points and, thus, allow for coherence. Since the slide is often postprocessed after the presentation event, these communicative objects also "survive" their situational performance and can be saved as "knowledge." What has been established in the presentation and identified on the slide can be referred to later (as "on the slide"), for example, in meetings, texts, or even examinations. As "knowledge," the communicative object is ascribed to the presenter. (There may also be a team, organization, or other social unit established as the author of "knowledge.") Since it includes speech, this "knowledge" needs only to be indicated by the text on the slide and remain very much dependent on the spoken words. As we shall see, bodily performance (as in pointing) may also add significantly to what "knowledge" is about. Finally, technology also contributes to the objectivation of the "thing" as the representation on the slides demonstrates.

The construction of communicative objects is, of course, not really "self-referential." Although it may be described as the mutual reinforcement of visual representations, written words, and speech, paralleling of speech and slides works on the basis of the technology. Whatever the presenter says can be related to what the presentation "shows." What the computer shows by means of the projector is visibly related to the speaker, who not only changes the slides but also – and this is the parallel – speaks at the same time. The paralleling of spoken language and slides depends on the technology: slides designed on a computer by means of presentation software and projected onto a screen (or the wall) by a projector. Even if they are not being pointed at, the slides still "show" something in a technical sense. Note that "showing" is here deeply ambiguous, for the "object" shows something while it is "shown," that is, projected, by a technology. This "showing" or implicit deixis cannot be called a gesture since it is accomplished by the technology and is used by the speakers when giving presentations. It is rather inscribed or, as one may say, institutionalized in the technology.[13] The technological chain of computer and projector is made to "show" something. Presentations, thus, not only consist of text, speaker, and audience, but also involve a computer and a projector as a part of the communicative action.

I will return to this active role of the technology, which is essential to the performance of the presentation, when analyzing audiovisual records of powerpoint presentations. Before that, however, we need to address the overall internal structure of the presentation, which is based on the establishment of communicative objects.

Slide 9: Objectives. Reproduced with permission from Zoll, German Customs Chemist Conference 2004, Dr. Dirk Meyer, ZPLA Berlin.

## 6. Lists and Seriality

As the examples have shown, paralleling builds on recognition markers within single sentences, paragraphs, or items as well as on the sequence of these items. It is at this point that we have to turn to how the bullet list plays a role in providing an order of reference for paralleling. As poor as the reputation of lists may be in the discourse on powerpoint, they definitely represent one important method for the production of coherence in talk (Lobin 2009: 78).[14] Drawing on the analysis of Schnettler (2006), one can state that lists serve, first, as a simple pattern of spatial orientation of words on the slide, that is, the projected surface (what occurs later is below). Second, lists also function as structuring elements of speech. Let us look at a slide presentation from the Customs Office. Slide 9 consists of a series of four bullet points subsumed under a title ("Objectives of XXX").[15]

It is quite common for slides that the text after the bullets is reductive in terms of fragmented or truncated sentences. The sentences on a list follow regularly similar grammatical constructions (e.g., they use either the infinitive of verbs without mentioning the subject, or the third person, or the subject only). Although one would assume that speakers just read and complement the sentences, real speech often turns out to be very different from the grammatical constructions, the serial order of the items, and even the text on the slides. Take as an example the speech (Fragment 4) relating to Slide 9 (translated from German):

**Fragment 4**

| 1 | S: | [Switch to the new slide (see above)] |
|---|---|---|
| 2 | | Yes, again the objectives of this committee, |
| 3 | | (1,0) |
| 4 | | Erm a primary objective is first of all to that the diverse standards existing in |
| 5 | | the different European countries be harmonized; |
| 6 | | (1,0) |
| 7 | | And erm, a further objective is the greater involvement of all participating |
| 8 | | countries in the standardization process |
| 9 | | (1,0) |
| 10 | | Well, in addition a contribution should be made to formulate the European |
| 11 | | position on the international level, as for example at ISO, the International |
| 12 | | Organization for Standardization and also when codices are designed. |
| 13 | | (1,5) |
| 14 | | and the aim is to for standardization and regulation to closer cooperate, and |
| 15 | | (1,0) |
| 16 | | erm, and we find again as I mentioned before in the regulatory texts of the EU 17 which are binding investigations and our evaluations… |

Fragment 4 shows that the spoken text is not just repeating the visualized text but produces a series of words that have also been called paralleling. The peculiar feature of this paralleling is that the presenter uses words spoken in German paralleling words that are written in English on the slide. Since the text on the slide is in English, whereas the speech is in German, the speaker not only seems to assume that audience members understand the English slides; he also assumes that the recognition markers are identified bilingually by the nonacademic audience. Although the cue words are set apart by additions and parentheses (such as "national standards" and "harmonize"), they are still used. In addition, the speaker translates the acronyms (e.g., CEN/TC into "these committees"). Furthermore, the fragmented sentences from the slide are completed, so he orally adds subjects to the verbal constructions on the slides, and finally he augments them by additional information.

Paralleling is not only produced on the level of items and sentences. The structure of lists can also be used to relate speech and slides. This

**Fragment 5**

| | | |
|---|---|---|
| 1 | S: | that's when I gave up trying to say something about eh substantive trends ( ) on |
| 2 | | trivial statements like gender and deviance is still quite strong and consumer |
| 3 | | culture is picking up |
| 4 | | (0,5) (Next slide) |
| 5 | | uhmI won't go through uhm three sets of remarks (.) and overview |
| 6 | | of institutional context of … |

relation can be established by "builds," that is, "building" items sequentially one after another. Yet, even the use of pauses in speech may fulfill this graphic function of segmenting text.

When looking at the relation between text and speech across a number of slides, one can observe that paralleling can also exploit the transitional pauses. Take Fragment 5, from an academic presentation at an international conference.

As we can see in line (4), the presenter leaves a pause when switching the slides. As opposed to presentations with overhead projectors, where, as we shall see, pauses account for the manual intervention by the presenter, pauses between slides in powerpoint are technically not necessary. Here, they serve instead to mark the reference of oral communication to slides. Talk before the pause refers to the former slide, talk after the pause to the new slide. Although the slides do not exhibit a list structure, the juxtaposition by such pauses turns them into units following one another. In this way they become serially related to one another and to the oral communication.

By *seriality* I want to refer to the simple fact that slides are shown one after the other so that the presentation includes a series of slides. As a result, the slides are taken as units to which one can refer before and after. Speech and slides are, thence, not only related on the level of one slide only; there are also relations between both levels across slides. As the relation between bits of talk and elements of slides can be indicated by pauses, these form a strategy to indicate the relationship between bits of talk and different slides. The simultaneity of the pause and a new slide seems to establish a kind of rule saying, "What is being said next is to be understood as relating to what is shown next (unless indicated otherwise) within the slides and across slides." Paralleling thus allows for synchronizing not only speech and the slides, but also what the speaker "means" or "knows."

## Fragment 6

| 1 | S: | you can see it here, |
|---|----|----------------------|
| 2 |    | (.) ((slide switch)) |
| 3 |    | and here;            |
| 4 |    | (.) ((slide switch)) |
| 5 |    | and here.            |
| 6 |    | (.) ((slide switch)) |

This rule, however, differs from what Rendle-Short (2006: 101) proposes as the "display rule," that is, "that [an] image is made visible to the audience before the presenter commences the topic talk – either during the pause between the sections of talk or during the orientation." As true as this may be in some cases, in many of the cases studied, speech precedes the slide if, for example, the recognition markers used on a slide not yet shown are already formulated orally. Also recognition markers mentioned in earlier slides are often repeated (as one of the most important strategies to create coherence).

Marking off by pauses is one of the ways of synchronizing series of slides and text. The synchronization can also be accomplished by overarching structures, such as lists. As we have seen, list constructions are not reduced to the single slide but can be extended across subsequent slides. In the following example (Fragments 6 and 7) taken from a medical presentation, for example, a speaker presented his evidence in three consecutive slides, which he showed while talking in a way used for lists (raising his voice first and then lowering it step by step at the end of the sentence).

While showing different slides representing visual demonstrations *ad oculos* (reproductions of visual representations produced by computer tomography and magnetic resonance tomography inserted into the slides), the presenter obviously produces a list both of visuals and of words spoken, which he takes as supporting an argument. Note that the visual evidence here should not be understood in a positivistic manner, for, on closer inspection, it is (probably by mistake) exactly in the case quoted previously that one and the same image is used twice for different recognition markers, that is, for the two different technical methods of producing representations that are under discussion.

## 7. Macrostructures

As we have seen, presentations are not only synchronous combinations of single slides and speech. They also include series of slides and spoken words. In order to grasp the series of slide and the accompanying text and talk exceeding the level of the single slide, one may compare them to the "macrostructures" van Dijk (1980) refers to in language texts. Since presentations include visual slides and talk, however, macrostructures cannot be restricted to text but require a look at the synchronization of text, spoken language, and visual slides.

In addition to an intricate synchronization of text and speech and single slide or items of slides, presentations can be shown to exhibit strong coherence on the level of macrostructures. Without discussing the multiple ways that coherence can be produced on the level of macrostructures, I want to focus on one example that shows how an argument is produced across a series of slides. The example stems from a medical talk that has been analyzed by Brinkschulte (2008: 24ff.). Because of its length, the argument will be paraphrased rather than reproduced by transcript, and the paraphrases will be related to the respective slides.

The presentation starts with the thesis that spontaneous medical cures were already the subject of the first international cancer congress in 1906. To begin with, the presenter claims that this thesis is still worth debating. The corresponding slide (Slide 10) represents the name of the speaker who had put forward the thesis, the title of his 1906 paper, and a short abstract – which is neither quoted nor referred to in the spoken presentation.

When showing the next slide, the presenter starts his talk with the question why medicine lost interest in the issue of spontaneous cures of cancer. The slide shown (Slide 11), however, is not related to this question but already anticipates, as we shall see, the next topic the presenter talks about, monoclonal proliferation, which is named on the slide and illustrated by a model.

The second slide includes a slide built of two parts shown consecutively: a model of "monoclonal proliferation" of cancer cells, and a photographic reproduction of an avalanche of snow, which is added when the presenter continues, to make a metaphorical comparison between the avalanche and the proliferation model.

For the next stage of his argument in the talk, he makes a reference to Albert Einstein and stresses his idea that theories determine our perception. This reference is not mirrored on the slide, although it serves as a kind of logical backing for the general proposition. He concludes that the

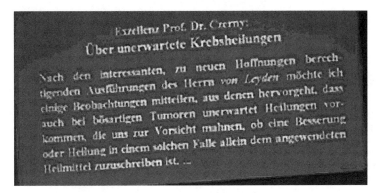

Slide 10: Introductory slide. Reproduced with permission from ICC KK Kappauf.

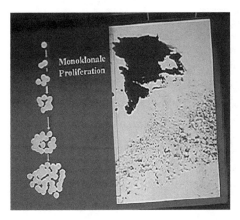

Slide 11: Second slide: Monoclonal proliferation. Reproduced with permission from ICC KK Kappauf.

neglect of spontaneous cures derives from ignorance about this phenomenon. The slides only represent what now appears as the consequences of this ignorance, such as slide (Slide 12) quoting a book on the "problem of cancer" from 1949, in which the lack of evidence for spontaneous cures is stressed (Slide 12), and it presents the results of a quantitative study with a table of numbers supporting the idea that there are no spontaneous cures (Slide 13).

Again, there is a nonlinear relation between the series of slides and the speech relating to the slides. Yet, as complex and nonlinear as the argument is, the synchronization of speech and slides makes perfect sense so that the presentation can be understood to make a point already mentioned: we have ignored the role of spontaneous cures so far, and because of that,

Beim Krebs gibt es eine natürliche Heilung nicht. Eine
Gesundung aus eigenen Abwehrkräften des Organismus,
eine sog. *Selbstheilung*, ist zwar immer wieder behauptet (s.
dieses Kapitel, S 612), aber so gut wie *noch nie einwandfrei*
*bewiesen* worden. Aber selbst wenn sie vorkäme, so wäre das
angesichts der wenigen Fälle behaupteter Selbstheilungen
im Vergleich mit den schätzungsweise 2 Millionen
Krebskranken je Jahr vielleicht eine Chance von 1 : 1
Million. Krebs ist eben wie schon GALEN sagte, ein morbus
contra naturam. So gibt es keine sanatio naturalis, sondern
nur eine sanatio curativa medici

DAS KREBSPROBLEM
Berlin 1949, Springer, (S 532-533)

Slide 12: Third slide: The quote. Reproduced with permission from ICC KK Kappauf.

Interferon gamma-1b compared with placebo in
metastatic renal-cell carcinoma.
Gleave ME et al. *N Engl J Med* 1998;338:1265-1271

| Therapie | IFN-gamma-1b N = 91 | Placebo N = 90 |
|---|---|---|
| Remission | 4.4 % | 6.6 % |
| CR | 3.3 % | 3.3 % |
| PR | 1.1 % | 3.3 % |

Slide 13: Fourth slide: Evidence. Reproduced with permission from ICC KK Kappauf.

the scarce evidence only supports ignorance instead of producing new insights.

Although the synchronization between the slide and the speech is not uniform, this nonlinearity should not be seen as redundant. On the contrary, it is related to a change in footing. Whereas the first slide supports the presenter's view and thus represents his arguments, the third and fourth slides represent not his but others' voices: the presenter "quotes" these slides and takes them as representations of a view misled by a wrong assumption. "Quoting" here is one case of what Goffman (1981a: 124ff.) calls "footing," by which he refers to the different stances a speaker may take toward his or her own utterances. In the preceding case, it is by way of this change of footing that he deviates from a linear argument yet produces a dialectical argument between "his" arguments and those of "others." Note that although the presenter illustrates the extent of research that has been misled by the avalanche, the major switch of his footing is not part of the slides at all. It is the explicit verbal reference to Einstein and his claim that theories determine perception that produces the new footing and turns his argument into a part of his knowledge.

We shall later turn to footing as the framing of the source of utterances, for it usually demands that additional aspects of the communicative actions, such as body movements or technology, are taken into account. Here we have to note, first, that slides and text take on a certain meaning in the context of a series of slides, and, second, that the coherence of the argument is dependent on the complex interplay between spoken text and slides (the dialectical argument earlier is only one example of this complexity). Although this complexity deserves more detailed study, for the present purpose we have to content ourselves with the observation that presentations cannot just be considered as a linear series of slides. Just as there are many differences between slides, so are there many different ways they can be be synchronized with speech. Nonlinearity not only refers to the fact that hyperlinks may be used (which, at the time of our recordings, was rarely the case). It refers also to the fact that by cross-references speech does not need to follow the order of slides, and that the order between and in the slides can be changed and rearranged. (Pointing, to which I turn later, also plays an important role in this – as does the mere nonreference, or, as it is called more elegantly in rhetoric, "ellipsis.")

The nonlinearity of slides in macrostructures is supported by the corresponding use of what one may call simple forms,[16] such as narrations, jokes, gossip, and arguments, each of which can be synchronized in various ways to the slides. In addition to these minor speech forms, one can discover more or less fixed speech-slide forms, such as short or lengthy quotes printed on the slide and recited from it, lists and bullet lists, and comic strips, cartoons, or pictures that can require very few spoken comments and "speak for themselves" *ad oculos*. Thus, in a presentation on bowel diseases, a cartoon and a media quote of an (iconographic) pop star (Anastacia) are used to illustrate the role of public personas as identification figures for health issues. Whereas the cartoon is not addressed in the speech at all, the picture of Anastacia is detailed by way of a narration or gossip. Other types of minor forms can be the use of statistic tables as single slides that are then elaborated verbally, a photographic image that may serve to "make a point," a quote by a famous person, and so forth.

Rather than a linear structure, macrostructures of presentations, therefore, exhibit an *aggregate* character, constituted by a variety of different elements and following different, quite complex paths. The coherence of these aggregates is probably even more complex than the coherence of

**Fragment 7**

| | | |
|---|---|---|
| 1 | Speaker | So it's       /uhm (1,5) sort of /difficult |
| | *Hand* | *((/ RH to sheet/ sheet to LH       /TH to slide* |
| | | *1,5* |
| | | *((Slide and sheet together))* |
| 2 | Speaker | /SO HOW DOES THE /UH |
| | *Hand* | *((Slide and sheet to pile on pile))* |
| 3 | Speaker | /(2,5) how does the:: /model |
| | *Hands* | *((/RH to new slide       /slide on OHP))* |
| 4 | Speaker | and /the algebra /help you do that |

linguistic texts because of their additional visual mode and the many ways in which they can be synchronized with speech. In addition, of course, the very seriality of slides provides a formal coherence to the presentation. This formal coherence is often expressed in speech by "continuers," such as "and then" and "the next slide shows," or by reciting the title of each slide.

The formal coherence of the presentation can best be illustrated by comparison with its predecessor, the overhead presentation. Consider again the change of a transparency in an overhead presentation as taken from and analyzed by Rendle-Short (2006: 104).

While the speaker talks, he is busy coping with the materiality of the slide. Indeed, he has to leave a series of pauses in order to change, adjust, and readjust the transparencies by using one, sometimes both hands. As this example demonstrates, overhead presentations, on the one hand, demand that one copes with "the more complicated task of taking an old slide off and putting on a new one. There are four discrete actions that occur when changing a slide: taking the old slide off; putting the old slide on the pile of old slides; picking up a new slide; placing the new slide on the overhead projector" (Rendle-Short 2006: 69f.). In powerpoint, on the other hand, a new image is easily produced by just clicking a mouse or a remote control button (to which a huge range of visual transitions provided by the software can be added). The only hand activity consists of a click, which may be invisible to the audience when using a wireless remote (possibly combined with a laser pointer). Thus, the presenter's hand is almost completely free.

The result of the free hand can be seen, first, in the astonishing role of pointing to which I shall turn later. A second result is an impression of continuity, seriality, and, thus, formal cohesion: speech and slides are related to one another so that they are considered as part of one performance; they are serially related to one another and set in an order, and this order set can be labeled, printed, and stored so that it can be turned into an objectified product as a "document": a deck, an online slide show, a podcast, or any other of the "document formats" or "corollary genres" transcending the situation.

The coherence of presentation is, additionally, supported by the "skeleton" (Stoner 2007): basic template elements, such as running heads, footers, or page numbers, and the graphic "theme," that is, the collection of colors, fonts, and graphic effects of slides. By using the same template or master slide or just reusing a slide used earlier, this theme is repeated so that the graphical style of the slide is reproduced.

The coherence of macrostructures is also reflected in structuring slides introducing, organizing, and terminating presentations. Thus, for example, in books, films, and other objectified "works" of communication, titles form an essential part of the presentations. As Slide 14 illustrates, they regularly include forms of identifications, such as the name of the presenter, the institution to which the presenter belongs, and the date, location, and occasion of the presentation.

Title slides may already include the structure of the presentations. Often, but not necessarily, there is a distinct slide that introduces the structure of the presentation, frequently a text slide using bullet lists. Sometimes, the bullets are highlighted by various graphical means or even hyperlinked so that they function in a nonlinear way. The structure may also be rendered visible by means of graphical elements within the presentation slides, for instance, by reference to the subtitle, the chapter, or the step on the margins of the slides. The *final slide* (Slide 15) may consist of a final "summary," a "conclusion," or a final expression of gratitude to the audience, such as "Thank you for your attention" or, as in Slide 15, just "Thank you" for listening.

Whereas the title is a regular part of powerpoint presentations, final slides or summaries need not be part of them. As with books or films (which need not necessarily have an explicit hint to "the end"), presentations are closed forms (although the decks can leave options, as, for example, hidden slides or additional slides after the end of the presentation), for in almost every case they are terminated by performative means, and as we shall see, even the audience's final gratification applause is less dependent on the slide than on the performance. Even if some presentations may miss a closing slide, there is at least a last slide in the decks, that is, presentations made available on printouts or on the internet.

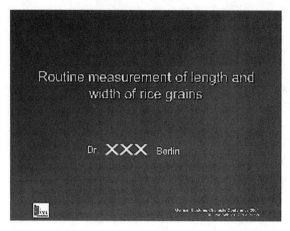

Slide 14: Title and name (anonymized as xxx). Reproduced with permission from ICC KK Kappauf.

Slide 15: Thank you for listening.

The macrostructure of the presentations is (in older versions of the program) additionally supported by PowerPoint's infamous "AutoContent Wizard" and similar software organizing content. It recommends certain orders according to presentation types (such as business plans, financial overviews) or communicative purpose ("recommending a strategy," "communicating bad news," "brainstorming"). In PowerPoint 2000 the AutoContent Wizard template for reports, for example, suggests an introduction, an argument, and a conclusion. It also makes certain recommendations, as they are known also from rhetorical advice books, such as "clarity of expression," use "verbal or visual illustrations," and make "logical connections between the arguments."

The AutoContent Wizard has been one of the weak points attacked by PowerPoint's critics. Thus, as Parker (2001: 76) remarks, "It's hard to shake off AutoContent's spirit: even the most easy-going PowerPoint template insists on a heading followed by bullet points, so that the user is shepherded toward a staccato, summarizing frame of mind." Yet, as infamous as the AutoContent Wizard may have been, hardly any of the presentations we have been recording followed its pattern in toto (at a time when it was still part of the application). This may be related to the fact that there were few presentations from business recorded; it may also be related to the fact that the types of presentations offered in the program are not present in many of the contexts we studied (such as academia or public administration). Thus the academic presenters we videotaped, for example, succeeded quite well in producing academic genres, such as the lecture or the disputation, although PowerPoint's AutoContent Wizard provided them with no templates for these formats.[17]

To sum up, one must concede that powerpoint presentation slides exhibit a certain structure, just as, for example, Tufte would have it. The analysis of their form shows that they are characterized by the surprisingly important role of text on the slides, and they seem to follow quite typical patterns with respect to certain basic design elements. Although the structure of the slides may even correspond to what presenters are projecting when preparing the slides, the analysis has shown that they "acquire" more specific meaning through the presenter's speech. This acquisition is not just a result of adding or combining speech and slides; it is, rather, an effect of the enactment of both in communicative action. Therefore, I suggest calling the subject matter or the themes of what a presentation is about the "communicative object". It is the communicative object that counts as the "knowledge" communicated by the presenter. The structure of "knowledge" presented, therefore, is not just determined by the technology (as, for example, the argument for "linearity" claims); it is rather coconstructed by the way that speech and slides are enacted by communicative action. Communicative action, however, is not restricted to these two modalities. They have only been selected as part of the internal level since they can be isolated by stills, audiotapes, and transcripts or manuscripts. In these forms, they can be made subject to analysis (visual, linguistic, etc.) and thus yield a specific form of evidence. In order to understand powerpoint presentations and the way they objectify "knowledge," we have to turn to the more encompassing process and acknowledge the relevance of visual conduct, on the basis of audiovisual data.

# 5 The Intermediate Level: Pointing, the Body Formation, and the Triadic Structure of Powerpoint Presentations

Without any doubt speech is no less a social phenomenon than are the slides analyzed. When focusing on the internal level of the communicative genre, the intentions of the actors, and the visual and verbal objectivations they produce, one is necessarily abstracting from the contexts in which this is done. The analyses on the intermediate level compensate for this abstraction by focusing on the performance of interaction in social situations. The notion of situation indicates that the observations on this level orient toward the interactive dimension of the communicative actions and include the "other" of interaction, the presumed "recipients." In order to account for the reciprocity of the interaction, I use Erving Goffman's notion of "situation," which also serves as a title for the designation of this level of analysis. We shall see that the situation also opens the way to include the more encompassing so-called macro-structural aspects of the communicative action, to be analyzed later.

As these remarks again make clear, the distinction between levels of analysis is analytical. It also follows the order of data, for, as we have seen, slides, as products of communicative actions, for example, can be studied independently of the context of their performance. In this chapter, I shall draw mainly on video recorded data. Although the earlier analysis of speech also used video records, in this chapter I shall mainly rely on a method called video analysis. This method is sketched in the Appendix. Here, it serves to focus on the interaction between different modalities of communication. As we have seen, the synchronization of slides and speech (as the relation between types of signs) is needed to account for performative aspects, so that this part of the analysis may be seen as a junction between the internal and the intermediate situative levels. The same may be true for the first part of this chapter. For pointing, to which I turn later, could also be analyzed as a form of social action or as a structure of (gestural) signs, that is, as part of the internal structure. However, we shall see that the analysis of pointing not only allows us to acknowledge the role of the body. Moreover, it is essentially part of the "body formation," which includes the various forms of interaction with and by the audience as well as with and by technology. The body and its formation already refer to the setting and objects that relate to the external level of the analysis.

## 1. Pointing, Gesture, and Speech

The synchronization between speech and slides by deixis, paralleling, and the use of recognition markers is based on the institution of pointing provided by the technological chain of projector, computer, and screen. This is nicely caught in the "powerpoint" metaphor. Given the importance of technology and the relevance of linguistic deixis, one should not ignore that pointing is also performed in a very literal sense by the human actors as a form of bodily conduct. Pointing as a form of action refers to the performative aspects of bodily conduct restricted neither to linguistic deixis nor to the use of the index finger. As we shall see, it is not even necessarily accompanied by linguistic deixis. Pointing is a form of communicative action not only because of its performativity. In addition it exhibits distinctive social characteristics.[1] Pointing is one of the basic ways of intentionally orienting to something else and, at the same time, orienting to someone else. As Tomasello (2008) argues, it constitutes one of the most pristine forms of communicative action specific to humans (and different from primates), for by performing it we constitute a shared intentional reference. As simple as the form may be, it presupposes complex processes of intersubjectivity that allow that person B not only recognizes the finger or pointing device of person B but also recognizes that B is pointing to some "thing." This "thing" must not just be an invisible meaning but suggests most often a spatial and objective reference. On these grounds, pointing may be said to be one of the procedures for producing a communicative object. As with many communicative actions, the performance must not be planned or projected each time. It can be habitualized and applied routinely. Thus, Hanks (1990) also stresses that pointing belongs to those forms of routinized practices actors are able to perform without necessarily having explicit knowledge about when and how they execute this action.

One of the most noteworthy analyses of pointing has been undertaken in the context of what is now called "gesture studies." In one of the most encompassing studies Kendon (2004) suggests that the meaning of gestures is reconstructed by identifying the particular gestural forms "carrying" meaning. On these grounds, he distinguishes pointing from, for example, iconographic gestures that appeal to visual images or mimetic gestures that mimic other processes.[2] Indeed, if we look at the various video data of powerpoint presentations, we can easily detect the frequent use of different forms of pointing. Most popular, of course, is pointing with the index finger. In addition, pointing may be done with palm downward (Still 1), the hand forming a triangle (Still 2), or the hand forming an U shape (Still 3).

The signification of pointing, however, is not unequivocally correlated to its manual form, as Kendon (2004) seems to suggest. We cannot determine the meaning of a pointing gesture only by the form of the hand and its movement. Rather, the meaning of pointing gestures is established in relation to other aspects of communication. Let us first consider its relation to oral speech with respect to a case recorded during an academic powerpoint presentation to some forty people. While the orator speaks, he is gesturing (single lines) and pointing to the slide (double underline):

**Fragment 8**

1      we have done a very <u>intense cartography</u>? And (-) one sees virtually in spaces
       *wir ham dann sehr <u>intensive Kart\*ierung</u> gemacht? und (-) man sieht eigentlich in Räumen*

2      <u>like the east Thames region</u> which is very close to the centre; in which city planning
       *<u>wie dem Aach\*eeraum O\*st</u> der sehr z\*entrumsnah ist; in dem die Stadtplanung eigentlich*

3      would like to have some <u>kind of Liverpool Place</u>; that <u>these</u> are absolutely vital spaces for
       *so 'n zweiten <u>Münchner Pl\*atz</u> äh vorsieht; dass <u>d\*as</u>; absolut vit\*ale Räume sind für n*

4      ehm a large bandwidth ehm a large spectrum of different usages
       *ganz äh großes unterschiedliches Spektrum ähm n großes Spektrum an unterschiedlichen Nutzungen.*

5      (3,3)

The transcript (Fragment 8) illustrates how frequently pointing may occur during speeches. In this short stretch of talk, the presenter three times employs a pointing gesture. The first two gestures (lines 1 and 2) are pointers with the forehand, which are linked to a movement of the arm resembling a wiping gesture. In line 3 ("these"), we encounter a typical pointing gesture with palm downward. In addition, there is a discursive gesture[3] that does not point but follows the linguistic stress ("Pl\*atz"). As the fragment also shows, these pointing gestures must not be linked to linguistic deixis. In fact, only one of the pointing gestures is associated with a deictic pronoun (line 3: "these"). By using two different signs (single and double underlines), the transcript suggests a clear distinction between deictic gestures and "discursive" gestures accompanying talk. Yet, the fragment also shows that this difference is not dependent on the gestural form, as Kendon (2004) assumes. Thus, an extended finger may point to something,

Stills 1–3: Pointing gestures. Reproduced with permission from Aktien richtig handeln, Tobias Tenner.

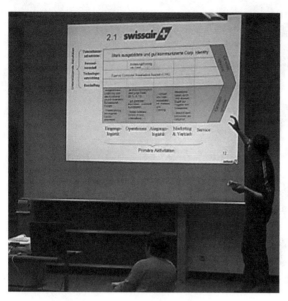

Stills 1–3: (*cont.*)

but it may also, when moved as in line 5, function as a rhythmic stress in speech like a "beat." A pointed finger could be emblematic for a "warning" gesture as well.[4] In the transcript, the difference between discursive gestures and the deictic becomes clear only through the tight coordination between the gestural form, on the one hand, and the communicative context, on the other hand. These are related by the temporal coordination of the gesture and, as can be seen here, speech, that is, the references to locality (such as "Thames region" or "Liverpool Place").

As a result we find that, first, pointing is not necessarily linked to linguistic deixis. Second, it can be said that the meaning of a gesture is not determined by its form but rather by the way it is embedded in other odes of communication. While in the last case we have only considered its relation to speech, later we shall also see how visual elements of the presentation provide for a meaning-bestowing context for gestures. Gestures, then, cannot be read on their own, and they are not only "related" to other modalities of speech, for example, spoken words, body posture, or visuals. The meaning of such a gesture emerges, as Hindmarsh and Heath (2000: 558) argue, "within the developing course of action and interaction; their objective and determinate sense is intersubjectively and momentarily accomplished ,here and now'." Therefore, I would like to consider pointing as not just a gesture that "complements the spoken utterances in order to possibly disambiguate the gesture that comes with them" (Streeck 1994: 249). Since here the synchronization of the action goes beyond speech and the technically projected slides, including the body movements and, as we shall see, the social formation of the body, Schnettler (2006) suggests the notion of *orchestration* of interaction. This notion has also been used by Kress (2010: 162), who defines it as "the process of assembling/organizing/ designing a plurality of signs in different modes into a particular configuration to form a coherent arrangement." Orchestration refers, indeed, to the role of slides, text on manuscripts, speech, body, technology, and so on. Yet, it would be inadequate to define it by just combining these levels. Orchestration is not just the combination of signs but their interplay in communicative action. That is to say that the temporal performance of action, as registered by the video recordings, produces its meaning (and allows meaning to be understood).

The argument that the meaning of pointing is not defined by the exact shape of the finger or the hand is supported by the fact that in presentations the manual forms of pointing are often substituted by other technologies: sticks, pens, and pencils may be used, as well as the computer cursor. Although most software allows the cursor to be enlarged so as to fulfill the pointing function, in the data analyzed we found no evidence for the use of the cursor as a pointing device. The most popular technical form of pointing with powerpoint is the laser pointer. From the perspective of a formal description of pointing, as suggested by Kendon (2004), the laser pointer poses a serious problem. For this technology reduces any iconographic aspects of pointing to a minimum: instead of a hand, or an arrow, or any other iconographic form of "deixis,"[5] the laser pointer does not even produce a line; it consists only of a dot of light visible on the screen. The laser pointer may be considered, therefore, as the "purest" form of pointing since the iconographic elements are minimized very strongly (as opposed to an "arrow," which itself is iconographic).[6]

## 2. Pointing, Space, and the Objectivation of Meaning

Although the laser pointer does not relate the presenter and the pointed object visibly to one another, it only makes sense if the audience knows that it is part of a communicative action, that is, that the presenter is the origin of the light spot produced by it. As opposed to involuntary light effects caused, for example, by changes of sunlight, pointing meaningfully links speech and slide by relating it to the pointing body. Supported by the technology and the audience, this orchestration allows meaning that is

## Fragment 9

1    ehm this is now like the classical (-) equipment which is available 1
     *ähm das ist jetzt so die::klassische (-) Ausrüstung die einem zur Verfügung*

2    if one wants to scrutinise rice..°(You may see here)
     *steht wenn man eben Reis untersuchen möchte, (°sie sehen hier)*

3    on therighthandside such a° eh *magnifyingglasswhichserves=to
     *auf der rechten Seite eben sone° äh *Lupe die °dazu=dient°*

4    in which one may the rice grains or under which one may put the rice grain
     *in die (-) Reiskörneroderunter der man die (-) Reiskörner halt entsprechend*

5    that is on=the=one=hand now=these ehm two hundred rice cors
     *auslegenkann=also=zumeinenebn=dieseähzweihundertganzenReiskörner*

6    that one need for this investigation in order to determine the=length=and
     *die man für die Untersuchung *braucht um eben die=Längen=und=*

7    breadth and then on the left hand side (-) now
     *Breitenverhältnisse feststellen zu können und dann links daneben(-) eben*

8    meter screw which we use as a reference procedure because
     *jetzt die *Messuhr die wir als Referenzverfahren .hhähm verwenden und zwar*

9    on the grounds because this is now ehm a gauge clock.
     *aus dem Grund weil das eben ähm ein- eine geeichte Messuhr ist*

not present in any single modality to be produced. In order to show how orchestration produces meaning and contributes to the construction of a "communicative object," I want to focus, first, on the interplay of pointing gesture, speech, and slides with respect to another example.

The following fragment, Fragment 9, stems from a powerpoint presentation for twenty listeners during an informational meeting in a public administration organization. (Stretches of talk during which the speaker is pointing with the laser pointer are double underlined; the special termini are pseudonyms.)

The presenter coordinates use of the laser pointer with certain stretches of his improvised fresh talk. The interplay between the talk and the slides consists in the effect that certain aspects of what he says are illustrated by what he points at, and that certain aspects of the slides are what he talks about. Moreover, he not only points at certain elements, as we can see when we look at the way he is pointing, but makes movements while pointing. One should not mistake the somewhat shaky movements with the laser pointer as involuntary trembling of the hand. For if one looks closer at these movements, one discovers that the patterns they form are utterly meaningful. Thus, if one looks at the pointing movements of the laser pointer spot during the talk in the preceding fragment, one can identify the patterns represented by the following diagrams (see Diagram 4).

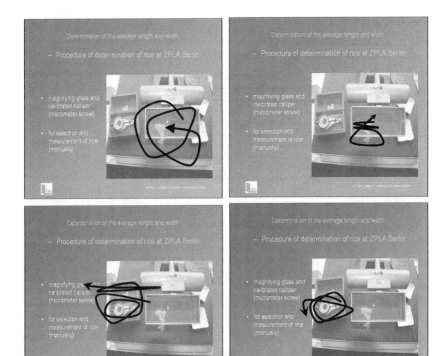

Diagram 4: Sequential reconstruction of laser pointer movements: magnifying glass (top), micrometer screw (bottom). Reproduced with permission from Zoll, German Customs Chemist Conference 2004, Dr. Uwe Schlick, ZPLA Berlin.

As can be seen by the lines representing the movements of the laser pointer on the slides, the presenter makes various movements with the laser pointer on the slide. If one reconstructs these movements in slow motion from the video, they appear to be certain forms circumscribing, encircling, and underlining certain units. Obviously, these units are also recognizable elements of his talk as it was quoted earlier: "rice," the "magnifying glass," and the "micrometer screw." Indeed, in his circling movements at different locations on the slide, he creates a distinction that parallels what he says in his fresh talk. By talking, he is producing a spatial contrast between right (line 3) and left (line 7). While I shall return to the role of space later, here it is important to note that the distinction in pointing and the contrast in speaking are synchronized in time so that they are perceived as relating to the same thing: the magnifying glass on the right hand (including some rice grains lying below it) and the measurement watch on the left hand. Moreover, the duality of this structure

**Fragment 10**

1        *(1,0) The migration of lakedemons out of the vessels into the texture*
         *(1.0) die Auswanderung von Lakedämonen <u>aus dem</u> Gefäß <u>in das</u> Gewebe*

2        *has=been=studied=  quite well, one knows that the lakdemons first=need 'n*
         *ist=relativ=gut=untersucht, man weiß die Lakedämonen brauchen=zuerst n*

3        *<u>initial contact,</u> (has a reduced) affine adaption;*
         *<u>initialen Kontakt,</u> (hat ä / geringe affine) Anlagerung;*

4        *<u>roling motions</u> then support the circular movements contact=this=fixed*
         *<u>des Rollen verstärkt</u> dann den Kreisbewegung Kontakt=diese=feste=Anlagerung*

5        *<u>adaption then migrates</u>; and will then via the molecules it will*
         *<u>wandert dann raus</u>; und wird sehr <u>viel über die Moleküle in</u>*

6        *<u>control the interaction of lakedemons the flacocytecells and</u>=many of you may have asked...*
         *<u>Interaktion von Lakedämonen mit Europol</u>zellen steuern*

is supported in the utterances' construction: Both are introduced by what in rhetoric is called an "apostrophe," addressing the audience (in line 2 explicitly; in line 7 elliptically). Thus, the movements of the laser pointer can be understood as interpretations of what he is saying and what he is hinting at. Speaking, pointing, and the movements on the slide coproduce an understanding of the slide that identifies certain items and objects and their order. These items, one should stress, need not correspond to the structure on the slide. Rather, the structure (as the contrast between right and left) is produced by means of the verbal construction and the pointing movement and, so to say, projected onto the slide. In addition, the remaining text on the slide is not referred to either by talking or by pointing so that it seems to be made irrelevant. Note that the pointing gestures here are not at all only dots on the screen. Rather, the movements circumscribe, encircle, and underline while pointing. It would be a sophistic question to ask whether such gestures can still be designated as pointing or whether they should rather be called "iconographic" or "illustrative," for the most important observation is that the pointing gesture itself adds a visual element to the slide in its various movements.

The question of how these movements contribute to the meaning can be discerned in more detail in the next example. It will demonstrate how the interplay of temporal and spatial aspects of pointing creates new meaning. This kind of creative pointing has already been stressed by Haviland (1993: 27), who considers pointing gestures as "creative" in that they create their referent.[7] Let us have a closer look at this creative use of pointing in another example in which the movements while pointing are highlighted. The example is part of a life science presentation held before an audience of about fifty at a high-profile conference.

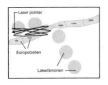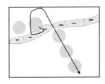

| line 3 | line 4 | line 5 | line 5f |
|---|---|---|---|
| "initial contact" | "roling movements" | "migrates" | "interaction" |

Diagram 5: Sequential reconstruction of laser pointer movements: "initial contact," "roling movements," "migrates," "interaction." Reproduced with permission from Zoll, German Customs Chemist Conference 2004, Dr. Uwe Schlick, ZPLA Berlin.

The presenter turns to the screen by leaving a pause (1) – as he did in his speech before quite frequently. The new slide he refers to in Fragment 10 opens a new topic, which is identified by the pseudonym "lakedemons" (a pseudonym used here for a biochemical structure analyzed by his research group). Already his introduction of a new topic is accompanied by discursive gestures of the presenter illustrating the direction of these "lakedemons'" movements ("aus" or "out," "in" or "in," line 1f) by two gestures of the hand, turning outward and turning inward. As the double lines (lines 3, 4, 5, 6) indicate, he points several times with the laser pointer at the diagram on the screen. Let us look at what is entailed by the ways he points at the screen by again representing the movements of the laser pointer dots as lines.

As can be detected, he points at the "lakedemons" represented by little gray circular forms, resembling balls, and the "Europol cells" by a continuous line on the slide. Moreover, he moves the pointer in different ways on the space of the slides. In relating these movements to what he is speaking about, it becomes quite clear that these pointing movements are particularly meaningful: as Diagram 5 shows, the "initial contacts" (line 3) of these biochemical structures with the "Europol cells" (pseudonym) are underlined by a vertical movement between two circular forms on top and the "Europol cells" (a), their "rolling" by a circular movement (b), their "migration" by sudden straight movements (c), and their interaction by loop-shaped movements (d). His pointing movements seem to mimic the movements of the microscopic objects referred to in the text. They not only "illustrate" what is being said or shown but add movements to these graphically static elements. Further, they bestow an additional sense by the narrative structure of his speech. The speech starts with "first" an initial contact, "then" there is the "rolling," "then" they "migrate" and "will be steered" by the "interaction" between the former. Quite obviously, the difference between these movements corresponds to different parts of the talk ("first," "then," "will then") in such a way that the pointing movements complement the narrative structure of the talk and add meanings: the movements of the laser pointer are dynamic as he moves across the slide relating to the various "objects" in space so that he adds temporality.

Note that the temporal structure is not identical to the temporal sequence of the talk with its "first," "then," "then," and "will" sequence. Rather, it refers to the temporal processes within each of the verbal steps, which are related temporally to one another ("then," "then" ...) As a result, what appears as a simultaneous structure on the slide is turned into a temporal sequence of processes that are characterized by the movements. The orchestration of slide, speech, and pointing results in a kind of imaginary dynamics transforming the diagram into a sequence of diagrams (by the talk) and mimicking the spatial movements of objects on the diagram, which is essentially and basically static.[8]

Obviously, pointing does much more than just indicating something represented on the slide. It relates speech and visual representations in a creative way that allows the production of new meaning. This is to say that the meaning of the presentation cannot be detected from the visual representation alone. In fact, what can be talked about must not be represented in any way on the visual slide. Neither must it be in the words only; rather meaning results from the interplay between speech and slides orchestrated by the pointing body and technology. The orchestration of speech, slides, and pointing creates new meaning. As a consequence, this meaning is not fixed either in a linguistic notion or in a visual sign. The communicative object is, rather, a result of their interplay and, therefore, as elusive as any communicative action in time. Although it may be deciphered by means of slides and text as "knowledge" and can be stored and transmitted as information, this elusiveness results from the fact that communicative action happens situationally in time – and passes in time. (It is, in this sense, also a way of producing the impression of a "fresh" presentation, i.e., of "liveness.")

The fact that the identification of such an "object" cannot be done linguistically demonstrates to what degree pointing contributes not only to the designation but also to the creation of meaning.

At this point, and before we go on to look at the ways in which the body figures while pointing, one should stress that this finding has serious consequences for the criticism of powerpoint as exemplified with respect to Tufte. For the example demonstrates that the meanings communicated in slide presentations should not be reduced to what is represented on the slide. Rather, the meaning is accomplished by the interplay of spoken words, slides, gestures, technology, and son on, which we have called orchestration. By means of this varying interplay, the meaning communicated can greatly exceed what is represented on the slides; it can even differ from whatever "information" is encoded on the slides.

The creation of meaning depends on an additional dimension neglected when talking about the slides. Pointing is not simply a "visual" act relating to a "point." It is, rather, the spatial enactment of the visuals already indicated previously. Objects named verbally are visually identified by relating them to a certain location in the space of the slide. Pointing transforms a visual representation into a spatial object or, to be more precise, into a set of objects ordered in space. Their spatiality is marked by circumscription, and they are positioned in relation to one another by setting them "right" or "left," for the reference to a certain area on the slide allows what is represented there to be highlighted and to be distinguished from another area and the respective "things" represented in this area. Thus, by pointing both presenter and audience are coordinated in time, as in a lecture, and in space. Pointing movements create positions on the slide and relations between these positions, both temporally and spatially. Spatially, the positions and movements pointed to are related to "objects" identified by words.

The relevance of space becomes clear when one considers that what counts as communicative object here needs to be pointed at in the ways described: circumscribed, highlighted, related to, and so forth. One should be aware that spatiality is not restricted to the representation of spatial objects. Rather, pointing may also refer to words, signs, and other abstract elements of the visual repertoire of powerpoint. Everything, including "imaginary objects" not visualized (and indicated or formulated by words), can be treated as a communicative object to which one can point. In this very basic sense, the presentation exploits spatiality in order to create objectivity. In doing so, pointing can be seen as an objectivation in the very elementary sense mentioned: we do not just talk about something that passes by after it has been said. What we talk about can be referred to also in another mode so that we can "point at it" and "go back" to it in the course of the presentation or even "remember" it (as paper or electronic copies) after the event.

This kind of objectivation resembles what Kress (2010: 166) designates as *ratification*: "Something that has been done by another mode is 'ratified' through its naming in speech." Although orchestration is a situative accomplishment that is quite fugitive and ephemeral, by drawing together speech, gestures, and slides it not only serves to ratify meaning; pointing contributes to the objectivation of something that is put at the intersection of the different modalities by action. Thus, an object results from the pointing gesture toward some space, the naming of words, the signs on the slide (both visual representations as well as words), and, not to be forgotten, their interaction and the technology that does the projection. Pointing adds a kind of animation to objectivation in time and space. As does paralleling, objectivation also contributes to the construction of something which is neither "real" nor purely represented and simultaneously "there," that is, the communicative thing. This is what is created by the orchestration in the situation and what counts as "knowledge" that is transmitted in the situation and "held" by the presenter.

Objectivation by orchestration as part of the construction of communicative things depends on an additional dimension related to pointing that needs to be explained. Slides are not spatial in any literal sense, and the screen or the white wall, on which the slide is projected, is to be seen more as a surface than as a space. The spatiality and the communicative objects are not produced like manna from heaven. They are directly linked to what the pointing finger (or the hand holding the laser pointer) is linked to: the body. Seen from the perspective of an extension of the finger and the technological devices used for it, the body figures prominently in the orchestration of the performance. It gets in, so to say, by using concrete things, such as the laser pointer, the hand holding it, and the body related to it. For as abstract as even laser pointing may be, it requires a body to move. In light of this, let us now turn briefly to the role of the body in pointing, which is rarely acknowledged in research (but cf. Hindmarsh and Heath 2000).

## 3. Body Formation and the Triadic Structure of the Presentation

The body performs a hitherto neglected role while pointing. Understandably, pointing requires more or less extended body movements and a reconfiguration of the body, which, however, only comes into sight if one extends the study of it beyond the "gesture unit" (Kendon 2004: 111f.). For only then does one observe that pointing involves the body to a degree that may belie our focus on the finger, the hand, or the forearm. In most cases, pointing includes the posture of the body.

As Still 4 from an academic presentation shows, the presenter not only points to the slide with his finger. He also turns his arm and, quite visibly, his whole upper body around while pointing. The postural change in this case is quite extensive. The presenter, in a way, follows his finger. In this case, this leads to a dramatic turn of his upper body because the

Still 4: Pointing and postural change.

presenter stands very much in front of the slide rather than, as we shall see later, being decentered as most other presenters are. For this reason, the presenter in Still 4 twists his body more than usual, but this demonstrates even more clearly to what degree spatiality is constructed by body and body movements. Consider how, in principle, it would be quite feasible for most presenters to point into the projector's lights so that the shadow of their hand could serve as a (so to say) two-dimensional indicator. Although we might also adapt to visual effects (such as fingers and hands appearing larger than normal), this easy way of pointing has not been found in any of our data. Instead, presenters prefer generally to exploit the space between their body and the projected slide when pointing.

This body movement makes a clear difference to classical oratory, speeches, and talks where presenters turn their body front clearly and exclusively toward the audience and sometimes toward the text they are reading. In powerpoint presentation it frequently happens that they turn away from the audience to the screen. Since pointing can already be considered as a turn toward the screen by the presenter, the turn to the slide on the screen or the wall (to which I will refer as screen) extends this movement to larger parts of the body and, if turning to the screen, to the whole body. Next to the relevance of the slides, these movements indicate the relevance of the body to the performance (while performances vary to the degree that the body is engaged). This role of the body is an additional reason for the difference between a speech or talk and a presentation. It is the performing body that turns the speech into a presentation.

Although the reference of the body may be not very exact, it makes clear the relevance of the screen or the slide when it turns toward it, and the additional movement of pointing to the slide (on the screen or wall) allows the presenter to relate to what he or she is attending to. This way, the pointing gesture, the spatiality of the body, and its position in space (a) engender the spatiality of the slide, (b) make movements of the body into references to objects on the slides, and (as we have seen), finally, (c) allow movements of the body to be turned into movements of the "objects" referred to. The character of spatiality is enhanced by the fact that the slides often are as large as the presenter's body or even larger.

That is to say that the turn away from the audience toward the screen must not be an indication of disengagement from the audience, as Rendle-Short (2006: 41ff.) suggests. On the contrary, the turn toward the slide is, rather, an indication for the engagement of both, the presenter and the audience, as assumed by the presenter. There are, furthermore, good reasons for this assumption. As opposed to the lecture and the reading of a manuscript, where the audience would not have access to the text, the powerpoint presenter is being seen while pointing and turning to something, and this something is seen by the audience, too.[9] While the manuscript in some sense serves as a backstage for presenters who read, inaccessible to the audience, the "content" of the presentation is part of the audience's "public" stage, the common environment of both, presenter and audience. Rather than interpreting the focus of the presenter toward the slide as disengagement from the audience, it can be seen by audiences typically as an indication of also turning toward them (particularly obvious when presenters and screens are placed at different ends of the room so that audience need to move their heads). Therefore, already the sheer act of turning the presenter's body may be understood as a pointing gesture toward the screen or back, and in some positions even a mere turning of the face can be understood this way. In this manner, body movement is an essential part of the communicative action for it not only expresses an actor's attention toward the slides, thus enhancing the objectivation; the body (and its movements) also anticipates the fact that the presenter is monitored by the audience and reflects the ways this occurs. The body helps to establish what may be the focus of the interaction the presenter is addressing – knowingly being watched by the audience.

Note that this kind of objectivation presupposes the processes of inter-subjectivity analyzed by Schutz and sketched previously in the theoretical Chapter 3. Pointing and the respective body movements only make sense if one assumes that actors presuppose being seen while acting; by assuming that the audience will look at what they refer to from their position in space, in addition, they presuppose the "exchangeability" of standpoints analyzed by Schutz, while their assumption that audience members will look at where they point implies, finally, the reciprocity of motives. In this respect, the body is an essential part of the communicative action. One should, however, not forget the subjective dimension of pointing as action. For turning to the screen must not only be relevant to others; it may, simultaneously, allow the presenter to recognize, possibly even remember or reconstruct, items represented on the slide that he or she may have forgotten. In this sense, it functions as a mnemotechnique. Yet, even if this were the primary reason for the presenter (and if not stated otherwise explicitly), interactively, the body's turning can be perceived by the audience as an indicator. In this way it acts as a device that indicates the presenter's focus of attention and the focus to which he or she seems practically to draw the audience's attention. In doing so, it is quite clear that he or she also considers the body as public. Indeed, the public visibility of the body is an essential part of performance.

It should not be forgotten that the body, here, is first of all a presenter's body. By relating to something, the body relates to what is on the screen (and what he or she talks about) and what is also seen by the audience. Since, in pointing, the body is also presupposed to be seen by the audience, body movement establishes a *triadic relation* among the presenter, the screen or slides (and everything referred to here as informational technologies), and the audience. As already mentioned in the Introduction, this triadic relation is of the utmost importance to seeing powerpoint presentation as a communicative genre. Without determining the genre, one could say that it is the backbone that determines its essential features both on the intermediate level and on the external level of analysis. We should, therefore, delineate the triadic structure in further detail.

The triadic structure can probably best be exemplified with respect to the middle position. By middle position I mean a position of the presenter's body in relation to the screen and the audience that is characterized by the body's being only slightly turned toward the screen and, simultaneously, slightly toward the audience, as in the example in Still 5.

Still 5: The middle position.

In front of a small audience the presenter stands in such a way as to be able to turn his face from the screen to the audience easily without turning his back to the audience. At the same time, his body posture tries to "face" both, the audience and the screen, halfway toward both.

The middle position is typically linked with a phenomenon one may call the *decentered presenter*. Whereas screens are often located in the center of one side of the room, the podium is moved to the side. Although familiar in many academic lecture halls and churches, where lecterns or pulpits are mostly positioned away from the center, decentering is sometimes intensified by dimmed light (often in locations not equipped for any or equipped with older presentation technologies). Enhancing the objectivation process, the common stage is centered on the screen and the slides shown. As Still 6 shows, presenters even tend to extend the side position by moving desks to the side, so that the "middle" position" prevents the presenter from turning his face and body away from the audience.

The decentered position does not signify a removal of the presenter out of the focus. Rather, it gives space to the screen in such a way that the relation of presenter, slide, and audience reminds one of a triadic "face formation." According to Kendon (1990), the spatial positioning of faces in an interaction indicates the kind of involvement of participants and the kind of attention they confer upon and expect from coparticipants. In interactions between two actors they confront each another face to face, setting their faces in such a way that they are visible to each another.

The face formation indicates speakers' "addressability" as well as their attentiveness to the communication. Moreover, it also affects their ways

Still 6: Face formation[10].

of acting. If the number of interaction partners increases, the participants tend to configure their faces in a format close to a circle so that each person is able to see the others' faces. The circular configuration would also influence further steps as any movement would necessitate certain rituals – as when leaving the circle, entering its core (O), or including new participants in the circle or on its fringes (R).

Looking at the face formation, it appears that there are striking parallels to presentations. By moving their bodies in certain ways, presenters establish a relation between the various elements that works like the face formation: the reciprocal monitoring of faces and bodies allows the participants to coordinate their engagement, their actions, and their mutual understanding. However, as the analysis of pointing has shown, the notion of face formation may be somewhat misleading. In addition to the face, the whole body, or at least those parts and movements that are visible to the audience, is of importance in presentations. On these grounds, it would be more apt to talk about a *body formation*, referring to the position of the body with respect to other bodies and objects and the orientation of attentiveness indicated by the body and its parts. Thus, while the face can be oriented to the audience, the upper body may take a middle position as one hand and the fingers may be turning toward the screen. The body may also move into the middle position, the upper part of the body towering over the lectern may be turning, or the whole body standing decentered beside

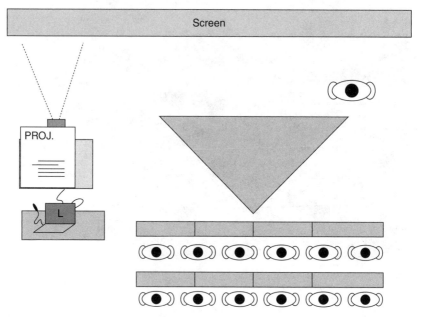

Diagram 6: Presenter/audience/technical chain triangle.

the lectern can get into a "screw position" so that the feet remain facing the audience whereas the rest turns over to the screen.

Given the similarities to the face formation, with respect to the presenter, the triadic relation is not just based on the face formation or even on the relation between the participating bodies. It is constituted by the presenter's whole body, the audience, and the slide or screen that represents the technological chain of projector, computer and monitor or notebook, remote control, as well as other technologies necessary for conducting powerpoint presentations. This means that the slide and whatever is needed to show it (in the case of smooth operations without technical failures, such as a nonoperating projector) function as the third party of the presentation. The basic structure of the presentation consists of a triadic relation among three elements in which the screen and the slide do appear in the position of the third party in an interaction. This "party" becomes involved through the pointing function of the slides, by the sequence of slide, and, not to be forgotten, by the activities of the body that set the stage for it as a third party.[11]

As Diagram 6 indicates, the body, its parts and technical extensions (like fescues or laser pointers), is not only an "indication" of the presenter's focus of attention. It also allows the presenter to relate to the slides and the audience. As we shall see, the meaning of the presenter's performance does not just depend on his or her actions but also on the relation to, and the performance of, audiences and technology. Here, however, I want to focus on the presenter's bodily performance.

The most mobile part of the triadic relation during the presentation is ordinarily the presenter, who can move his or her body (or, in some settings, only part of the body, such as arms or fingers). Given the presenter's inter-subjective anticipation of being seen by the audience and the knowledge of the spatial setting, his or her body exhibits his or her orientation toward the audience and the slides. It is an essential part of the communicative action for it serves to indicate the presenter's attentiveness and, simultaneously, to guide the audience members' attention. Presenters turn to the slide in such a way as to indicate the relevance of what is being said to what is being shown and to draw attention to certain points of their talk. It is for this reason that presenters appear as the *subject* of presentations, that is, as those who are presenting. Yet, one should note that, first of all, the knowledge that actors use when moving (more or less accounting for the similarity of the presentation to the face formation) is deeply habitualized knowledge so that their movements are often performed routinely. (Presenters lacking experience with powerpoint quickly learn to move their bodies accordingly even if neophytes exhibit some clumsiness.)[12] Second, it is not just the actions that take on a certain meaning. As the meaning of any communicative act needs to be objectified, here it is the presenter's body that is the focus of attention (as is the screen). For this reason it takes on a focal role and functions as a pivot. The movements of the presenter's body exhibit and steer attention between the slide and the audience.[13] Intentionally and routinely, the body employs pointing and other gestures, the turning of the face, and its reorientation, as well as its movement within the space of audience and screen.

Even from the presenter's perspective, the presentation cannot be seen as a kind of monologic action toward the audience as passive recipients. By the movement of his or her body, the presenter accounts for the audience members and their monitoring of her or his movements. Since she or he is actively prompting, orally referring to, and bodily orienting toward the slides, the presenter enacts the triangular relation to the slide or screen (projection surface) and the audience. Of course, presenters performing lectures also turn to their notes as a kind of a "third part" while reading and, thus, open a third point of reference. However, this reference to a text remains "backstage" (Goffman 1980/1980), not accessible to the audience. Although the back stage may be seen as a third reference point, at least to the speaker, that may become relevant in the temporal course of speeches, it typically does not become a spatial object for both speaker and audience. Exceptions to this rule are, of course, failures, for example, when a speaker realizes he or she has missed a page or when a draft blows notes off the lectern. The same holds for other types of notes. Recent versions of PowerPoint allow annotations to the slide that remain hidden from the audience. Turning toward the screen slide differs in this respect, for the body as well as the slide projected on the screen form part of the shared "public" environment of all participants, thus allowing objectivation.

The presenter, his or her body, and the movements (including sounds) produced by it are the pivot of the triadic relationship; moreover it is the only agent that acts intentionally and has intentions ascribed to it by the audience. The presentation is, therefore, biased toward the presenter. From the perspective of the triadic structure one may also say that it is *asymmetrical*. Nevertheless, asymmetrical as it may be, one must note that the presenter is dependent on the other two aspects of the presentation, the slide and the audience, for his or her performance. In this sense, the triadic structure lies at the core of powerpoint presentation as communicative genre.

The dependence on the triadic relationship can most easily be inferred from the fact that the body's position within the triangle and its exposed relationship to the other elements not only have significance for single action steps but can determine the "frame" of whole presentations. Goffman's (1974) notion of frame refers to what a certain situation means to the actors. Particularly if presenters move to different positions during their presentations, it becomes clear that these moves take on some significance, for example, the common switch between the position toward the screen, which accommodates pointing to the screen, and the frontal position, in which the presenter faces the audience. It is quite clear to anyone that in the first position the speaker relates to the elements of the slide, whereas in the second case, the presenter highlights what is being said. One could say that the presenter frames what he or she says by moving and, thus, turning to either the audience or the technical chain. Goffman's frame, thus "refers to a sense of what activity is being engaged in, how speakers mean what they say" (Tannen et al. 1987: 3). For our purposes, the notion of frame is still too broad since it may also refer to "ironic" presentations (as in powerpoint karaoke or rather playful "dry runs," i.e., rehearsals of presentations). In order to catch the specific significance produced by the relationship within the triangle, it would be more precise to specify the frame by another notion Goffman (1981a) has suggested: production format. Accordingly, the *production format* of an utterance differs (and with it what Goffman calls "footing") depending on the way a speaker is related to the utterance. While Goffman restricts himself to the consideration of relations of speakers to their spoken utterances, I want to extend the discussion to any bodily communicative performance involved in speaking and presenting and its relation to the technology. Production format can refer to oral utterances, but also to a text or diagram on a slide or a gesture, such as pointing. In indicating and expressing an orientation, the various positions with relation to the other elements of the triangle frame can be regarded as different production formats. Presenters may turn to the written text and perform a reading lecture, that is, "read"; or use a hybrid of talk and "pointing" and performing; or they may speak freely and rely on or ignore the paralleling of the words and the slides (which functions as indirect pointing).

If words are orally directed to the audience, the production format differs from words relating to slides and visual representation, which, thence, must be considered as part of the participation framework. Although there is a huge range of body movements performed by the presenters, the focus on the triadic relation and the fact that presenters take certain positions for longer periods facilitates observations. For most presenters not only switch continuously among various positions but take what may be said to be their preferred position: very few would, during their speech, turn around and orient toward the screen and show their back to the audience. Many more (and some of them for longer stretches of time) sit facing the monitor of their notebook; others turn only slightly away with the upper part of their body, in this manner alluding to a turn to the screen rather than actually pointing. Some presenters again may face the audience for almost the whole presentation, whereas other presenters may read from a text, their face switching from text to notebook to audience.

As diverse as the various postures may be, there are three major positions we have already encountered in talking about types of presentations: positions oriented toward a text or monitor, positions oriented toward the screen or slide, and positions oriented toward the audience, as well, forming, it is important to note, the triadic middle position. As the monitor or *manuscript orientation* as well as the audience orientation can be found in lectures based on written texts or fresh talk and screen orientation in black- or whiteboard teaching, the middle position seems to be prototypical for powerpoint presentations, that is, the middle position. It is one of the corroborations of the basic nature of the triadic structure of powerpoint presentations that the positions are framed by a triadic structure, which, thus, defines the production format.

The usefulness of the production format becomes even more obvious if presenters remain for a longer period in a certain position, sometimes exclusively. Some presenters, for example, prefer the frontal position facing the audience. One must concede that sometimes presenters are coerced into this position by spatial orders and objects, such as fixed lecterns, desks, and microphones. I shall turn to the role of the objects in space later. With respect to the production format, there are also presenters who hardly ever turn to the slides or point at them. (Some may be doing it because certain instruction books for powerpoint presentations suggest not looking at the slides or pointing at them.) Of course, the presenter's body does not disappear in these presentations; it is still visible to the audience but at the same time denies its focal relevance to the presentation. Instead of an idealized triangle formed by presenter, audience, and slide, the body formation turns into a parallel setting, where the presenter stands in front of the slide facing the audience.

Thus, the triadic structure provides the grounds for the various types of presentation, which appear like empirical cases of typically different production formats.[14] A first type is characterized by presenters who turn their face to the written text or the monitor only, large parts of their bodies hidden behind a lectern. During these *manuscript-oriented presentations* the presenter reads a text written in advance, while a slide presentation accompanies the presentation. Here, speech and (rather formal) written forms are dominant, while the slide may parallel the speech or, as in some cases in which the paralleling is minimized, provide a background to it like a tapestry. There are also presentations in which slides dominate. In these *visual presentations*, the presenter often or exclusively turns toward the slides, either only with his or her face or with the whole body.[15] In rare cases in which the presenter is decentered by dimmed light, this can also be considered as a visual presentation. The *presenter's type of presentation* is characterized by his or her turning to the audience with the whole body front moving and gesticulating without frequently referring to the slides. If he or she is also not oriented to a manuscript, the presenter appears to talk "freshly," as often expressed in an informal style.

In between these types, there is the mixed type, which is characterized by the middle position. In fact, this seems to be most usual manner adopted in powerpoint presentations, in which presenters move between the types mentioned. They are typically linked to forms of footing like commenting, paraphrasing, or relating the text and a style labeled previously as "formal informality." Thus, as most presenters switch positions, the types indicate extreme cases of presenters sticking to a single major position for the duration of their performance. As extreme as these types may be, they illustrate the role of the triadic structure for the production format: thus, the visual presentation not only relates to a certain kind of presenter but sets the audience member in the role of spectator. That spectator is watching slides, continuously turning his or her head toward the screen, whereas the manuscript oriented presentation casts the presenter in the role of the speaker and turns the audience member into a listener who may look in other directions or turn to his or her own notes.

The importance of the triadic structure lies in its hints of the boundaries of the communicative genre. Thus, if, under certain circumstances, a presenter ignores the projector and the computer and unpacks a manuscript to be read, she or he is transforming a possible presentation into a talk or a more formal speech, even if, as may happen, the organizers project a slide mentioning her or his name, the title of her or his presentation, and the organizational affiliation. This case occurs quite frequently when organizers expect invited presenters to give a presentation only for them to prefer lectures to other genres. Also a presentation that includes only photographs and has no "text" relation will be felt to be on the boundary of what we may call a presentation and to be, instead, a (picture) slide show. There are, of course, more factors that may cause us to hesitate to define a particular event as a presentation. Yet, considering the powerpoint presentation, the triadic structure seems to be constitutive for the genre in the sense that it is a necessary condition of a presentation. (Other aspects identified in this analysis contribute to the definition of the communicative genre.) That is to say that the meaning of communicative actions is not just dependent on the linguistic or visual signs produced by the presenter but also on their relation to and in the triadic participation framework.

Given the importance of the triadic structure and of the presenter as the most mobile element and pivot within this structure, it also seems necessary to address the other two termini of the triadic structure, the "audience" and the slide, that is, the technology.

## 4. Audience Interaction

The interest in the participation of the audience is based on its relevance to the presentation as a communicative genre and, therefore, as we have seen, as part of the triadic structure. It is also motivated by the widespread criticism that powerpoint denies interaction between speaker and hearer by introducing a sharp hierarchical relationship between them (Lobin 2009: 182). As commonly as this argument is voiced, there are hardly any studies supporting it. Most empirical investigations of powerpoint presentations addressing this issue only deal indirectly with it by way of interviews or abstract standardized observation codes. One must mention that the empirical analysis of audience interaction in natural settings within the social sciences in general is still a much neglected topic. Although audiences and the public in general are of the utmost importance not only to sociology, but also to rhetoric or the political sciences, there are few studies that focus on the communicative forms in which audience members "react" to speakers or presenters in natural settings. Among these studies is, for example, Atkinson's (1984) study of political oratory, Goodwin's (1986) application of conversational analysis to the interaction with audiences, or Knoblauch's (1987) study on the sales speech interaction between sales representatives and audience members. In the only naturalistic study considering audience interactions in (academic) presentation, based on audio-visual recordings, Rendle-Short (2006) supports the view that there are, indeed, few interactions.

With this background and in trying to identify the role of the audience, I want to show that the audience can easily become an active part in powerpoint presentations. By locating where they occur within the presentations, I aim to identify several forms of audience interaction. On the basis of this, I will then clarify the general role of the audience as part of the basic triadic genre structure. In doing so I thus want to argue that audiences are not passive recipients of presentations but are actively oriented to both the technology as well as the presenter, thus coproducing the triadic structure. In addition, audiences are not just "collective" actors. Rather, members of an audience interact with presenters and the rest of the audience in various ways, some of which account for the fact that they need to coordinate their own actions simultaneously. Although this is sometimes referred to as "audience reaction," it consists of conventionalized forms of action that are oriented toward technology and presenters as well as toward the other audience members.

In order to refer to the active form of interaction in audience formats, the notion of primary speaker is widely used. The primary speaker is the one who has a monopoly on speaking for a certain period. Indeed, considering the figuration of powerpoint presentation in which the presenter disposes of the speech monopoly and the technical means of projection, critiques of powerpoint have some reason to assume that presentations are in danger of severe asymmetry: the speaker as presenter disposes of the power to occupy the acoustic "stage" as well as the visual focus. As

## Fragment 11

1   S:   ...and hark back - a short question, before we begin; uhm, almost all of have been at the
    S:   *...zugreifen - kurze Frage, bevor wir anfangen, uhm, Sie waren fast alle bei der*

2     introductory event if I remember it right. Who has not been in theintroductoryevent
    *Einführungsveranstaltung, wenn ich das recht in Erinnerung habe, wer von Ihnen war nicht*

3     Technical Analysis?
    *auf der Einführungsveranstaltung. Technische Analyse"?*

4   A1:   ((Raises Hand))
    A1:   *((meldet sich))*

5   A2:   Me too.
    A2:   *Ich auch.*

6   S:   Oh, well (...) you have not been there and you neither...
    S:   *Oh, nun gut (...) Sie waren nicht da und Sie auch nicht...*

plausible as the assumption may be, the critique does, however, not correspond to the findings of empirical research. If one looks at active forms of interaction, one can easily observe that powerpoint presentations do not exhibit a stronger tendency to elicit participation or prohibit participation in explicit interaction.

### (a) Interaction at the Beginnings of Presentations

It is an essential feature of presentations as forms of focused interaction that they are temporally embedded, both before and after, in less focused forms of interaction, as, for example, in introductions or farewells, discussions or comments (but mumbling and conversations between audience members are also typical forms). Interactions of this kind, in which audience members are visibly, audibly acting and so becoming the audience's focus of attention, can also be discerned if one looks at the video data on powerpoint presentations. Take as an example a seminar for professionals by a presenter using powerpoint to teach the creation and understanding of economic diagrams. The presenter already starts to talk when he suddenly turns to the audience.

At the beginning of Fragment 11, which stems from a seminarlike presentation, various inquiries and similar interactions between presenter and audience members occur. But it is not that the interactive episodes are suppressed as soon as the initial phase of presentations has passed. In the case discussed, the pace of participation did not change even ten minutes later. Although the presenter is performing in front of a powerpoint slide, he is still inviting members of the audience (who are unknown to him) to participate, and this is quite easily facilitated.

## Fragment 12

1   S:   I have seen that there are problems with using the web page, did I get this right?
    S:   *Da' hab ich vorhin wahrgenommen, dass es einige Probleme gab mit der Bedienung dieser Internetseite, hab ich das richtig verstanden?*

2   A3: Yes
    *A3:Ja*

3   S:   Trade signal
    S:   *Trade signal*

4   A3:Yes.
    *A3:Ja.*

5   S: OK, if there are any questions…
    S:  *Ok, wenn da Fragen sein sollten*

While referring to a Web page on the slide (see Fragment 12), the presenter is asking the audience about their experience with this page. Obviously, the representation of the slide allows a reference to the audience member's experience of the Web page, so that here the slide allows the presenter to ask a question – and to trigger an answer and a consecutive embedded side sequence with the audience member.

This is only one short sequence out of a presentation during which the audience is continuously active and participating. The experience of such interactive seminars may be quite common for many readers, too. It must be stressed, therefore, that the use of powerpoint does not obviously obstruct the interactive nature of such events.

### (b) Audience Interventions

Interactions with audience members are not restricted to those presentations in which at the beginning active participation is encouraged by the presenter's eliciting responses. Active participation of the audience, or intervention, can also occur in the course of presentations that are characterized by a more formal style, that is, with an audience silently listening to a presentation and watching it. By "formal" (a notion refined later in the analysis of the setting) is meant that the slots for audience participation are clearly marked by an introduction, possibly a moderator, and a discussion at the end. Take as an example a presentation given in the frame of a large medical conference. In one of the sessions at this conference the presenter, after having been introduced by a moderator, talked for almost fifteen minutes monologically in front of an audience of about thirty people before the following sequence emerged:

The presenter is in the midst of his speech when a woman in the audience demands attention to her question. This demand is quite unexpected

**Fragment 13**

1   S:  With the whole body- (0-5) MR are= of course even much worse (0.5= than /new slide
    S:  *Mit der Ganzkörper- (0,6) MR sind=die natürlich noch viel schlechter (0,5) ähm in*

2       In this moment; that does not make any sense. (0.7) something different if cancer of the
        *dem Moment, das hat also da: keinen Sinn. (0,7) Was anders=is beim*

3       prostate.
        *Prostatakrebs.*

4       (1.4.) that is
        *(1,4) das ist-*

5   F1: May I ask a question?
    F1: *Ich habe da mal eine=Frage*

6   S:  = please
    S:  *= bitteschön*

7   F1: Concerning the prot- con- concerning this MR mammography
    F1: *Zu dem Schutz- zu=dem- zu=diesem MR Mammographie*

8   S:  Mhm
    S:  *Mhm*

9   F1: Many professors recommend…
    F1: *Viele Professoren empfehlen doch…*

since no such intervention occurred before the "monological" presentation. It may be for this reason that the question is introduced ritually (Goffman 1981b: 17f.), for she first formulates a presequence (5), followed by the ratification of the presenter (6). Only in the next step (7) does she begin her question, clearly relating it to the topic of the presenter's speech.[16] The fragment does not include what happens after the intervention (9) when another member of the audience joins in the discussion. While the presenter still gives his answer to the first woman, a second woman starts another question, leaving out the ritual introduction and speaking in medias res, "May I say something, the health protection…." This second intervention almost transforms the whole format of the speech into a discussion. This interpretation is corroborated by the ensuing move by the moderator, who, after the second question, joins in and proposes that the presenter answer this questions, since, he argues, there will be no time left for discussion after the talk. After having answered the question, the presenter returns to his presentation by changing his body formation.

These examples demonstrate that powerpoint presentations do not necessarily obstruct audience participation. On the contrary, the chance of opening direct interactions is built into the genre itself. This can be seen with respect to Fragment 13, quoted previously. Scrutinizing the visual conduct before this exchange, one can observe that the intervention does not "come out of left field" (4). Before the first woman starts to talk, she is moving her body and her hand quite visibly. Exactly at this point, the presenter, standing in the middle position, starts visibly to face her. Having "caught his eye," she looks back to him and then starts to ask her question. Obviously, the spoken part of this interaction is built on the mutual forms of monitoring one another and the body formation. It seems that because of the visual orientation of the presenter to the audience (which differs from the manuscript orientation of lecture reading), the presentation allows for the interventions by the two women.

### (c) *Presenters and Audiences*

As the previous case has shown, interactive sequences are not restricted to presenters and audience members. They may also be oriented toward moderators. Since sometimes there are several people on the stage giving one presentation together , the interaction between presenters becomes an issue for analysis. There are various ways that the multiple presenter format can be produced: temporally, presenters may displace each another, each performing a section of the presentation. (There is no case in which the text has been spoken simultaneously.) In these cases, presenters leave the space in the front when they are no longer talking: some move a bit to one side and indicate their changing participation status by handing over the computer, the computer mouse, the laser pointer, or the remote.[17] It is then quite clear that the next person takes on the role of the presenter. What, however, happens to the previous presenter?

Fragment 14 is taken from a university seminar in which students were asked to give very short presentations based on the results of small group work sessions.[18] The group presenting consists of three people, a female and two male students. For the purpose of their short presentation, the group had designed four powerpoint slides. The first introductory slide follows the pattern used by all groups, containing the group's name, the names of the group members, the "subject," the "method" used for performing their task, the "product" that resulted from their work, and the customers it is targeting. The second slide (below, slide X2) shows the "product" they developed during their group work session. The third slide (below, slide X1) includes a structured diagram of the process that is initiated by the product. The last slide, dominated by three colored question marks, draws a conclusion and indicates some pending questions. Now have a look at the three presenters while they are showing the slides.

The text of presenter S 1 is obviously prepared in advance since he reads from a manuscript. It is not quite clear whether the performance is

**Fragment 14**

Speaker 1 Speaker 2

S 1:    ....to diabetics, heart cases, the needy
       and elder people

2    *an Diabetiker, Herzkranke, hilfsbedürftige*
     *und ältere Menschen*

3    Ehm our product
     *ähm, unser Produkt*

4    do you go on
     *machst Du weiter*

5    S 2: our product guarantees permanent

     *S 2: unser Produkt gewährleistet eine*        *permanente &*

6    datatransfer of individual patients         *Patientendaten*
     *Datenübertragung    der    individuellen*

planned in advance or just follows the pattern of the other presentations: all "authors" are standing at the front but only some are speaking. After finishing his part on his slides (Still 7), S 1 hands over to his colleague in the center (S 2) using deictic gestures pointing at him with the card he was reading from. This sign is also perceived by the third presenter on the right, who immediately initiates a movement toward the laptop computer, presses a button, and changes the slide. In this moment, S 1's head is turning around and he is focusing the screen and the female presenter, while S 2 begins to address the audience (Still 8). Presenters, thus, may divide the role of presentation, so that one is talking and the other clicks the buttons. If they do, it is quite interesting to see that those presenters who are momentarily not performing are oriented to and guided by the current presenter's speech, pointing, and body formation in a similar way to the audience members – yet in a more exposed position, since they are part of the focus of the audience's attention.

## (d) Endings and Applause

Presentations vary with respect to the degree to which they allow for explicit or visible audience reaction. Whereas some formats are highly participative in being accompanied by expressive audience reactions, in other cases audiences are less participative. The degree of participation as well

(a)                                        (b)

(c)

Still 7:  Presenter leaves.

as the degree of preparation are strongly related to formality or informality, to which we will turn in the next chapter. Whatever the formality of the presentations, they all exhibit what conversation analysts call a "transition relevance place" where the speech (not, as we shall see, the presentation) comes to an end so that the audience is expected to take the floor.[19] Presentations are typically framed in such a way that when the monological part ends, the presenter receives credit with some kind of applause. Typical forms of audience action include clapping with the hands, knocking on desks (in the German academic context), nodding while looking at the presenter, and sometimes smiling gratefully at him or her. Applause is sequentially referred to by the presenter, for in all cases they turn away from the audience while being applauded. This may even hold if they do not mark the end of the presentation. Consider the following example, which represents a somewhat "deviant case."

In this case, the presenter does not announce the termination of her presentation verbally. Although she lowers her voice in the final sentence and drops her gaze (Still 7a), she does not say a word indicating the end of her presentation. Instead, after finishing her last sentence (read from the manuscript), she turns away (Still 7b) and leaves the lectern (Still 7c). It is at this point that the audience starts to clap. Although the presenter does not mark the end of the presentation, it is at this juncture and as the presenter leaves the lectern that the audience realizes the presentation is finished. This holds for most presentations: the applause sets in as soon as the body indicates inattention to the audience, even if a presenter does not produce any sign of having reached the end. The rule also holds for deviant cases. Thus, in one case a presenter looked into the audience while receiving applause. The presentation before, however, had been characterized by extremely long pauses, and when the presenter finished and offered to answer questions, nothing happened. Only when she had expressed her gratitude did clapping start, somewhat reluctantly, while she was looking at the audience.

This almost timid kind of inattention while receiving applause is quite different from other performative formats, such as theater, music, or dance performance. In these cases performers openly look at the audience while being applauded. Instead, actors after powerpoint presentations typically turn their head or their body away when applause is offered. The most likely interpretation is that the event has not ended; the presentation is followed by a discussion or any other kind of action that allows the audience to appreciate, assess, or evaluate the performance. The presenter, one may say, stays in the role, while artists leave the role when they bow with thanks.

Since the advice books and texts recommend a closing slide, it is quite legitimate to look at the interactive functions of these slides at this point. Quite frequently presenters use the final slide to request responses or questions or to express their gratitude for the audience's attention (often using witty cartoon diagrams). However, in many presentations, the closing slide is not in sync with the spoken text so that it is already visible while the presenter is still talking or it is shown after the applause has already begun. Still, in our data there were some cases in which a speech somehow ended simultaneously with the slide. In none of these cases was it the slide that "triggered" applause. Instead, in all empirical cases analyzed the audience always waited for the presenter to give some verbal (or, as we have seen, behavioral) indications for the termination of the presentation before the audience started to clap.

In summary, we can quite clearly see that powerpoint does not obstruct interaction between audience and presenter. The analysis has shown that, instead, there are peculiar forms of interaction. One might even say that

powerpoint facilitates the forms of interaction to the degree that presenters are not oriented toward a text or a manuscript but to a slide visible to
both presenters and audience simultaneously, and to the degree that they
are monitoring the audience and are seen to be monitoring it. This is found
consistently in, and is, simultaneously, constitutive of, the "presenter type"
of presentation.

If one asks whether and, if so, how interaction is linked to powerpoint
presentations, one is not restricted to looking at the frequency of the forms
of interaction analyzed. Even if one may find that certain types are crucial
whereas others are more marginal, it would be misleading to reduce the
notion of presenter- audience interaction to these explicit exchanges of
individual presenter utterances. As the example of the final applause shows,
audiences display their own forms of expression, such as clapping, knocking, smiling. Utterances of an audience may be nonlinguistic but sum up a
collective communicative action, as, for example, if several audience members are murmuring sotto voce or simultaneously produce an expression
of surprise (such as a collective "wow").[20] Moreover and more importantly,
as the presenter forms part of a body formation, the audience's members'
bodies also "speak" in a sense: Faces look up to the screen, turn to the
presenter or to their documents, hands start to write, or mouths to yawn.
Leaving aside the hard work that is often required in maintaining the signs
of attentiveness (for example, keeping the eyes open or even not sleeping
during presentations and speeches), one should not mistake these indications as being merely "passive." Although these acts are not uniform and
although they may be semantically ambivalent (such as yawning, which may
be read as "natural" exhaustion or a social "reaction" to the presentation),
they are also aspects of interaction. Here, again, the triadic structure plays
a decisive role. Whereas in lectures the process of hearing remains largely
invisible (so that hearers may be allowed to turn away from a presenter or
close their eyes), presentations demand attention from audience members
through watching and, often (particularly in the presentation type), switching (and being seen switching) between watching the presenter and watching the slides. It is because of the triadic figuration that audience members'
movements are typically taken as "signs" of their awareness, their attention, and their participation. ("Sign" should not be understood as static but
rather as a bodily performance in time that becomes significant because of
the orientation toward what else is happening, mainly with respect to the
triangle.)

The relevance of the triadic structure can be seen in the fact that the
presenter and the slide provide the two major points of orientation for

the audience. The audience can, of course, also orient to themselves, for instance, in writing down what is heard. (In the next chapter, we shall encounter a case in which a collective action by the audience is oriented to audience members' subsequent actions.) The triadic structure, thus, provides the background or, as we have said, the participation framework for the understanding of the various actions in the presentation. As mentioned, this not only holds for the presenter and the audience. Technology also "figures" as a major aspect in the figuration of presentations. It is, therefore, also necessary to have a closer look at how technology contributes to presentations.

## 5. Technology, Failures, and Footing

In recent years, the relation between technology and action has stirred controversy and debate. Because of the rise of new information and communication technologies, particular questions have been raised regarding the "agency" of technology. Whereas traditionally technology has been considered as "means" that are subordinate to human actions and the goals set by humans, the increased delegation of tasks to "socio-technological systems leads to questions as to whether these systems' performance must also be considered actions" (Rammert and Schulz-Schaeffer 2002), and whether objects are to be treated as actors (Latour 1993). This question is not only of general interest. Because of the importance of technology for powerpoint presentations, it applies here as well: are presentation programs set in the role of actors who not only structure ideas but also determine the course and order of presentation as action? Instead of relying on participants' or observers' descriptions and narratives (which often are used in order to reconstruct the "agency" of things and technologies), I want to answer these questions by analyzing the ways in which technology contributes to the performance of the presentation.

Up to this point in the analysis of powerpoint presentations, it has become quite clear that "technology" refers not only to the slide as it is projected on the screen or wall. Although this is made relevant by the middle body formation, presenters – being the most mobile part of the pivot – can easily redirect attention from the slide. Technology may refer to the visuals produced by the computer-notebook unit; it may refer to the sound produced by a computer loudspeaker unit, as in the case earlier; or it may refer to the "noise" produced by microphones, loudspeakers, or the human voice apparatus (Goffman 1981a). Although the slide plays a decisive role in the presentation, it remains shorthand for the chain of technology involved in it. The chain of technology also includes software, the computer, mouse, computer screen, canvas, projector, laser pointer, possibly a microphone, and other objects. In fact, any technical item involved in the production of the presentation (including the human body and the paraphernalia involved, such as desks, lecterns, reading lamp) may be considered as a link in the chain of technology. In this section, I want to focus on those technologies essential to the powerpoint presentation.

The question of what technology is essential for a powerpoint presentation is not just of academic interest. Powerpoint technologies offer quite a range of situations that provide what one may call experiments at the boundaries of the genre: quite often, and more often than presenters and organizers would presume, the technologies cause problems, and in many cases, one may even talk of a breakdown "caused" by technology. I have put the "causal" attribution in quotation marks for it is one of the questions of how and why technology contributes to the powerpoint presentation. The analysis of technical failures should help to show how technology figures in presentations. In order thus to identify the role of technology it is useful to look at those cases in which the technology does not work smoothly, causes problems, or breaks down. It is such moments that produce a kind of symmetry between technology and presenter, foregrounding it and demonstrating *ex negativo* the role it plays in the "normal" routine cases.[21]

My major thesis is that the chain of presentation technology, which has as its major elements projectors, computers, and screens, is essential for the presentation genre. This technology contributes to it by framing the action by actively doing something. Instead of calling it an "actor," it seems, however, much more pertinent to consider it as the part of the communicative action that, paradoxically, helps to create something immaterial by its very materiality.

### (a) Technical Problems and Technical Failures

If one looks at the data on powerpoint presentations, one observes that problems and technical failures occur quite frequently. To be more exact, failures are quite frequently rendered observable in a more or less conspicuous way. In order to demonstrate this, let us first look at the following case, in which a presenter shows a new slide before suddenly realizing that one diagram is turned upside down (Fragment 15).

While speaking (1), the presenter realizes visually that there is some problem with the slide. The problem he encounters is not only indicated by the pause (lines 2 and 4); he provides an explicit description of the

**Fragment 15**

1    S: that vessels actually provide the nutrition

2    (1,0)

3    and,

4    (2,0)

5    yes, so, this is now upside down,

6    But=basically=one may say that in the

7    moment when nutrition is provided

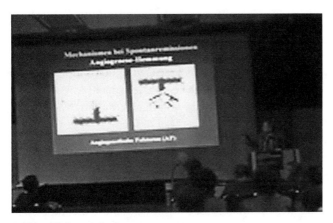

Still 8:  Slide upside down.

problem, specifying that what is seen is "upside down" (5). Moreover, he continues his talk by taking up a recognition marker, repeating "nutrition" and "provide," yet leaving out the vessels in the now-passive construction. The sequence referring to the technical problem (2–5) are side sequences (Jefferson 1972) in that they do not continue the text started in line 1 and continued in lines 6–7. Although the presenter uses a continuer between them (3), he indicates the kind of relation via the "yes-but" construction and the generalization "basically" and the passive construction that leaves out the vessels that are supposedly represented on the upside-down slide.

Note that the technical problem is not just a technical problem. The slide could be turned upside down, for example,. for rhetorical reasons.[22] On the other hand, there may simultaneously be other "technical" problems which are not accounted for (e.g., the laser pointer might not work) – but they do not become part of the communication process and therefore are not socially consequential. Most importantly, the technical problem can become part of

**Fragment 16**

| 1 | S: | Ladies and gentlemen, you see, they are busy working, these are the preparations for |
|---|----|--------------------------------------------------------------------------------------|

1   S:   Ladies and gentlemen, you see, they are busy working, these are the preparations for

2        the next presentations. I would respect this, and I would ask if you consent that we

3        leave them another 5 minutes before we start. Do you agree?

4   A:   yes.

5        (2 minutes pause, the projector is turned off, the technician leaves the room)

6   S:   Well, we have postponed the technical tinkering to after the presentation, and

         want to use the occasion to again cordially welcome you…

the performance. The way this happens can be compared to what Goffman (1981b: 3ff) calls "talking out of frame": the presenter is not following his "text" but changes into someone who is watching the slide without speaking (during the pause) – and thus turns the audience's attention to the issue. So we find that the presenter not only produces a side sequence by which he accounts for the technical failure; the slide simultaneously serves as a frame for the utterance that allows us to read it as "out of frame."

The fact that the presenter only makes a side sequence and continues speaking may be called an explicit *technical problem*. The problem is accounted for in that it plays a prominent role in the side sequence, in which it is in the focus of both, the presenter and the audience. By explicit technical problems, I mean problems that arise within the presentation and remain only a topic for the presentation. Although out of frame, they still form part of the presentation. Such "minor problems" occur in presentations, for example, when presenters leave out bullets (particularly in builds, i.e., series of animated items within one slide), skip slides, miss a slide, and so on. There are, however, other kinds of technical problems, which are usually not just accounted for by embedded insertions. Consider Fragment 16 from the phase just prior to a presentation.

In the case shown here of a technical problem, the presenter gives an account of the problems he is facing: after an earlier presentation by a prior presenter, he is preparing for his presentation. Since he refers only to the "the preparation for the next presentation," the problem here is not seen as part of the presentation. The problem becomes "visible" to the audience witnessing his actions by the fact that the projector is turned off and the person in charge of supervising the presentation technology leaves the room. The problem, here, is not only inserted "out of frame," but is outside the general frame or, one may say, beyond the boundaries of the presentation as a genre. This out of genre character is accounted for by

Stills 9 and 10: Audience members volunteering for technical support. Reproduced with permission from DPMA_Pisatzky.

the audience, whose focus disintegrates, who start to engage in subordinated conversations and even more literally to "dissolve," that is, move, leave the stage, or even leave the room. In various cases, members of the audience volunteer to help, moving toward the technical equipment and giving advice, thus also obstructing the focused character of the event. In the case quoted, people from the back stage go up to the front, so that it is now only the technology that is the focus of attention. This focus can quickly dissolve so that audience members start to volunteer, to talk to one another, or to pursue other activities.

**Fragment 17**

| | | |
|---|---|---|
| 1 | S: | (2,0) What=s=now=happening? (2,0) |
| 2 | | Hm? =this=is=not any more my computer? |
| 3 | | (5,0) ((laughing)) |
| 4 | | Okay |
| 5 | | (4,0) |
| 6 | | Well |
| 7 | | (3,0) |
| 8 | | okay ''(we will turn to this later') |
| 9 | A: | (Audience mutters) |

Although one might expect that the preparation or technical problem would be a back stage problem, the Stills 9 and 10 clearly show that the notion of back stage is as metaphorical as the notion of frame. The presenter and some volunteers are trying to make the technology work, but they do so in front of the audience. It is in order to defocus the audience's attention that the presenter asks the audience's permission to consider the time as a "preparation" phase.

As opposed to explicit technical problems that are part of the presentation, one may consider the kind of technical problems that are (or have to be) handled outside the presentation proper as failures. Unluckily, such failures occur not only before presentations but, sometimes, within presentations. Take the example analyzed by Schnettler (2007): We are in the midst of a highly formal presentation on the results of a natural science project to an audience of about fifty people (including representatives of her funding organizations) when the following sequence occurs:

As we can tell from the presenter's account (1f.), something unexpected has happened halfway through her presentation: The presenter states, "This is not any more my computer." She realizes that the slide shown is not hers, and, assuming that the computer is somewhat identical with the slide, she infers that the projector is showing the slide from another laptop prepared for the ensuing presentation. In her account, the presenter, again, describes what is happening and accounts for the change with pauses, laughter, and more pauses. In the part following the extract, she turns to her assistant, who rapidly leaves the room. In the meantime and in the sequence happening after Fragment 17, the presenter tries to reframe the presentation. She first attempts to describe what is supposed to be seen on the slides she had prepared; simultaneously she tries to handle the technical problem by fiddling

## Fragment 18

| 1 | S: | third reflection – we wanted from dive- |
| 2 | | (5,5) |
| 3 | M: | I suggest, I suggest you turn that off for it is diverting from what mister M. is saying, |
| 4 | | right (when the assistant closes the program and moves backwards, waiting until it is |
| 5 | | turned off) |
| 6 | S: | third we wanted to move from… |

Still 11: Technical failure: No slide on the screen. Reproduced with permission from BMBF-Forum, Prof.Stock.

with the computer. While she is handling the computer, the audience witnesses long pauses. After realizing that she has not succeeded, she again changes the frame from a spoken lecture to another format at the boundary of the genre: she takes her notebook into her hands and turns it toward the audience in an attempt to "show" the slides by way of the notebook's monitor. What works in a two- or three-party presentation, however, is considered inappropriate with an audience of this size – the monitor is too small, and it does not constitute a focus for the audience. This inappropriateness is expressed quite clearly by the audience: some members start to talk to her, suggesting she should continue the speech without slides. Luckily, the failure ends. Her assistant returns and tells her that the technician is back in the media room, from which the presentations are supported, and the desired slide finally is seen on the screen. The presentation can then go on, leaving the technical failure again as a kind of embedded "intermezzo."

Although the presentation could be continued, the example shows quite clearly that the technical failure is not just a "side sequence." The speech does not go on, and attention turns to the technology; some audience members become inattentive, and the presenter starts and restarts her talk in between a number of pauses while she is handling the technology. This interpretation of the failure as a side sequence is best supported by the observation that after the slide reappears, she starts where she left the presentation before the technical problem occurred.

In this case, the failure of technology disrupts the presentation. If we look for technical failures, we can even go a step further. In the next case, the technical problem also occurs after the presentation has already started. To be more exact, the presenter begins his introductory comment while a technician is still trying to get the slide presentation started (1). At this point, the moderator interrupts the presentation (2f.) (Fragment 18).

After the first words by the presenter (standing behind the lectern) and a long pause, the technical problem (the slides are not on the screen) is accounted for by a side sequence of the moderator, who is not visible on the still (3f.). In the long pause (5.5 seconds) that follows, the assistant (Still 11, right, beside thelectern) tries to handle the technical problem. After that sequence, during which the problem is not solved and no slide is seen, the presenter resumes his talk (5).

Although the situation seems not to have changed, the genre is quite different. Instead of observing a presentation, the audience now witnesses a kind of lecture, and instead of a presenter, it is faced with a reader. Because of the failure of the technology, the genre is transformed. Since the transformation of the genre from a presentation to a lecture also transforms the production format of what the presenter is and does, one can infer, *ex negativo*, that technology plays an important active role in defining the production format. The smooth working of the technology may allow for a presentation; its failure, however, denies the use of visuals and, thus, demands a different frame, such as the lecture that had been prepared by this presenter.

In the face of the smooth transition between the genres in the preceding case one may realize that the frame is of little importance, as the differences between the genres are minor. But this impression is quite deceptive given that the presenter in this case had not only prepared a presentation as document; obviously he also had prepared a written manuscript. If this is not the case, matters are quite different. Take the following example, from an international social scientific conference. As the last of a series of presentations, the presenter who had appeared late, after the first

## Fragment 19

| | | |
|---|---|---|
| 1 | S: | abetted by, eh |
| 2 | | enable one to grasp the reference |
| 3 | | in terms of one's own experience |
| 4 | | (4.0) |
| 5 | | eh:: |
| 6 | | (19.0) |

Still 12: Technical disaster.

presentation in the series had already started, learned only shortly before his presentation that the technology provided did not accept the data carrier (a diskette) on which he had stored his presentation. In his despair, he tried to give the presentation without a projector and computer. He took his paper printouts of the slides and started to talk in an improvised "fresh" manner. The phrase "fresh talk" must be in quotation marks, since, unluckily, the printouts included a lot of text that he had to read from the paper (Fragment 19).

As the transcript shows, the moves between the different orientations caused long pauses: since the presenter tried to "show" the printed paper copies of the slides while reading them (as shown in Still 12), he held them in front of his body. Despite his attempt to take a middle position, reading was hampered since he had to read the text from an awkward angle almost upside down. Moreover, most audience members could not identify what was pointed to on the paper. Since, finally, the presentation took much longer than the time scheduled, audience members afterward designated the presentation a disaster and quite embarrassing for the presenter. For these reasons, Tuma and Schnettler (2007: 176) refer to this case as a "frame break."

It is because this presenter had not prepared for another genre than a presentation that the thrust of technological failure can be felt and its role assessed.[23] Technology can be seen to be framing the presentation in a quite fundamental way. As the failures *ex negativo* show, it takes an active part that also affects other aspects of the genre, for, as in the preceding case, the failure of technology affects the audience. Moreover, it clearly affects the presenter as, in this case, and in the other cases, failures are typically related to feelings of embarrassment. In some cases, this feeling is quite visibly expressed as presenters start to stumble and even on the videos one can see their faces flushing. If, however, technology was an actor on its own, as it is asserted, why, one can ask, should presenters be embarrassed in cases of technical problems?

One important reason for this embarrassment is that presenters are considered to be responsible for their presentations. Whatever may happen, presenters are expected to have prepared the presentation, which includes having tested the operation of the technology before the event. As we have already found with respect to the asymmetry of the triadic structure, the technological failure also corroborates the idea that presenters are seen as the subjects of the presentation. This is not restricted to a digital format as having been "produced" by the presenter (and his "team"); it also includes the presentation as event to be performed by the presenter. It is of some sociological importance that presenters are expected to work competently with the technology. Presenters not only have knowledge, they must be able to "show" it competently, so that failing to do this causes embarrassment.

There, is, however, an additional aspect to embarrassment that can be discerned in cases in which the failure evidently cannot be ascribed to the presenters, which we see in Fragment 15. In this case, the presenter made it very clear from the beginning that the technical failure was not her fault, and the fact that the technician was absent proved that there was someone else in charge. In order to explain why the presenter was, nevertheless, embarrassed (and flushed) it seems quite plausible to follow Goffman's (1967) suggestion that embarrassment occurs when actors deviate from the image they have projected for the situation.[24] In the case of the presentation this means that the person who prepared for the preparation does not succeed in acting as a presenter. As the deviant case shows, one may save

Still 13: Text and sound (rat tat tat). Reproduced with permission from Zoll, German Customs Chemist Conference 2004, Dr. Dirk Meyer, ZPLA Berlin.

face by moving to an alternative genre, an alternative production format, and a respective alternative identity (i.e., as a speaker). Yet embarrassment remains as the actor cannot live up to the expectation of at least a neighboring genre, particularly since the mishap is "on stage."

In this sense, the technical failure is not just a failure. As the technology contributes to the participation framework, its failure urges the presenter to change her or his identity. He or she is no longer a presenter in charge of the presentation but a "speaker" or someone in need of help. It is this unexpected change that may be considered to be the reason for the embarrassment. In this case it is less the identity of someone who does not know how to handle the computer, the projector, or the slide – for this is definitely what the technician is there to handle. Following Schnettler (2007: 301) one could say that it is "the situation itself that is threatened," for the presentation as a triadic genre is at stake.

### (b) Projection Is What Technology Does

The consideration of failures seems to indicate that technology is only foregrounded if problems arise. However, technology can also become a more symmetric element in the triangle in cases not considered as problems and not related mainly to the presenter. As odd as it may sound, technology can also act on, and interact with, the audience. Take the following example, from an internal presentation in a public customs office. The presenter tries to transfer information to his coworkers by means of a powerpoint presentation.

**Fragment 20**

| 1 | Presenter | Am I may welcome you here now cordially |
| | | *Uh ich darf Sie also dann jetzt herzlich begrüßen.* |
| 2 | | (0,8) |
| 3 | | / [PPT: Sound of a type writer] |
| 4 | Audience | / WO:::::W |
| 5 | Audience | Uhh |
| 6 | Audience | Hahaham          / Ha |
| 7 | | / Haha |
| 8 | | (2,0) |
| 9 | Presenter | Yes, European standards for cereals |
| | | *Ja europäische Standardisierung (.) für Getreide* |
| 10 | Presenter | and corn production (.) that is now the topic of |
| | | *Und Getreideerzeugnisse (.), das ist also das* |
| 11 | Presenter | my presentation (1,4) and I work here (.) |
| | | *Thema des Vortrages (1,4) und ich bin hier seit* |

Let us have a look at the initial sequence of the presentation (Fragment 20).

After the presenter starts to welcome the audience cordially, we hear a noise emitted from the computer that sounds like "rat tat tat," that is, a traditional typewriter (3) which ends at the point represented by Still 13. Shortly after this sound starts, a few members of the audience begin to express their astonishment and (as we shall see, somewhat ironic) admiration (4–7) with their "Wow" pronounced like an (extended) American "Wow" (an expression loaned from U.S. English quite frequently used nowadays in Germany). Along with the subsequent utterances, this audience "reaction" lasts about two seconds. If we consider the utterances sequentially as interpretations of previous sequences, we can hardly relate them to the rather conventional introductory sentence and the performance. Instead, it is quite plausible to consider the "Wow" (4) as an interpretation of the "rat tat tat" sound produced by the notebook that is mimicking a typewriter. At this point, we can easily see that and how the audience interact with the technology itself for the audience takes the floor for several turns without the presenter involved. Indeed, he does not show any sign of appreciation of the audience's turn but moves his head away from the paper to the screen in order to repeat (after the pause) the title that has been produced by the sounds of the typewriter.

Looking more closely at the subsequent turns, the case displays an even more complex pattern relevant to the study of audience participation. Listening more closely, the "Wow" exhibits a slight exaggeration so that it sounds somehow ironic. As problematic as the acoustic evidence may be, this interpretation is supported by the subsequent acts of other audience members. Instead of appreciating the gimmick, some start to laugh in such a way as to invite others to laugh (Jefferson 1979). In this way, they ratify the interpretation of the "funny" use of a gimmick rather than the appreciation of the technical competence represented by it. As such, it is not only that the audience reacts to the technology in sequentially reacting to it and interpreting it in this way; moreover, the audience takes the floor in that it acts in turn and thus takes the floor. It is quite understandable and sequentially sensitive that only after this sequence the presenter repeats the title – now without the sound of the typewriter – and thus gives it the status of a sequence embedded in and thus different from his talk since the audience interacted with the technology.

At this point, one should remind the reader that the triangle is, of course, an abstraction and that the slide is what is important in the technology. As Latour claims, it is especially in the event of crisis that the black box of technology is unpacked. Latour (1994: 38ff.) explicitly refers to the overhead projector, which, when breaking down, reminds us of its existence. While in the situation described the crisis makes technicians identify the problem, it thereby points at various technical "actors" who normally do the work. Although powerpoint failures rarely require mechanical repair procedures and the "deconstruction" of the black box by technicians, embarrassed presenters, volunteering audience members, or technicians usually dissect the problem into different parts (computer software, projector, cable, etc.). It is very common that human actors at this point address the technical chain involved in powerpoint presentation: the "screen" can turn out to be a problem if we are not able to erect it manually, the projector may not show the slide, the file cannot be uploaded from the stick, the computer does not have a CD drive on which the presentation as document is stored, and so forth. Thus, there is a whole technological chain with respect to the slide that appears to be acting "behind" the scenes, becoming visible only in the case of problems. Should we then consider all these different objects and technologies as actors, and do we have to extend the triangle to a network of actors? Can we even maintain the thesis that the triangle constitutes the basis for the genre of the powerpoint presentation?

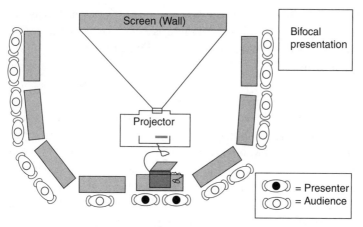

Diagram 7: Bifocal presentation setting.

In order to answer these critical questions, it may be useful to consider again a case that, though somewhat "deviant," is empirically quite frequent. It is the type of presentation we call "bifocal."

As Diagram 7 shows, by representing the spatial constellation of a presentation in a university seminar, the two presenters sit at the lower end of the room. The screen on which the slides are projected (which is actually only a wall painted white) is located at the other end of the room, some fifteen feet away. Because most members of the audience can see only the presenter or the slide, I would like to call this spatial order "bifocal." Bifocality does not refer to a form but to the kinds of performances by the audience. Because of the two foci, quite a few of the audience members move their heads regularly when monitoring the presentation. Because they have to switch between the presenter to the left or right of them and then to the screen at their respective other side, the movements of their heads resemble those of spectators watching a tennis match. Particularly when presenters point or parallel, audience members indicate their awareness by moving their heads from the speaker to the slides, whereas further gestures by the presenters make them turn their heads back to them. These movements from left to right, respectively, and from right to left, are optional and neither mechanical nor sequentially determined. Some audience members may stick to one end while others move, some may take notes while others switch sides, and others might move although there seems to be no clue triggering it.

Despite this irregularity, the example makes a simple, even trivial but crucial point: it is not only the talk and the presentation, but the projection that can draw the audience's attention. Whatever technology contributes to (framing, contributing to production formats, or filling sequential turns), it does so by virtue of the fact that it is projecting. Projection should not be reduced to the projection technology. Since projection implies the PowerPoint software, the computer hardware, and the projector, it encompasses the whole chain of technologies. The question as to the various actors in the network is not really essential, and even in the case of failures it is mostly the method of trial and error along the whole chain that is applied in order to solve the problem. Nevertheless, as the case of bifocality shows, one has to say that technology *does* something, that is, projecting, that is essential to the presentation.[25]

Although technology plays an active role, it would be inadequate to ignore the human actors designing and triggering the slides and the audience watching it. Following Latour (2008), one could call this a network of actors, including both, technologies and humans. This description, however, would decisively ignore the triadic structure that is defined by it. Rather than being just a network of human and nonhuman actors (Latour 2008) or, more specifically, a sociotechnical ensemble (Bijker 1995) or a sociotechnical constellation (Rammert 2006), the technology forms part of communicative action within the genre of the powerpoint presentation. This is, by far, not something new. As the voice is a somewhat technical part of speaking, chalk and the blackboard features in traditional teaching presentations, technologies like projectors, and presentation software are the kind of objectivations that are enacted in powerpoint presentations. The important point about these technologies is not that they are actors different from the human presenters, as Latour believes, but that they are enacted as part of the communicative action of and by the presenter in such a way as to become part of the genre.

As the communicative genre is an institution, we may follow Rammert (2006) and Pinch (2008) in also addressing technology as an institution or, in this case, as part of a communicative institution. It is important to note at this point that communicative genre as an institution is embedded in the social structure because of both its human actors as well as its technology and objects. While actors become presenters and audience only in the situation, the technological chain extends to software companies (like "PowerPoint"), to computer networks (like the Internet, where many text elements, diagrams, and visuals seen on the slide originate), and to hardware producers (of computers and projectors). These extensions of the communicative genre shall be pursued in the next chapter. With respect to the role of technology in the situation, it is important that it in some sense represents not only a technical black box but also a division of labor: before powerpoint had been invented, the role of technology had been fulfilled by human actors, such as designers who drew the diagrams, the projection assistants, who projected the slides, and the technicians, who set the projectors in the presentation rooms. In performing these "roles," available technology contributes to stabilizing the features of the communicative genre and, by way of its own dissemination, to reproducing it as a communicative "institution."

From the historical background it is quite obvious that these roles are being inscribed into the technology. From the perspective of the actor acting not in the *longue durée* of history (and the path of technological development – which is not at issue here) but in the interactive time of the presentation, the historical "black box" of various elements built into the presentation is of no immediate concern. To the actor and to the genre, it is much more important that the technological chain becomes invisible. As we have seen, the performance only runs smoothly if technology is seen as contributing to the action instead of becoming the dominating topic, as is the case with failures.

The "invisibilization" of the technology in routine performance of the communicative genre is not only accomplished by the smooth operation of the presentation by the human presenter. It is, paradoxically, achieved by successful visibilization. For the slide projected successfully (as the product and result of technology) is in itself not to be considered technology. It is, in fact, an almost immaterial representation. This representation does not even need a material screen; nor does it depend on a material slide, if it is, for example, just projected against a white wall.[26] Although it can be seen and depends on technology, it is an immaterial "picture." This material carrier is, in principle, nothing more than some "bits" used in electronic information processing. I have already stressed the ambiguousness of the slide (Chapter 2.1.), but one should stress again that the "materiality" of slides is virtual: it is based on informational processes and reproduced by information technologies. It is by means of these technologies that slides can be produced in situations and become part of presentations as events, and it is by virtue of these technologies that slides can be presented as documents and used anywhere informational technology is available.

In this chapter on the intermediate dimension of the presentation as a communicative genre, I have analyzed the communicative actions by the presenters, focusing in particular on their bodily conduct. Pointing and the body formation turn out to be essential features of the presentation that shed light on the role of audience and technology. Presenters, audiences, and technology constitute the core of the communicative genre. While audiences actively contribute to the performance of presentation, technology also takes an active role not only by providing visuals but also in "doing showing." As the interactions among all three elements exhibits a certain asymmetry within the presentation, they transcend the situation in various ways that also characterizes the genre. How they transcend the situation of the presentation and characterize the genre shall be analyzed in the next chapter.

# 6    The External Level: Settings, Meetings, and the Ubiquity of Powerpoint

Since it seems quite obvious that powerpoint presentations include technologies, presenters, and audience, the stress on the triangular structure of the genre may appear trivial on the surface. However, the data shown so far demonstrate that the structure is much more complex and specific to the phenomenon. Powerpoint presentations are not just presentations plus technology, and they are not just some multimodal combination of talk, text, and visualization.[1] The forms analyzed are more than just the sum of the triangle's three termini. Rather, one could say that the interplay among these termini results in an emerging structure, or, to put it in other words, the communicative genre of powerpoint presentations is constituted by the specific kind of enactment of these three elements. As the complexity of the form is methodologically accounted for by distinguishing among different dimensions, one can discern it most clearly on the internal and intermediate levels as the performance of communicative action by the triad of technology, audience, and presenter. Previously, I have analyzed the interplay of the aspects of the triadic structure during its performance in terms of synchronization, coordination, orchestration, body formation, audience interaction, and projecting. As we shall see, the triadic structure also extends beyond the performance: the interaction of audiences and presenters is embedded in organizations, and the format of the meeting, objects, and the chain of technologies is built into a larger infrastructure that, finally, coincides with what we have called the "information society" in the Introduction. Even the "presenter" is dependent on the predecessor of the powerpoint presentation, the recently developed genre of presentation.

The difference between the internal and situative level, on the one hand, and the external level, on the other hand, touches a crucial issue in the social sciences. The "internal" and "intermediate" levels of the analysis of communicative genres correspond to what Goffman (1981b) has called "interaction order." In turning now to the external level of the analysis of powerpoint presentations as a communicative genre, it may again be useful to draw on a distinction suggested by Goffman, who distinguishes between the "situational" and the "situated." By situated he refers to "any event occurring within the physical boundaries of a situation" (Goffman 1963: 22). Within the situation, there are elements that "could not occur outside situations." "Some of the meaning of words conveyed in conversation is merely-situated; the coloration given to these words by bodily expressed emotion, however, is distinctly situational" (Goffman 1963: 22). What Goffman designates here as "situational" corresponds very strongly to what I have tried to emphasize as the performative character of communicative actions. As communicative actions, however, rely on bodies and objectivations for communication (materialities, media, technologies, objects), communicative genres also build on situated aspects. Both kinds of aspects are not cut off from one another, but are scrutinized in two different ways, that is, by the methodological distinction between levels and their corresponding data sorts.

One has to mention that the relation between the "situational" and the "situated" is not just of methodological relevance but has a quite strong theoretical bearing on the social sciences. Whereas representatives of "microsociological" approaches, such as ethnomethodology, would stress that the "situational" is only relevant insofar as it is made relevant in a situation or a "situated action" (Suchman 1987), more "meso-" or even "macrosociological" approaches would hold that the situation is determined by general rules that can be analyzed in terms of social structure and its constituents, such as norms, values, and institutions (Parsons 1964). The relation between the situation and the social structure is, indeed, a major problem in sociology, also known as the "micro-macro" problem (Knorr Cetina and Cicourel 1981): What is the relation among actions, interactions, and social structures, such as institutions, organizations, and social classes? Or indeed, as Knorr Cetina (2001) adds, what is the relation among the social structure, objects, and technologies?

This question applies quite obviously to our case: for even if the triadic structure emerging from the performance is situated, performance depends on things that are introduced into the situation of the presentation, such as slides, texts, computers, and projectors. In addition, buildings, objects (such as chairs and lecterns), and the human actors exist before, after, and outside the situation and relate to the social structure, to available resources (such as information technology and infrastructure), and, thus, to persons and their power. Since these situated elements are "introduced into" the situation, they become part of the situation and, thus, are a crucial part of the meaning of communicative actions. But the question is not only how they become part of the meaning but also how they enter the situation. Why is it computers and not record players, why projectors and not blackboards, why presenters and not speakers only?

Goffman's (1981b) solution to the problem of the situational and the situated, or between micro- and macrostructures, consists of the suggestion that they constitute two different entities governed by their own logics: the social structure, on the one hand, and the "interaction order," on the other. Although Goffman allows them to be connected by "interfaces," Latour's (2008) critique of the assumption of two separate spheres seems to me quite plausible. "Micro-" and "macrostructures," he claims, are not separated; rather, they are mediated actors and their networks. Latour (1994) is also quite right to claim that objects and technologies play an important role in linking situations with the "social structure." Technology indeed forms an important element in the performance of the genre of the communicative action, for "powerpoint presentations" connect the situation of the presentation directly with the infrastructure of the information society. The same holds for the presenters and the audiences, who must literally, that is, spatially, "enter into" the situation before they can perform situationally, and who must, formally, "come to terms" with what is called the presentation. The "external" level, thus, is not a different world from the presentation but mediated by actors, objects, and actions. Objects, technologies, and organizations not only mediate the "external" context but are part of the situative context in that they "contextualize" the communicative genre: that is, they provide an objectified material context for the performance of the communicative action.

As Latour (2008) suggests, one could, indeed, follow the path of these mediations from the context of presentation to other situations in an ethnographic manner. However, as useful as the notion of mediation is in this case, and as important as it is to acknowledge the role of objects, it seems rather misleading to conceive of their relation to actions in the simplified terms of (correspondingly dense) "actor-networks," as Latour (2008) proposes. Considering the powerpoint presentations, first, the notion of network seems too unspecific. If one follows the path of actors (objects, technology, human actors), one does not just discern diffuse "networks." Instead, we find a very specific structure that is highlighted here as communicative genre. This structure consists of situated elements (structured by the triad) linked with, mediated by, and contextualizing other elements,

such as objects, spaces, and organizations. Second, it seems utterly misleading to focus only on objects and ignore the semiotic meaningfulness of
objects, such as slides, manuscripts, visual representations of bodies, and
gestures. Finally, the fact that the objects and signs are enacted in processes
rather than structures, that is, communicative action, seems to be absent
from the notion of actor network.

Nevertheless, the idea of mediation is extremely useful when looking
at how the situated and the situational are interrelated. Mediation can be
pursued transcending the time, space, and situation of the performance.
The situative performance takes place in certain spatial structures, that is,
settings, characterized by a certain form shaped by more or less typical
objects. As technology is an essential feature of the performance, it is also
very important on the external level. It is here that we encounter again the
information society (mentioned in the Introduction) and its hardware, software, and infrastructure. Moreover, if we follow the temporal path outside
the situation, we discover that presentations are part of a well-organized
event, very often designated as a "meeting." The meeting is, again, part
and parcel of organizations and networks of organizations that need to
communicate in order to produce the event. Finally, the presentation as
something performed by the presenter also presupposes a large degree of
"competence" of the human actor. If I may coin a formula: he or she needs
to know how to show what to know. The meeting serves as an important
interface between the presentation and the patterns of situated actions
called formal organizations and organizational communication. As numerous as these situations and patterns are, the analysis of the external level
necessarily needs to become more abstract with respect to the descriptive
categories.

It may be worth reminding the reader that the distinction of an external
level of communicative genre analysis is not due to an ontological cleav-
age. As stressed previously, the distinctions among the levels account for
the differences of data used in analysis and, thus, for the different modality
of evidences. Thus, for example, in the following chapter, I shall draw on
statistical data in order to characterize the external level. These numbers
should not be considered as representing a different level of reality, but
as "shorthand" and, more often, indirect and very abstract indications for
processes of communicative actions. Thus, the indications for the number
of powerpoint presentations refer, of course, to the performance of these
presentations in communicative actions. Also the organization of meetings
is an intricate communicative process, often summarized in organizational
structures (which depend on the order of these communicative processes).

Even the numbers for sales of projectors or software, which allow an estimation of the societal relevance of powerpoint presentations, refer in principle to communicative processes in which transactions occur. Other data in this part include interviews with representatives of various organizations, analyses of dictionaries, and, again, advice books. These types of data are selected in order to address a question formulated in the Introduction: are powerpoint presentations really ubiquitous, and if so, in what sense?

This chapter not only provides evidence for the ubiquity of powerpoint presentations, that is, their social distribution across society. It also serves to answer a second question: how did powerpoint presentations come to be distributed in the way described? While the first question focuses on the "social structure," the second sheds light on the temporal process by which powerpoint presentations became socially distributed, or, to put it differently, diffused as a communicative innovation.[2] These processes consist of the institutionalization of the meeting, the diffusion of the technology, and the proliferation of presentations. As the answers to both questions, and particularly the data supporting them, cannot always be separated accurately, both will be addressed in this chapter. As such they will serve as a basis for the concluding chapter, in which I will try to explain the reasons for the kind of ubiquity powerpoint presentations exhibit, which will be demonstrated in this chapter. Before analyzing the "larger" picture offered by the numbers and structural indications, let me first turn to the tangible forms to which they refer.

## 1. Objects, Settings, and Spaces

As mentioned, the three elements, presenters, audiences, and technology, are constitutive of the presentation in the sense that, irrespective of the context, the interplay among these three elements could be considered a powerpoint presentation. As crucial as the three constitutive elements may be, however, powerpoint presentations involve a set of other objects that are less constitutive for the presentation, less in the focus of the audience's or the presenter's attention, and that offer instead a varying background for presentations.[3] As already mentioned, the chain of technologies involved in projecting can be extended enormously, particularly in the more formal modes of presentations. This extension involves projectors fixed to the roof, media boards with computers and relay stations, mobile media trolleys, loudspeakers, or portable laptops and portable projectors. There may also be older presentation technologies present in the setting, such as blackboards, overhead projectors, flip charts, slide projectors, and video players.

In addition to these technologies supporting the task of projection, there is a range of other objects that form part of presentations, such as fixed or mobile stools, chairs, fixed desks, and fixed microphones. Flags, heraldic devices, or company logos may function as decorations. Note that all these objects are "given" to the situation of the powerpoint presentation, sometimes fixed in advance, sometimes literally taken in. At this point one should not forget the most permanent form of objects given to the situation, that is, rooms, walls, and buildings. From their historical origins, presentations have been set in rooms specially set up and even built for this purpose.[4]

Following Goffman (1980/1959: 32f.) and Lofland (1971), all these objects can be said to constitute the *setting*. The setting involves "furniture, décor, physical layout, and other background items which supply the scenery and stage props for the spate of human action played out before, within, or upon it." Rapoport (1994: 465) stresses that one of the major dimensions of setting is space: objects are related to one another in space; the larger objects, such as rooms, walls, or stages, give a form to space. Because space is not only constituted in the communicative performance but also "introduced" into the situation, I shall look at the order these objects take in presentations.

Given the large number of presentations considered, one must, first, admit that the spaces vary significantly between, for example, a powerpoint presentation in a church and a presentation in a business environment. If one scrutinizes the visual depictions of the places of presentations represented on our video recordings, one can indeed discover some recurring elements. When analyzing the technological chain, I have already mentioned that the technical elements of the triadic relationship can be expanded, extended, or differentiated. Speech may be supported by a microphone, the slide may be projected on a screen that itself includes interactive features, and the audience may be seated in rows or in other geometrical arrangements. The triangular structure is underlined by a common spatial arrangement in many settings specializing in public talks. Be it in Christian churches, festival halls, or large university lecture halls, very often presenters are not placed in the very center of the focus or the stage created by the division between presenter and audience and their gaze built into the space by chairs, and blackboards. Instead, most spaces position the presenter slightly off-center of the front the audience is facing, mostly left or right of the center, and in many cases, the screen is installed in the center of the audience's focal point, that is, in the middle of the surface the audience is facing.

As shown previously, this *decentered presenter* is rigidified by the body formation, which follows the spatial division of central screen, audience, and presenter. Other technical aspects of the presentation add to this de-entered positioning. In a number of presentations the electric lights are dimmed and curtains are drawn closed in order to prevent daylight from outshining the slides and to improve their visibility. As a result, present-ers are visually faded out. In these cases, presenters appear only as talking shadows and are set in contrast to the highlighted slides, a visual impres-sion not only witnessed in video recordings of presentations but also in real life presentations by the audience.[5]

As the decentering of the presenter seems to be related to the triadic structure, a set of other features of settings are much more independent of the presenter's performance. Settings differ with respect to the size of the audience, the order of the spatial setups of furniture, and the technological endowment of the facilities. Despite the huge variations, one can discern a relatively clear-cut difference between two major types of settings. The first type of setting for presentations is most often characterized by a kind of stage, created by means of different objects – a heightened podium, a lectern, a microphone, for example – that serve to set the presenter and possibly other members of the podium apart. Special light effects or visual emblems also add to the impression that space is divided into a stage and an auditorium. The other type of setting for presentations does not require a marked stage. In these settings, the presenter sits beside other presenters without being marked off spatially or or having access to any additional technical equipment, such as a microphone. Occasionally, even the pre-senter's notebook must not be a specific feature of the setting since audi-ence members may turn up with their own laptop and set them up visibly in front of them. Not even the projector needs to be monopolized since presenters may talk one after another. In these cases, the "stage" is instead a metaphorical notion reserved for the temporary "monopoly," which consists of the fact that one person is given the right to talk for a certain amount of time, and that the presenter has the right to decide about the slides to be shown for this period. In these cases, the stage format of this spatial order is not only due to the objects but also to the relation between two essential units located at different ends of the space: the audience, on the one hand, represented by chairs, stools, and spaces left empty; and the presenter, on the other hand, who has access to the pointing technology and may be marked by other features, as, for example, an upright position.

Although one must admit that the two types are not segregated sharply but blend into one another, they can be distinguished at their extremes quite clearly. I shall refer to them as the *meeting type* and the *conference type* of setting. Often, both types already differ with respect to the kind of built spaces. Conference type settings like these are to be found in private companies' meeting roomsand in conference rooms in hotels but also in some universities and bureaucratic institutions. Conference type settings typically offer fixed technical support such as projectors on the ceiling, outlets, loudspeakers, plugs, electrical light control, a fixed screen, a public address system (mixer, operator), microphones, and other technical equipment as well as adequate furniture, such as stack, swivel, or upholstered chairs; permanent stages; and lecterns. In addition, the conference type is often linked to some markers of formality,[6] such as name cards, notepads, flags, table coverings, and, in addition, technical personnel working at the scene (aiding the presenter to link to the projector) or behind the scenes (allowing the presenter to use only the remote without having to set up his or her own laptop). As Stills 14 and 15 demonstrate, the formality of these objects is often also mirrored in the formality of the participants' "façade," that is, their clothing style (Goffman 1980/1959).

The conference type of setting differs quite clearly from the meeting type. Although exhibiting all the essential features of powerpoint presentations, this type lacks many or most of the additional features mentioned. First and foremost, the meeting type appears more provisional. Projectors are put on chairs or desks and informally adjusted by means of books. Instead of fixed screens, there are portable screens, or the slides are projected onto a white wall, and the audience is free to arrange their stools as they like.

As can be seen in Stills 16 and 17, the differences are not restricted to the technical equipment, the setup, and the furniture. They also sometimes refer to the "façade." Whereas in formal presentation settings participants typically wear more formal dresses and suits, as the first two pictures demonstrate, the second pair of pictures is characterized by a rather informal clothing style, of course depending on the style of the institution. Thus, the tie worn without a suit or a jacket by the presenter (in Still 17) does appear informal in the business environment where the presentation is given, whereas in most academic environments neckties would indicate formality. Frequently, the difference between the two types is also related to the size of the audience, although one must concede that, as with other features, there is a continuum: smaller events tend to be more informal, and larger events tend to be more formal. One of the reasons for this is that it may be more difficult to establish order by interactive negotiations with larger audiences without certain formalization and conventions; indeed one may say that the degree of interaction between presenter and audience is also

Stills 14 and 15: Audience of two formal presentations.


part of the degree of formality, so that informal presentations tend to be more interactive.

However, formality is not restricted to large meetings. We may encounter highly formalized small presentations in business organizations, associations, or universities. These situations are often linked to decisions relevant to the organizations and therefore often institutionalized in highly formal meeting rooms. I should also repeat that the types are nothing but extreme examples on a spectrum on which various aspects mentioned can vary and different objects and technologies can be supplemented or removed. As

Stills 16 and 17: Two rather informal presentational settings. Reproduced with permission from Wieder Tobias Tenner, Aktien richtig handeln.

different as the types are, one should also stress that we are not only refer-ring to ideal types, which serve to inform many real settings.

Given this caveat, the types can be said typically to relate to the very basic spatial features of the presentation, the body formation highlighted previously. Thus, conferences tend to exhibit a frontal order in which the screen is in the focus of a fixed audience and the presenter is a decentered part of a stage marked off spatially as well as by other objects and boundar-ies. Empirically, the frontal setting must not necessarily be linked to other formal elements. Yet even if presenters attempt to make informal presenta-tions in such a setting, the milieu tends to place them in a frontal relation to

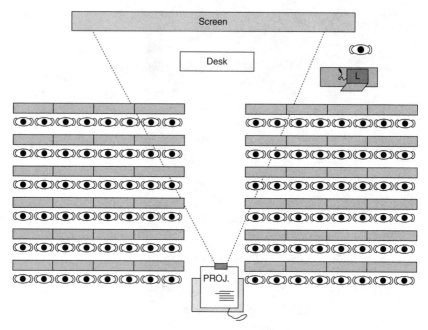

Diagram 8: Conference type setting.

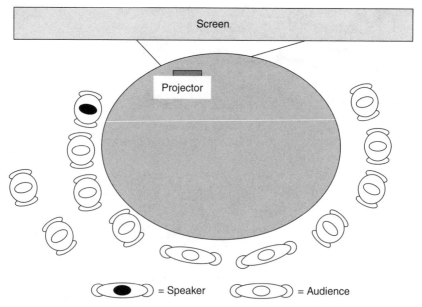

Diagram 9: Meeting type of setting.

the audience. The frontal type is quite currently (yet not at all exclusively) encountered at places with prefixed architecture for presentations, such as conference sites. (That is one reason for calling it the conference type.)

The conference type of setting, represented by Diagram 8, can be sub-divided; there is, for example, an auditorium- or theater-style setting with a raised stage.[7] Yet it differs in this respect significantly from the spatial order characterized by the meeting type, as it is known in schools, universities, and small business meeting rooms.

The difference between the types can easily be discerned if one com-pares the diagram of the conference type (Diagram 8) with the sketch of a small informal meeting's setting (Diagram 9). The meeting is typi-cally small and often, but not necessarily, includes improvised elements. Although bodies can be arranged in rectangular form, its specific differ-ence from the conference type becomes much more salient in circular set-tings. For whereas the rectangular form (as portrayed in Diagram 8) puts presenter and audience in a rather frontal position, presenters in meeting settings can face members of the audience and, thence, reduce the stage elements of the presenter. Presenter and audience are sitting on the same level and share similar face orientations. In order to minimize the differ-ence between presenter and audience – an essential tendency of meetings – presenters sometimes sit down to perform at eye level with the audience. The circularity of the seating arrangement supports the spatial equality of participants since everyone can look in the face of everyone else. Of course, the notion of equality should not conceal the fact that in presentations presenters have, at least for the course of their presentation, asymmetrical control over certain technical means, particularly access to the other major elements of presentation, that is, the primary speaking right and the access to the slides projected. As equal as everyone else may be, the projection puts one "face" relevant to the participants' activities in an extraordinary position: the canvas or the slides as shown on the wall.

While analyzing the "petrified" meaning of objects and their order in the setting, I should again stress that they do not determine the performance of presentation. For as Rapoport (1994: 462) stresses, "spatial organization is at least partially independent of the hardware, the plans of settlements, buildings or rooms as defined by walls and the like." Indeed, by means of their actions' performance, participants can transform the spatial order of built spaces even to the degree that they obstruct the preestablished type of setting. Thus, there are some cases in which the conference type setting is counteracted and undermined by a spontaneous kind of speech. In some conference settings, audience and presenters decide to sit closer to one another, improvising an informal meeting setting with close proximity of their bodies. In these cases, presenters may refuse to position themselves behind the lectern and stand – or better, sit – beside the audience to indicate symmetry. There are also cases in which the presenter sits down in a formal frontal setting, ignores the microphone, and tries to create an atmosphere of equality through direct audience address.

Note that this seating format contradicts the deterministic view that powerpoint necessarily creates an asymmetrical relation between presenters and audience. As the formal types of settings show, the asymmetry is instead due to other objects than the powerpoint technology, which can be also created in informal settings. Thus, in meeting settings, presenters can set up a table as a lectern to create some distance between themselves and the audience. The informality of the built setting can be further undermined by addressing the audience in a formal speech style. Sometimes, the presenter compensates for the decentered position by moving closer into the projector's light, thereby supporting the impression of a stage. In some meeting contexts characterized by informality (for example, certain university seminar rooms), the formality necessary for dissertation exams or lectures by invited speakers is produced by mixing the presentation with a manuscript lecture written in a very formal style and with an audience refraining from any intervention until the end of the presentation.

All these examples demonstrate the relative autonomy of the situated order of performing powerpoint presentations. They also attest to the crucial role of the triadic structure. At the same time, they corroborate the enduring relevance of the objects and their spatial order or, in other words, their "meaning." Thus, if a microphone is fixed in front of a large audience, its use may be preferable to such a degree that ignoring it may not be appropriate. Also the existence of a lectern may "urge" the presenter to use it for her or his presentation. The meaning of spatial structures has already been demonstrated with respect to the bifocal presentation, where slides and presenter are positioned spatially in such a way as to constitute two different foci for the audience members.[8] While the audience reactions acknowledge the active contribution of the projector, they also demonstrate the effects of the spatial order.

The meaning of objects and the spatial order, thus, is not only created in the situation. In other words, the situation builds on objects ordered in space. Since they are already in the setting, are introduced into the setting, or will remain in the setting after the course of the performance of powerpoint presentations, they belong to the "external" level of the communicative genre. That is not to deny that they are part of the situation and can be made relevant by the actions. Yet, they also "transcend" the situation.

The notion of transcendence here does not mean something that is "beyond" the actual situation of interaction. It also does not mean that the objects carry meaning as a material sign relates to a signification. Transcendence here can be understood as something that is not present in the situation but only referred to by something present. It is, to use a term more strongly related to the communication process, an objectivation mediating among spaces, times, and actors, that is, contexts.[9] Thus, seating arrangements of settings for presentations, such as, for example, the built environments, transcend *pars pro toto* in that they are part of larger spatial structures, such as buildings, places, streets, cities. In this sense, buildings and built structures serve as spatial mediators. They are "there" and, simultaneously, part of something that is not perceived in the situation (such as the street in which the building is located). The same holds for the "information," which is on the notebook, yet, at the same time, on some other carrier or even on the "cloud." Even actors are transcending, for they all gather at a certain time and space yet relate to actors who may (or may not) be approached later. Again, these mediating structures are not mere "networks"; rather, the spatial settings of presentations are typically institutionalized in certain kinds of built environments, most prominently business office buildings, hotel conference rooms, or university halls. By providing a material stage, buildings and objects allow the performance to be contextualized.[10]

Of course, powerpoint presentations do not necessarily need this kind of building. The common example for the broad use of powerpoint given by many interviewees is a mother who shows her slides on the organization of household matters. Thus case only requires a living room – and the triadic structure of the presentation. One could even imagine a presentation to be held in the open air (requiring in addition only power and a screen). For this reason, the external features we note are not as essential to the genre as the triadic structure itself. Nevertheless, the setting refers to some spatial structures that are institutionalized in a way that is specific to powerpoint presentations. With respect to space, the (formal) meeting in the conference type setting nowadays typically provides one of the common spatial structures, including the technical infrastructure necessary for powerpoint presentations. In conference hotels, universities, and business and public agency offices we increasingly find a number of rooms built for powerpoint presentations. Contemporary office architecture accounts for the meeting format by providing space in the two formats observed previously: small meeting rooms with a circular arrangement and larger meeting rooms.[11] As we shall see, this is part of and results from the institutionalization of the meeting.

Although one may hypothesize that the empirical relevance of the two types of settings is a result of the path already institutionalized in the early phases of "meeting mania," I have to admit that there are no satisfying grounds for this hypothesis.[12] Even if we have to leave this question open, the analysis demonstrates that the buildings and the objects provided, such as chairs, lecterns, and screens, are not "external resources" to the presentation. Rather, they shape the presentation with its basic triadic structure by providing a locale and a spatial pattern for it and thus contextualizing it in a wider spatial and material context. Space, buildings, and objects, however, are not the only means of transcending the situation, but materially mediating it to other situations and simultaneously materially contextualizing the performance. Interestingly, there is also an important temporal context it is embedded into and by which it is transcended.[13] This temporal dimension will lead us to the major social context of powerpoint presentations, that is, the meeting.

## 2. The Temporal Order of Presentations and the Meeting

Buildings are a very "heavy medium" of communication (Fischer and Delitz 2009) that transcends the situation in a lasting, yet nondetermining way and thus provides the context for many diverse situations. Bodies are a similar heavy, but more mobile "medium." Their mobility refers to another dimension of transcending the setting: time. Like space, time has proved to be an essential feature of the performance of presentations; indeed, performances are defined by the temporality of the communicative actions in talking, showing slides, and interacting.

The presentation as a whole genre exhibits a temporal structure with a clear beginning and end. In addition, however, the presentation is embedded in actions transcending its performance temporally. Importantly, these actions can take various forms that do not affect the question of whether what has happened before was a presentation or not. Before the presentation starts, the presenter may be introduced by someone else. After the presentation and the applause (as well as the subsequent expression of gratitude by the presenter), another person may act as an anchor and comment or moderate the talk. Frequently, the talk is succeeded by discussions, that is, comments and questions by the audience, followed again by comments and answers from the presenter. In other cases the presentation may be succeeded by a process of decision making, for example, of a board constituted by or separated from the audience in which judges, referees, or lawyers give speeches relating to the presentations. In some cases, the evaluations or decisions may be made directly, in written or in digital form. Depending on the context, presentations may be evaluated by audience members, assessed, or subjected to a decision.

In this temporal perspective, presentations form part of a series of presentations that again may affect the genre's internal macrostructure. Following the law of the series, introductions can be collected in the beginning of the series, applause can be postponed to the end of the series, and discussions can be deferred to the end after several presentations. In this way, the presentation forms part of a larger temporal unit (e.g., presentation and discussion, presentation and evaluation, series of presentations within introductory and concluding remarks) in which the same people are gathered at the same location in the same or a similar spatial order – yet without someone presenting.

From the perspective of the presenter, any presentation requires some prearrangement in a phase of "staging" (*Inszenierung*) (Lobin 2009: 40): a manuscript has to be written, slides have to be designed, and possibly handouts need to be prepared and copied or created (for example, by means of "Create Handouts in Microsoft Office"). As stated earlier, the preparation of slides turns the presentation into a more or less "rhetorical" action project by a presenter or team who, then, appears as subject and, consequently, as "author" and origin or "principal" of the presentation. Whereas the performance of the presenter, as one terminus of the triad, has been analyzed before, it is worth stressing again that the presentation temporally precedes the situation and is taken into the situation materially or by means of the digital document, one of the pillars of the triadic relation, using the technical infrastructure identified as the "information society."

Before I turn to the technological infrastructure, I wish to emphasize that the presentation has to be organized so that it "can take place" at a certain time. As we have seen, presentations transcend the situation not only as products of media, that is, as slides, decks, printouts. The prearrangement and scheduling are not restricted to the presenter and her or his action plan. Other aspects of the presentation as an event also have to be prearranged. Times have to be coordinated and fixed, rooms have to be reserved and equipped with objects, collaboration with helpers has to be coordinated, and potential audience members need to be informed and attracted.

In addition to their preparatory phase, presentations are postprocessed. They can lead committees to decisions with lasting consequences, they may result in the promotion of people within organizations, or they may be documented in "knowledge" or "information management systems." Spoken texts become protocols, manuscripts, and articles, or the performance can be shown by means of video records. As stressed throughout, the way presentations are preserved is, of course, summarized in the formula "presentation as document." Indeed, it is one of the specific features of powerpoint presentations that they can endure beyond the situation as information (by means of information technologies). They can be saved on computers, stored on intranet systems, put on homepages and learning platforms, attached by e-mail or just handed over as a deck to the audience members, who may take them home. Although the slides can be published on paper, too, the designation of the "documents" as "publications" (Lobin 2009: 40) may be misleading in two senses. On the one hand, they are mostly virtual objects that form part of the electronic infrastructure, and, on the other hand, many of these decks are not available on the Internet but are stored in intranets by means of information management systems within the boundaries of organizations and organized networks of communication. Since slides are often used, copied, and transformed into new slides and integrated into new decks and presentations as documents, extended to written texts, the notion of postprocessing seems to be more apt (from the perspective of the presentations).

Postprocessing refers, for instance, to the huge number of presentations as documents put on the Internet. In addition, however, presentations are stored in other ways. It is worth mentioning that they are considered to be "information" or "knowledge" processed on the intranet and made available to the employees. "Information" or "knowledge management" assumes that documents should be made digitally accessible to company members in order to allow them to learn from previous actions, assuming that this "knowledge" is saved and "organizational memory" is maintained. One of the few studies of postprocessing has been undertaken by Schoeneborn (2008), who analyzed data on knowledge management in a multinational consulting firm. He shows that, indeed, 87 percent of the documents stored in the knowledge management system in this company consisted of powerpoint presentations. (Note that presentations as "documents" are considered as "knowledge" and as products of the "presentations as events.")

The preparation as well as the postprocessing of presentations depend on some kind of organization not identical with the situative organization of the performance. This organization may be based on loose networks of communication, yet in any case it requires the provision and coordination of the three core elements of the presentation, that is, presenters, audiences, and technologies, as well as objects, buildings, and settings. Drawing on the notion of event elaborated earlier (Hymes 1974), presentations are indeed events. More specifically, because of the requirements on the setting, the presence of an audience and the availability of a presenter who has prepared for the presentation (and has a presentation as document available), powerpoint presentations are pre-organized events. Preorganized events of this kind have been generally referred to as "meetings in a very broad, anthropological meaning." Thus, Schwartzman (1989: 7) defines a meeting as occurring whenever there are "three or more people who agree to assemble for a purpose ostensibly related to the functioning of an organization or group" (Schwartzman 1989: 7). Moreover, the meeting is characterized by the fact that people pursue a certain goal. Since the performance of a presentation may be such a goal, powerpoint presentations doubtlessly qualify as meetings. Whereas events may just happen, meetings are prearranged and thus require organization and organizational communication. Since they occur at fixed times and spaces, they require a formal invitation, they include an internal order, and they relate to some kind of common task or goal.

Meetings do not just signify a very general anthropological type of event, to be found wherever human society takes the form of a gathering communicating in a more or less focused way. "Meeting" is also the name of a more specific modern kind of event that forms the frame for powerpoint presentations. Both types, indeed, share some features. As any type of meeting they also exhibit a double order of organization. As performances, they are organized by the synchronization, coordination, and orchestration of and by presenters, audiences, and technologies. In addition, all three elements must be provided for in a preparatory stage and postprocessed by actions and in situations different from the meeting itself. In addition, the current form of meeting is regularly (yet not necessarily) linked to a specific type of performance, that is, the powerpoint presentation. Both kinds of organizations, the organization of the presentation (or of the performance in general) and the organization of the meeting, are related, since the kind of participation as presenter or audience is agreed upon beforehand by means of telephone calls, e-mails, or meeting organization software. The organization of the meeting may include a meeting agenda, meeting minutes, presentations as documents, and so on.[14] Although the organization of the meeting is itself done by means of communicative actions, these need to be less focused and can be dispersed across space and actors. There are, however, very few studies on the communication of meetings, and fewer studies even on powerpoint presentations (Betz and Hitzler 2011).[15] To undertake a systematic study of their organization as communicative process would have extended the parameters of this study too far. For this reason, I will rely on selected interviews and information from other ethnographic data on meetings and the organization of presentations in order to identify some external features of the genre. In this way, the meeting will serve as the social structure in that it relates the presentation to organizations and its role in organizations as well as the role of organizations in shaping the genre.

As an example for the latter, the "purposes" or "goals" set by meetings and their relation to presentations, we can draw on Brooks's (2004) ethnography on the use of powerpoint presentations in a large systems engineering firm. She distinguishes different types of presentation that relate to different tasks set in the organization: "technical talks" serve to inform an audience about a new technology, "get acquainted talks" fulfill the purpose of introducing the presenter or the presenting group to another group in order to engender cooperation, and "project or program reviews" present projects or programs in order to account for resources. As Yates and Orlikowski (2008) show in a related study on advertising agencies and consulting companies, powerpoint presentations can serve as sales pitches or "pitch preezes" where members of the firm present their proposal to the prospective clients, or "job talks," in which presenters who are applying for a job give presentations that form the basis for the hiring decision. Also Farkas (2006: 166) stresses that powerpoint presentations serve quite varied purposes in different kinds of settings and meetings, such as official welcoming talk at a banquet, sales presentation to a potential customer, review of policy options, or scholarly presentations to an academic conference. Note that the kind of purpose Yates and Orlikowski take as an essential feature of the genre is, in fact, quite variable. It changes across different kinds of meetings, settings, and organizations while the features of what I call the communicative genre, that is, the powerpoint presentation, remain very much the same. The differences among these kinds of meetings vary with the kind of "goal" or "purpose." The "goal" or "purpose" or "task" should not be confused with the basic problem of powerpoint presentations as communicative genres; rather, goals, purposes, or tasks relate to the formal organization or organizational network and the task more or less explicitly set by the participants, ascribed to it by the organizers, or institutionalized in a kind of meeting, such as sales pitch, lecture or "technical talk." If powerpoint presentations may figure as part of these kinds of meetings, they are ascribed the respective "function."

A most instructive example of the tight connection among "purpose," "task," or "goal" of a powerpoint presentation; the kind of meeting; and the hosting organization is certainly powerpoint karaoke, of which we have recorded various performances on video. Powerpoint karaoke, which is an ironic comedy or parody of the powerpoint genre, is not set in office buildings, meeting rooms, or conference halls but in bars, pubs, or night clubs. Actors are members of the audience who join the event freely and who are allowed to decide on the spot whether they want to give a presentation. Of course, their occurrence in bars or clubs depends on the organization by certain staff, and on recruiting an audience, and it also requires all the elements necessary for a presentation. The crucial difference from other kinds of presentations is that presenters have not prepared the slides and do not know them before the performance. In this sense, powerpoint karaoke provides a kind of deviant case from regular powerpoint presentations since – as anyone in the situation knows as part of the genre – the presenters are neither the authors nor the principals of the slides. Instead presenters do not know the slides in advance; nor do they know the set of slides and or even the topic on which they are presenting. Only after they have entered the stage and opened the presentation do they see what it is about and start to improvise a speech. Because of this change, powerpoint karaoke leads to often awkward associations between the speech and the slide being produced, which, because of their awkwardness, appear as funny and trigger amusement and laughter. Powerpoint karaoke, therefore, very much resembles comedy shows not because the presenters are comedians, but because the performance appears to be funny (as in "science slams"),[16] particularly if some presenters are "performing well," that is, are, despite their lack of knowledge of what is on the slides, successful in synchronizing, coordinating and orchestrating.[17]

The importance of goals and institutions already indicates that, in addition to the presentations being framed by the meeting, meetings are embedded in, are mediated by, and transcend organizations and their institutional function. Thus, a powerpoint presentation within a religious organization will be framed as a sermon or another form of religious communication, whereas in legal settings powerpoint presentations may serve as evidence in lawsuits. In the political arena, presentations can be used as "demonstrations"[18] or as an argument in a decision process, as we saw with the famous example of Colin Powell at the UN.

## 3. The Multiplication and the Ubiquity of Powerpoint Presentation

Powerpoint presentations transcend the situation of their performance in another way. Whereas the situations of performance are, almost by definition, fugitive, powerpoint presentations are said to be a ubiquitous phenomenon. This means that the powerpoint presentation as a genre is being employed everywhere and all the time. Powerpoint presentations have multiplied. This multiplication, leading to its ubiquity, is one of the most impressive features of the external level. Starting with Gaskins's first PowerPoint presentation in Paris in 1992, presentations have become ubiquitous in the sense that an immensely large number are being performed at any time. In order to grasp the path through multiplication to ubiquity, it is, therefore, quite reasonable to look at numbers of presentations. Because of the frequent confusion between "presentation as document" and "presentation as event," there are, however, very few reliable numbers on presentations conducted. In order to compensate for this, I want to draw on indications of the major elements of powerpoint presentations: technology (computers, projectors), meetings (presenters and audience), and presentations (presenters). As announced in the introduction to this chapter, I do not just want to focus on the question of how ubiquitous these situations are. At the same time, I want to indicate how this ubiquity came about. This temporal process of multiplication will be reconstructed by observing the institutionalization of the meeting and the structural diffusion of the technology that contributed to the rise and stabilization of powerpoint presentation.

### (a) The Institutionalization of the Meeting

Just as there are manifold differences between organizations, so there are as many different purposes and diverse types of presentations, to the extent that meetings (and within them presentations) are very much routinized activities in the life of organizations. Meetings do not require necessarily formal organizations; they can be organized by any number of people as soon as they succeed in bringing together presenter, audience, and technology. Although meetings are not necessarily linked to presentation, they are a likely format for the performance of powerpoint presentations.

Therefore, the study of the meeting may shed some light on the role of powerpoint presentations in organizations and in society as a whole. Since powerpoint presentations depend on the organization of presenters and audiences, the institutionalization of the meeting is one of the prerequisites of this communicative genre, while the diffusion of presentation technology, which will also be treated, is another.

Building on the notion of institutionalization by DiMaggio and Powell (1983), the dispersion of the meeting can be seen to be the result of an iso-morphic reproduction of a distinct form of social action and its legitima-tion in an increasing number of organizations. The institutionalization of meetings, of course, implies a series of complex communication processes by which, for example, meetings are learned, organized, and protocolled. As meetings themselves are also communicative processes, the notion of "institutionalization" is, again, only shorthand for more complex commu-nicative processes. More and more organizations implement meetings as part of their "daily routine." The fact that, as part of their institutionali-zation, more and more presentations are conducted within these meetings shall be considered later.

The institutionalization of the meeting as a form of social action dates back to the turn of the twentieth century and, as Yates (1989) and Yates and Orlikowski (1992) suggest, lies at the origin of modern business cul-ture.[19] With the increase in the size of companies during the late nine-teenth century, business organizations started to establish meetings. The increasing necessity to integrate the horizontal flows and vertical coordina-tion in business organizations was solved, first, by depersonalizing written forms, such as "shop papers," in-house magazines, manuals, reports, and memos. In addition to these written forms, meetings (and, within meet-ings, presentations) were institutionalized in businesses. The early forms of such meetings were called "shop conferences" or "shop committee meet-ings," in which elected members of the labor force and the management met. At DuPont, in the vanguard of this form, a superintendents' meeting was established by means of unifying and systematizing the department as early as 1904. Later, a monthly meeting for all plants was established where personal pitches helped workers to learn about other plants and to mon-itor and adjust new rules, procedures, and records. "Many of the special reports delivered at the meetings by members of the headquarters staff (…) were intended to educate the superintendents in technical and managerial issues" (Yates 1989: 237). In 1906 different kinds of such meetings were already known, such as the "goodwill conference" held between the departments of a company, and the "supervision conferences" among foremen and department heads.

There are few indications as to the diffusion of meetings. As sparse as the information on meetings may be,[20] there is evidence that at the end of the twentieth century there was a massive leap in the number of meetings. Thus Parker (2001: 77) states that by the 1980s "America began to go to meetings." This proliferation of meetings as a form of social action seems to coincide with the establishment of a new form of legitimation. The analyses of management rhetoric by Boltanski and Chiapello (1999) provide one indirect indication of this "meeting mania," as they show that the organization of work in terms of projects became the most dominant way of legitimating work at this time. In addition to projects, the establishment of group work in industrial production, flexibilization of working hours, individual goal covenants, developmental plans, just-in-time productions, cross-departmental cooperation, and networking are cited as reasons for the increased coordination of activities. The meeting is quite obviously one of the social forms for pursuing this goal.

Further evidence for the proliferation of meetings is the development of the "meetings industry,[21] a specialized organizational field. This industry is composed of organizations specialized in meetings, incentives, conferences, and exhibitions (therefore also abbreviated as MICE). Although this industry represents conventions and exhibitions as well as meetings, and although the meetings referred to are not necessarily linked to presentations, the data on this industry may at least indirectly give some evidence as to how they expanded.[22] MICE is largely organized around two complexes, corporations and associations, and it is based on two major pillars, hotels and conference centers.

The numbers given by the various organizations differ significantly (HVS 2007; ICCC 2002). Although the institutionalization of these organizations of meetings goes back to the nineteenth century, Ladkin and Spiller (2000: 13) stress that "the development of the modern MICE industry is much younger." The first functional meeting facilities (such as presentation technology) in hotel chains had not been installed before the 1950s, a time when meeting planning also became part of hotel management. In 1978, there were a total of 156 large convention and exhibition centers worldwide. Centers and, with them, meetings multiplied from that date: Europe established more than 260 convention centers in 1995. The money generated by the U.S. meetings industry rose from $30.3 billion in 1987 to more than $50 billion in 1995 (Mieckowski 1990: 337; Montgomery and Strick 1994: 13). In addition to meetings supported by business firms and professional associations, a significant number of MICE events were sponsored by government, professional, social, and religious organizations. Given that only some restricted area of the universe of meetings is covered by these numbers, they are still quite impressive. In 2005 about 1,020,300 corporate meetings (attended by an average of 77 people) were organized. In addition, 210,600 association meetings were held, totaling 1,230,900 meetings. The number of people attending these meetings in 2005 was between 136 and 169 million, spending $107 billion to $131 billion for all meetings (Fenich 2008; K. Weber and Ladkin 2004; World Tourism Organization 2006).

Although the meeting industry represents only a segment of the meetings occurring in certain specialized settings (mainly hotels, conference centers), and although MICE surveys also include events other than those we might call meetings, such as conventions, its sheer existence and its development may be taken as, at least, some evidence of the successful institutionalization of meetings. This quantitative evidence can be complemented by qualitative data on the growing role of meetings mostly within organizations by Bolte et al. and by interviews conducted in the frame of our powerpoint project. Bolte et al. (2008: 62 trans. HK), for example, reported a representative of a company that specialized in planning and development as saying, "Today it is totally normal that if you meet with a small group you do a meeting. 'Come on, let's go to the meeting room where it is quieter. There is also a table, a projector. In any case I have my notebook with me.'" Another manager interviewed by us complains, "There are hardly any informal conversations anymore. As soon as three colleagues get together, and someone opens her notebook, there is a meeting." The meeting format transforms even informal encounters, and it does so, among other reasons, by implying presentations.

In all, six different companies of different size and from different industrial sectors were studied by Bolte et al. (2008: 137), and meetings were the most important means for the coordination of the major work activities within and across those organizations. The types of meetings they identified ranged from ad hoc to institutionalized departmental meetings, from informal communication to briefings, state of project reports, and association conferences. The meeting is tightly related to new kinds of organized work. Especially when employees form part of different projects at the same time (each share accounted by a percentage of their work time), the meeting proves to be the ideal "locus" of the project for it is here where the cooperating parties meet 'in real life." Although meetings are demanding with respect to time and energy, employees avoid being excluded and complain if meetings become a monopoly of management.

Due to their growing legitimacy, meetings have been increasingly accepted as a major instrument of coordination in the practice of management. The organization of meetings has been fostered by special software, such as Outlook. This kind of software helps in the coordination of participants in that it allows the booking of meeting rooms and of organization members via the intranet, the same network that is used for the storage of documents. As a result, organizations witnessed a "meetings euphoria," a "meetings revolution," that is, an "explosion of the number of meetings at which those participating are also not part of the management" (Bolte, Neumer, and Porschen 2008: 19 trans. HK). The same phenomenon is also framed critically as, for instance, "meetingitis," "Meeting Madness," and even "Death by Meeting" (Adams 1994; Lange 2004; Lencioni 2004). The quantitative evidence for the institutionalization of meetings is supported by the few qualitative studies in the field. Thus, members of a company studied by Brooks (2004) attended from one to three (middle level) up to ten or more presentations a week (in 2000). Also the manager of a German consumer product company stressed that presentations are part of everyday business. Meetings are so frequent that "you have to book two to four weeks in advance in order to make sure that people can join." Managers are involved in four to six meetings a day.

### (b)  Ubiquity and the Structural Diffusion of Technology

As the institutionalization of the meeting organizes the personnel who may also be necessary for powerpoint presentations with presenters and audiences, the growing availability of presentation technology, the third terminus of this communicative genre's essential elements, is not necessarily linked to the meeting. Computers, notebooks, laptops, and projectors are not necessarily part of meetings, and they are not exclusively accessible to organizations. It is, therefore, wise to assume that information technology follows a different path. I want to describe this path in terms of the "diffusion of innovations." By this term Rogers (1995: 5) means how and to what degree an innovation is communicated through certain channels among members of a social system.[23] With respect to powerpoint, this concerns a number of technological innovations, including the computer, the projector, and the presentation software. The diffusion of computer technologies, portable computers, and projectors can, then, be described in terms of their moving from a small number of early adapters through to their adaptation by a growing number of users and clients. In addition to its conventional meaning, the notion of diffusion used here is meant to account for the fact that these technologies form part of an infrastructure that includes political entities, big companies, and scientific paradigms (such as the U.S. government, ARPANET, the monopolization of the market, e.g., of Microsoft's PowerPoint). The critical role of political and economic actors in the social construction of the information society has been covered by a range of analysts.[24] Although these processes are not the topic of this study, their relevance is implied when referring to the "diffusion" of technology, and it is particularly relevant when addressing the structural diffusion of projection technologies.

Obviously, the ubiquity of powerpoint is related to the sheer diffusion of the computer as a communication device, the history of which is well known. Starting from a very modest level, the diffusion of computers exploded in the 1990s. Worldwide sales of personal computers rose from 325 million in 1997 to more than 800 million in 2005.[25] Sales of portable computers rose even faster, from $3 billion in the United States in 1996 to $7.4 billion in 2001.[26] The diffusion has exhibited severe traits of social inequality, addressed by the notion of the "information gap" or "knowledge gap," and, indeed, the differences in the diffusion of computers on an international plane are quite strong: besides the unequal social distribution within societies, mostly related to income and formal education, there are also inequalities between societies. From 2002 to 2007, the number of households with computers increased, for example, in France from 36.6 percent to 62 percent of all households, in the United Kingdom from 57.9 percent to 75 percent, in the United States from 59 percent to 70.2 percent, in Germany from 61 percent to 79 percent, and in Iceland up to 89 percent. In addition to these differences between Western societies, there is an immense gap on the global level, particularly when measured against African societies (International Telecommunications Union 2009: 101f.). In recent years, however, the "information gap" within technologically highly developed societies is diminishing, as it has between men and women and generationally between young and old. It is certainly one prerequisite for the success of powerpoint presentations that computers have become a ubiquitous technology and communication device for the majority of people.

The diffusion of computers went along with the creation of companies dominating the market. With respect to presentation software, Microsoft in particular was dominant, cutting out most other companies from the market.

The success of PowerPoint is, as a representative of PowerPoint states, due "to two things: One is it's easy to use, and two is, it is associated with Office."[27] The dominating role of PowerPoint is in fact related to the almost hegemonic domination of the software market by Microsoft. Revenues for Microsoft licenses were an estimated $300 million in 2003; the market penetration of the presentation software was then up to an estimated 96 percent.

As the software provides the basis for presentations both as documents and as events, the event also requires an additional technology, the projector.[28] The most essential invention in this respect was the liquid crystal display (LCD) projector, developed in 1984 by Gene Dolgoff. However, the technology then still had slight problems, and it was expensive until the beginning of the 2000s. "Projectors that plugged into your computer didn't become ubiquitous until the last eight years or so, and only in the past few years were there equipment that small departments could actually budget without raising an eyebrow in the finance department" (Bajaj 2008). In the last few years, LCDs, plasma display panels (PDPs), and in particular their portable counterparts have gained enormous ground. The sales of portable data video projectors have increased by almost 90 percent per year since 1993, while their prices have decreased by more than 40 percent per year. Between 1998 and 2004 growth in the business sector was 100 percent, generating a $12 billion projector market by 2004.[29] Although projectors are also used for televising and video, the numbers of worldwide shipments for font projection units from 2007 (including projections up to 2012) allow us to infer a corresponding rise in the number of projectors used for presentations.

From the sheer number of computers and projectors and the quickly rising number of presentations one may also infer that these are only one indication for the ubiquity of powerpoint presentations. A second indication can be found in the global diffusion with respect to both the number of national societies as well as the variety of categories within these societies. Increasingly, technologies are also available to those who had been considered to be beyond the "digital divide." In the next few paragraphs, I want to draw attention to a third aspect of ubiquity, and that is that powerpoint presentations are diffused across different institutional spheres and subsystems of modern society. Starting from the economic field, they entered the most diverse institutional spheres, such as science, primary and secondary education, the military, politics, law, religion, and the arts. I shall refer to this as the structural diffusion of presentations.

Although powerpoint presentations still meet with some resistance and criticism by scientists, *scientific organizations* started early to integrate them into their system of communicative genres, though various disciplines did so at different speeds. Some disciplines, such as information science, library studies, and business, have been using powerpoint since the mid-1990s.[30] With respect to business, Keller (2003: 5) states that by the mid-1990s, "more than 80% of the presentations given by business-school students rely on PowerPoint rather than the old fashioned flowing narrative" (2003: 5). Various reports and articles give evidence that powerpoint was established around 2000 in other scientific disciplines, such as geography (Mantei 2000), biochemistry (Parslow 2003), and machine construction (Winn 2003). Medicine also joined in around that time (Bellamy and Mclean 2003; Essex-Lopresti 2003), including the various medical subdisciplines, such as radiology (Dreyer 2001), cardiology (Feldman 2002), and dentistry (Halazonetis 2000). Pharmacists discussed powerpoint as early as 1998, while the humanities, such as academic history, also embraced it at this point (Pellmann 2002). If one looks for a general pattern, it is obvious that computer studies and business were first, followed by the natural and life sciences, social sciences, and, flater, the humanities, still with some resistance particularly in the latter fields. This chronology demonstrates how the critique of powerpoint presentations follows its diffusion across its original institutional fields in business and computing; moreover, the pattern of the diffusion of projectors indicates that the critique of powerpoint was triggered by the diffusion of powerpoint presentations as events rather than the diffusion of powerpoint presentations as documents (which existed before and could be easily disseminated by Internet, e-mail, etc.).

In *primary and secondary education*, the use of powerpoint is linked to an explicit stress on students' active participation, self-responsibility, cooperation, and project-oriented and self-initiated learning (Schulz-Zaner and Riegas-Staackmann 2004: 309). Together with videos, CD-ROMs, and other types of hardware and software, computers,, slide projectors, and overhead projectors are framed as "instructional design and technology," that is, "the physical means by which instruction is presented to learners," and used to support the process of teaching and learning (Reiser 2001: 54). In fact, computers had already been employed within education in the 1950s and expanded from the 1970s onward. By the early 1980s, computers were to be found in 40 percent of all elementary schools and 75 percent of the secondary schools in the United States. By 1995 there was one computer for every ninth student, and in 1998 one for every sixth (Reiser 2001). Although presentations are not covered in the statistics available, the use of projectors, as quantified in a German survey, may be seen as an indication. In 2003, projectors had been used twice a month across all school types (with a rise from 1.8% in 2002), peaking in high school as well as elementary schools. At this point, students had been only vaguely familiar with this technology, boys more so than girls (Schulz-Zaner and Riegas-Staackmann 2004). In the meantime, presentations have become formally accepted as an instructional form, and in some states and countries there are now special examinations to assess the quality of presentations. In the German federal state of Berlin, for example, there is a special "examination of presentations" for students finishing middle school.[31]

Although there are no numbers on the issue, the *military* is an institutional sphere in which the use of powerpoint seems to have reached almost epidemic proportions. As Pece (2005: 2) suspects, the military's distinct hierarchy of command and clear vertical stratification lend themselves to a "competitive briefing culture where every presentation is a performance that encourages endless hours of preparation." As empirical evidence, Yates and Orlikowski report (2008) that almost all documents of the U.S. Air Force are presented as powerpoint briefings, and Pece (2005: 55) adds that each student of the air force school is expected to present three separate speeches using powerpoint with fixed "main points." According to Miller, by 2000 no headquarters of the German army was without an expert on powerpoint. Recent reports (Bumiller 2010) support the view that powerpoint presentations dominate communication in the U.S. Army to such an extent that they have become one of the major activities of military personnel.

Evidence on the use of powerpoint in *politics* is scarce. Its importance, however, as has been previously noted, was famously marked by Secretary of State Colin Powell's presentation given on February 5, 2003, in which he made the case for war against Iraq. Furthermore, during the Iraq war, it is reported that every morning the defense secretary, Gates, reviewed piles of printed powerpoint slides, and this process continues with President Obama, who is also kept informed by being shown PowerPoint slides (Bumiller 2010). As our interviews show, presentations are used in all political administrations and at all levels. A German regional politician whom we interviewed stated that information on, for example, financial programs is passed on from the ministerial level down to the local levels in Germany via powerpoint presentations as documents and events. Presentations are held live, yet documentations in the political field are not restricted to slides and decks but, additionally, require other forms of texts and text documents.

There are a few indications that powerpoint entered the *legal system* particularly in the United States from early 2000. The case of Michael

Skakel, convicted for murdering the fifteen-year-old Martha Moxley in 2002, is considered a breakthrough for the "highly customized interactive presentation system." Although it is not clear whether PowerPoint or another software was used, there is no doubt that an electronically supported presentation was performed: "As witnesses were testifying, prosecutors displayed on a large screen photographic evidence, maps, diagrams of the murder scenes, and other demonstrative evidence that they were able to summon on demand from a CD-ROM" (Carney and Feigenson 2004: 23). Somewhat later, the lawyer Ricardo Cedillo from San Antonio won a $624 million verdict in a contract trial with the help of a computer presentation. Throughout the trial Cedillo used a powerpoint presentation in which all material evidence, press releases, photographs, and letters had been included. Since then, powerpoint has been so common a device in legal cases that there are special instructions for lawyers on how to use the software, design slides, and present them in courts (Brenden and Goodhue 2005).

Powerpoint has also come to be used in the *religious field*. First, powerpoint can serve religious organizations just as well as any other organizations in helping them perform their everyday tasks. Second, it is also used for specific religious events, such as church services, as our own recordings of three presentations in church services have shown. Also Hedahl and Hogan (personal communication) support the view that powerpoint presentations have become common in church services.[32] Although it is difficult to make guesses as to the numbers of presentations in this field, the existence of an Internet portal, EBibleTeacher.com, specialized in powerpoint presentations for various religious audiences, may serve as evidence: on the homepage the portal claims at the starting page (by July 2010) that more than 10 million people have visited the page, with more than 50 million page views. Given that the page attracts visits by religious clergy and professionals, this would indicate the enormous popularity of powerpoint in the field of religious institutions.

Powerpoint has been also adapted to other kinds of institutions, such as the *arts*. The former New Wave musician David Byrne, for example, tried to demonstrate that PowerPoint can also be a basis for the arts. "The software [PowerPoint]," he argues, "by making certain directions and actions easier and more convenient than others, tells you how to think as it helps you accomplish your task" (Byrne 2003: 3).

As selective as such evidence may be, it proves that powerpoint use has not been restricted to business and science. Instead we find a structural diffusion of powerpoint that is penetrating the most varied institutional spheres

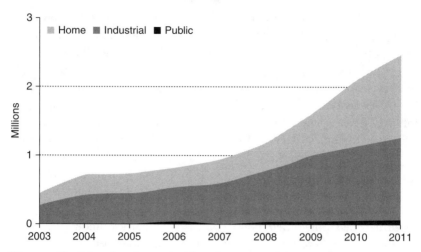

Diagram 10: Sales of projectors in Africa, Europe, and the Middle East.

of modern society. This penetration is not restricted to particular nations or even Western societies, but rather the notion of ubiquity, I want to argue, reflects powerpoint's use across different societies on a global level. Since there are no surveys on this level, there are at least some data on projectors that may again be used as an indirect indication for the use of powerpoint. This data show general sales numbers, and, moreover, indicate the numbers per global region and the distribution across institutional spheres. (As the use of projectors at home primarily serves entertainment purposes, their number can, again, only be taken as an indirect indication.) Take, for example, the sales of projectors, as documented across three world regions (Diagram 10).

Sales of projectors in general are here shown to rise about 25 percent in the first year and about 33 percent annually in recent years. Across the different world regions, we find a quite similar pattern for the diffusion of projectors, a diffusion that is not restricted to business and corporate sales but extends to public institutions and sales by private persons. Since corporate as well as institutional sales of projectors can be seen to serve presentations and meetings, we can infer the proliferation of an immense number of meetings and can assume that their number is growing. The cross-institutional diffusion on the global level is more detailed in another study according to which the number of projectors sold rose from more than 5 million in 2007 to almost 10 million in 2010, 70 percent of which was used for "conference and training," "education," as well as "sales and presentation," while only another 25 percent was for individual consumers and other institutional areas, such as government and religion.[33]

The structural diffusion of PowerPoint presentations that can be inferred from these data are quite remarkable. As its inventor, Austin et al., had stressed in 1986 (37, 48,), "Presenter [the precursor of PowerPoint] will sell directly to large corporations" and "managers and senior people." With respect to PowerPoint and its designers, this goal has not really changed, as in 2010 a representative of PowerPoint again stressed that large companies and major licensees remain the company's major target group. Yet, we found that powerpoint plays an important role far beyond the business world in the other institutional spheres reported, such as education, the military, and religion (and, probably, also in private life). So, quite obviously, this structural diffusion was not anticipated. As Robert Gaskins remarked later in an interview (*PC Magazine* 2007: 2), "What was unexpected was that the same hardware would also extend PowerPoint use into university teaching, children's school reports and science fair projects, sermons in churches, super-titles for opera houses, and many of the uses that its creator had never imagined." The fact that the broad diffusion into the most diverse institutional spheres was unexpected remains true today for the designers of PowerPoint (as document) still focus mainly on business users: "I don't know that we [i.e., Microsoft's PowerPoint branch] were focused on those additional users at all. I do not think that any of us sat down and said how the application would work better for schoolchildren."[34]

### (c) From Presentations to Powerpoint Presentations

Since projectors, computers, and meetings can only be considered as indirect evidence for powerpoint presentations, we finally have to consider some indications as to the proliferation of the presentation as event. As much as the situations of communication have been neglected in prior research, the very fact that "presentation" is used by the actors themselves as a designation for the genre may serve as another indication. In order to find this designation, Degenhardt and Mackert (2007) have examined twenty-six English and German language encyclopedias and fourteen dictionaries in English, French, and German.[35] As they convincingly show, the category of presentation came into use only in the last few decades, and its meaning differed from today's: in the 1962 edition of the *Oxford Illustrated Dictionary* (1962: 648), the word "presentation" is understood in terms of, for example, "presenting gifts," and of other semantic aspects, such as "theatrical representations," "formal introductions," and, interestingly, "phenomenological meaning." The *Webster Dictionary* of 1981 gets closer to the more recent meaning in defining one aspect of "presentation" as "the act of presenting to sight or view" (pictorial, etc.) (1981: 1793). In another dictionary from 1982, "presentation" refers to a "display or show (e.g., with slides), used especially in advertising" (as well as to "presenting a program on television") (Burchfield 1982: 765). Only in the 1990s is the now-popular meaning mentioned as, for example, by the *Cambridge International Dictionary* (1995: 1117): "The speaker gave an interesting presentation (= talk) on urban transport."[36] In 2008, the *Pocket Oxford American Dictionary* finally gets very close to the current meaning, calling a presentation also "a talk or a meeting at which a new product, idea, or piece of work is shown to an audience." Presentations as a form of communication were hardly mentioned until the 1980s, and only in the 1990s did presentations in this sense (and related terms, such as "presentational graphics") become part of encyclopedia entries. Another indication for this is that the "presentation" became a category in bookshops for the sorting of books (mostly beside "rhetoric" and similar categories that are thought to be familiar to the patrons). Both the representation of the category for organizing books and the encyclopedic category give a good indication of "general knowledge" of the "presentation," that is, what everyone knows or is supposed to know about it.

Encyclopedias may represent the general social stock of knowledge, yet they do not cover all lexical items in specialized social stocks of knowledge.[37] In our case, this distinction between a general and a special stock of knowledge is of some importance: well before presentations were reflected in the general knowledge collected in encyclopedias, they appeared in special fields of knowledge. We find them first in the field of business at a time when the meeting was starting to become an institution.[38] The word "presentation" can be found in practical advice books for business as early as 1921 and 1929. Such books gave advice on how to make business reports ("investigation and presentation"), referring only to written presentation and the visual display of mathematical information, that is, to information graphics. At this time, no mention was made of presentations as events (Saunders and Anderson 1929). "Presentation" at this stage referred to a form of document, such as a "graphic presentation of business statistics" (Holland 1921; Smart and Arnold 1947).

As with meetings, presentations were, one may say, originally a business genre.[39] The category is generally well known, yet the meaning of this genre has changed over time. In their analysis of forty-four how-to books on presentations, Degenhardt and Mackert (2007) have shown that in these books the word "presentation" is used for business communication as visually supported "documents." Earlier in 1975, Morrisey's "Effective

Business and Technical Presentations" was oriented predominantly to the printed form of "presentation as document." The importance of visuals for presentations as documents is expressed in a specialized magazine called *Presentations*, which began publication in 1993 in Minneapolis by a sales and management company covering topics like advertising, communications, graphics, and typography.

It was only in the early 1980s – a time when, as we have seen, the "meetings revolution" was presumably in its early stages – that a new aspect of the presentation became apparent in how-to books, namely, the visually supported "presentation as event." Hughes (1980), for example, gives instructions on "effective speaking with presentations." In *The Practical Approach to Business Presentations*, Morse (1980) defines business presentations as visually supported talk. Another advice book from 1988, directed at business and the professions, mentions multimedia settings as part of "presentations" and recommends special "multimedia rooms" with a separate soundproof booth behind the rear wall of the presentations room. This "nerve center" of any presentation is linked with a slot that allows for "the projections of slides, filmstrips and movies, and the television cameras used in videotaping" (Howell and Bormann 1988: 187). Presentations are in such cases no longer defined purely through the use of visual media in general but by special technical media, such as blackboards, magnet boards, white boards, flip charts, overheads and other projectors, print media (hand uts), video media (film), audio media, and computer supported media.

The strong connection between the meeting and the presentation has also been claimed by Yates and Orlikowski (2008: 8): "By the 1980s, formal business presentations with visual aids were commonly used to communicate information and arguments to an audience co-present in the same physical space as the presenter." This view is shared by Robert Gaskins, the inventor of PowerPoint presentations, who observed in 1986:

> A very large number of businesspeople make 'presentations' to other all the time as part of their work. These are semi-formal meetings to which an individual attempts to persuade others to make a decision, to approve a course of action, or to accept a result. Almost any manager, professional, or consultant considers presentations of this sort a major part of the job. (Austin, Rudkin, and Gaskins 1986: 5)

One should remember that at this time, most of these presentations were still based on overhead foils or 35 mm slides that had been outsourced and produced by graphics companies. In 1987, for example, shortly after introducing computers, a German based international American consumer product company had a contract with a multimedia company that produced slides for the meetings held by upper management. In addition, presentations were mainly restricted to the special multimedia rooms, which some organizations had been providing since the 1980s. These rooms included overhead projectors, film projectors, video systems, and slide projectors and were mostly used for special occasions such as the meetings of upper management and meetings with external members of the organization and with clients.

Also at this time, and using foils and slides, some presentations took on a more compact form with a beginning and an ending. Some of my interviewees recalled that already in the 1980s they had used "standard presentations." These presentations, which were the basis for the power-point presentation genre, consisted of a set of overhead slides that had been used for presentations on fixed topics, such as the presentation of one's own organization or organizational unit, its particular structure, goals, and visions. As later with PowerPoint presentations, these standard presentations were not only "documents": they provided presenters with a kind of "script" of topics and texts on which they could draw and rely when presenting live.

In the companies interviewed, PowerPoint and other presentation software came in use by the early 1990s. At this time, PowerPoint was linked to printers using special cartridges for different fonts and still in black and white. When color slides began to be used in the early 1990s, printing one slide took more than twenty minutes. The first projectors had been installed by the mid-1990s in multimedia rooms. The number of users increased rapidly while other forms of presentation still coexisted. In an interview study, Griffin (1995) asked 560 subjects randomly selected from a regional Training and Development Consortium in the United States about their use of PowerPoint. The questionnaire study revealed that 27 percent had experience with presentations by means of overhead, flip chart, and, third, electronic presentation. Overheads were still considered the most effective medium, but electronic presentations (already dominated by PowerPoint) grew in popularity (1995). A Web survey conducted by the company 3M in 1999 covering more than thirty-four hundred business, education, and government professionals showed that at that time more than 70 percent of the respondents still used overhead projectors. One in four said they mostly used multimedia projectors (Hanke 1998: 13). Interestingly, at this point it seems to have been used more for internal communication, for most of the respondents reported that the majority of presentations were held in the offices and classrooms where they normally worked (more than four-fifths). The vast majority of presentations (93%) were local with live audiences only. In another survey conducted by Hanke (1998: 13), more than 40 percent were said to use multimedia occasionally, while according to a survey by the journal *Presenter* in 1998, 94 percent of professional speakers claimed to depend on it.

This is also reflected in the how-to books. As late as 1996, an introduction to *Power Presentations* does not mention any presentation software at all but only handouts, slides, overhead transparencies, videotapes, and flip charts. The 1996 edition of *Communication at Work* only vaguely recommends the use of "new computer-assisted design of visual aids" as the most decisive "innovation" for presentations. Various software programs that allow the insertion of new visual forms (such as bullet lists, slides, and graphics) are mentioned without any reference to PowerPoint.[40] It is only toward the end of the 1990s that powerpoint started to play a more prominent role in connection with "presentations."

Obviously, presentations were in existence as a more or less formal genre before the advent of powerpoint. The inclusion of powerpoint in presentations happened only around, and mostly after, the year 2000. It coincided with the increasing availability of projectors and of laptops, and it was, from then on, characterized by the structural diffusion that led to its ubiquity, as document, and, with the increasing availability of projectors, as event. One should add that the dissemination of presentations was also subject to regional variation on the global level. Earlier adapters were found in the United States rather than, for example, Germany, or, even later, in the postsocialist societies. In addition, the adaptation of powerpoint followed the structural pattern of the diffusion of projectors. Early adapters were found in business and only later in other types of organizations, such as in science or education. To give an example, the manager of a large German fire brigade did not recall the use of computer projectors earlier than 2005. Even Microsoft had no projectors in their conference rooms on their campus before 2003. As delayed as the adoption of powerpoint presentation may have been, it became ubiquitous immensely quickly, to the extent that by about 2005 powerpoint presentations were routine in many organizations. As an official from a large (publicly financed) city fire brigade in Germany said: "PowerPoint is the Alpha and Omega of this agency; nothing goes without PowerPoint." It is used in meetings that occur regularly and at almost every organizational level. A representative of another German company specializing in industrial metal production saw powerpoint presentations as obligatory, right "down to the foremen." The manager of an American consumer product company asserted that

PowerPoint (and Excel) presentations provided the structure for regularly scheduled meetings, for routine meetings, as well as for executive meetings. As the CEO of a consumer product company (interviewed by us) confirmed, about 90 percent of his work was now done with PowerPoint and Excel, and similar statements have been made by members of the military. When a U.S. platoon leader based in Iraq was asked about what he was doing most of the time, he responded, "making PowerPoint slides": "I have to make a storyboard complete with digital pictures, diagrams and text summaries on just about anything that happens. Conduct a key leader engagement? Make a storyboard. Award a microgrant? Make a storyboard" (Bumiller 2010).

# 7    Conclusion: The Ubiquity of Powerpoint and the Communicative Culture of the Knowledge Society

Little known to the general public even as late as 1990, powerpoint presentations a decade later were ubiquitous as both documents and events. While in 2002, about 30 million presentations had been given daily (LaPorte et al. 2002), in 2006, Tufte estimated the numbers at about 35 million presentations per day. In 2005, Google listed about 4 million powerpoint decks on the Internet. In 2009, the number had increased to 8.68 million files of the format .ppt, and n April 2010 Google counted more than 59.4 million (April 12, 2010). In the same year (April 22, 2010) Google found more than 217,000,000 Internet citations for "presentation" ("religion" at the same date had 255,000,000 articles). At this point the most common definition of "presentation" in Wikipedia (April 22, 2010) was synonymous with "powerpoint presentation" – both as event and as document: "Presentation is the practice of showing and explaining the content of a topic to an audience or learner. A presentation program, such as Microsoft PowerPoint, is often used to generate the presentation content."

Having analyzed the phenomenon of powerpoint presentation as a communicative genre and having reconstructed how and in what sense it became ubiquitous, in this Conclusion I want to tackle the more difficult question of *why* powerpoint presentations became so successful and ubiquitous. The explanation of this phenomenon is not meant to invoke a notion of causality which would not fit into a theory of communicative action. Rather, it will draw on more extensive developments that establish the meaningful grounds for the ubiquity of powerpoint presentations.

As already indicated in the Introduction, the "information society" and the "knowledge society" – both in the sense of the socially constructed aspects of society highlighted previously – provide the conditions that explain the spectacular rise of powerpoint. To summarize it, powerpoint presentations result from the convergence of the institutionalization of the meeting (as an institution of "knowledge" organization) and the diffusion of information technology including its globalizing infrastructure. Both processes allowed presentations – the loose communicative form prior to powerpoint – to be turned into a stable communicative genre. The stabilization of the genre not only results from human action but depends on the standardizing effects of the technology (which, of course, are also due to the global hegemony of the organization owning it and the global accessibility of informational infrastructures). Thus powerpoint presentations link technology, objects, and human communication, with its specific focus on "knowledge" organization, or, in their specific societal forms, the information society and the knowledge society. The meaningful explanatory link between both is achieved by the simultaneity of mediatization and contextualization. Whereas the technology allows this situation to be connected to the information infrastructure and the standardized informational "data," it is also part of the situation and allows "information" to be contextualized and "situated" "face to face," overcoming the lack of situational specificity in standardized information. Since technology and human actors constitute the basic triadic structure, it serves both to contextualize the standardized forms of information and to mediate the situational forms of communication.

As Diagram 11 indicates, the invention and stabilization of powerpoint presentation as a genre thus result from the fusion of aspects of two different (but not contradictory) developments: the information society and the knowledge society. The "societies" are, of course, not different; they instead represent two institutional paths constructed by different legitimations, one technological, the other more related to humans. While the constitution of powerpoint as a genre is a result of these developments, it bestows a social form, that is, a genre of communicative action, on these structural developments. This form defines what has to be done in action and how it is supposed to look. As these developments are, however, are istorically prior (presentations, meetings, computers, even presentation programs), they serve as an explanation for its genesis.

As mentioned, neither of these "societies" is just an abstract entity. With respect to powerpoint, this is apparent in its two basic elements, the presentation as an event, on the one hand, and the presentation as a document included in the event, on the other. Both elements develop into a form of communicative action, that is, a communicative genre. Powerpoint presentation became a communicative genre because it linked the informational order ("presentations as documents") with the temporal work activities in their organization ("presentations as events"),

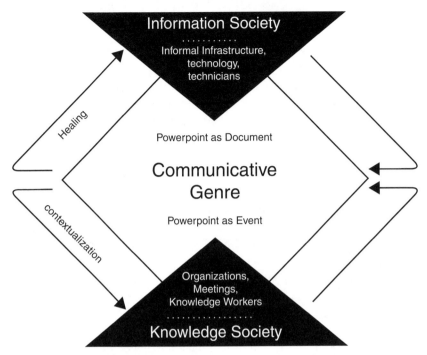

Diagram 11: Relation between powerpoint and the dynamics of the societal structure.

thus relating the standardization of informational forms of technically mediated communication, on the one hand, with the situational performance of face-to-face communication, on the other hand. The communicative genre is thus designed in such a way that communication is seen to present the presenters' or producers' knowledge in the situation or event while objectifying this knowledge as information or document. As much as they depend on "information," powerpoint presentations are communicative forms of the knowledge societies for two reasons: first, their inbuilt asymmetry leans very much toward the presenter, whose performance is seen as "knowledge" communicated to and by human actors. Second, the very fact that presentations are performed and that they are not (yet) transformed into social media demonstrates the relevance of this bias toward knowledge. Since whatever is acknowledged as "knowledge" must be communicated in a form (such as powerpoint presentations), this form itself becomes an essential part of the communicative culture of the knowledge society.

## 1. The Invention and Ubiquity of Powerpoint Presentations

Powerpoint presentations are based on several innovations, such as the computer, the laptop, and the projector. The invention of computer designed slides can be considered as a technological innovation that gave rise to the presentation as a document. Given this background one can say that powerpoint as an innovation originated in the "axis time of computing."[1] The 1980s was certainly the period during which the major directions for the design of computer systems were established. The development from large computer systems to the personal computer on which everyone could produce (and later project) presentations bestowed a certain form on what powerpoint presentations were to become.

As Gaskins's invention of the powerpoint presentation as an event in 1992 shows, the information technological innovation is only one source of the invention of the presentation. Powerpoint is the result of a marriage between the emerging computer technologies and business, providing a specific technical form, the slide software, to a specific business event, the meeting. While the meeting existed already for some time in business, the computer engineer culture was also already accustomed to the "technical project meeting" from the 1960s (Licklider and Taylor 1968). The impact of this encounter is due to the fact that this happened in the time when computing was in its formative developmental stages. Since computer developers had been in such close contact with business at this time, their solution to the problems encountered in the business world became fused so that their computers also were literally linked to the business world (as figuring in meetings). As we have seen, the pace of the diffusion of powerpoint followed this pattern – even to the extent that it transgressed the boundaries of the business world. For the availability of laptops, projectors, m and presentation software beyond business – the extension of the information society – also helped to "export" the communicative genre. Gaskins's idea of producing software for presentations is a direct result of this encounter.

The "presentation as an event" was invented in business and was hardly known anywhere else before the 1980s. This "presentation" was only becoming popular at the time when meetings became institutionalized within organizations, contributing to the rising role of knowledge. Also, it seems that, rather than the diffusion of the software, it was the projector and the generic combination of event and (digital) document that gave rise to the explosion of "presentations" in terms of number and ubiquity. The diffusion of the technology and the institutionalization of the meeting as conditions for presentation mirror the hybridity of presentations, in that they process both knowledge and information. The ubiquity of powerpoint, however, cannot be understood as a "simple" innovation. For, as Rogers (1995) suggests, innovations are diffused by means of communication. Here (and as I presume, in many other cases) the innovation is itself a form of communication diffused by communication. In this sense, powerpoint presentations as a genre are what Mead and Byers (1968) call a "communicative innovation" made of and by communicative processes.[2] It is the communicative character of the genre that lends itself to being a core element of the communicative culture.

Before turning to the communicative culture, we need first to consider the process by which this communicative genre became ubiquitous. From a more abstract view, this is linked to the developments of the information and knowledge society. As "information" and "documents," powerpoint presentations have participated in the diffusion of information and communication technologies, their growing market, and the immense financial investment in informational infrastructures by political actors, such as cities, nation-states, and the European Union. As events, powerpoint presentations to some extent follow the path of the institutionalization of meetings and the proliferation of presentations. As we have seen, the use of software and the presentation as document began to spread in the 1990s. Since it provides a communicative form for parts of the organizational communication both in situations as well as across organizations, the presentation as an event took a different, somewhat belated, path dependent on the institutionalization of the business meeting. Based on the crystallization of their predecessor, the presentation, powerpoint presentations created an elective affinity between the meeting culture, representing organizations producing knowledge, and the information infrastructure, representing technologies, their users, and producers summarized as the information society.

The ubiquity of powerpoint presentations exhibits additional features. Leaving aside the sheer number of presentations, both as events and as documents, they are ubiquitous on an increasingly global level. They are found all over the globe in almost every society (and most likely in those parts of the society linked with knowledge in one way or the other). In addition, the ubiquity is characterized by structural diffusion: Supported by the improved availability of projectors, powerpoint presentations moved out of the field of business and information technology at around the year 2000. Note that it was only at this time that the communicative genre became routinely a "powerpoint presentation," both as event and as document.

Technology, the growing hegemony of the software (PowerPoint), as well as the increasing availability of projectors contributed to the standardization of the "presentation as document" and thus supported the stabilization of the genre.

Obviously, the structural diffusion emanates from economic institutions. One may concede that the visual forms of the presentation as document are influenced by scientific precursors and that the presentation as event resembles somewhat (and can be compatible with) certain scientific types of events (such as the small conference or the seminar). Nevertheless, the communicative genre powerpoint presentation carries the traces of its origin in both information technology and the new organizational forms that satisfy the demands of the "new spirit of capitalism" (Boltanski and Chiapello 1999) with its new forms of projectlike organization and requirements for coordination and exchange of knowledge by communication. Therefore, one could suspect that the "new spirit" of capitalism leaves its traces on the communicative genre.

This suspicion becomes explicit even in the scientific critique of powerpoint. Without having to look for the "spirit" of this invention, there is a simple reason for this suspicion, as the critique of powerpoint sets in only at the point in time when powerpoint presentations move out of business and into other institutional spheres. Such criticism is almost exclusively voiced in the spheres outside those where powerpoint originated. The critics of powerpoints react, one may say, to the expansion of the emerging communicative genre from business and computer industry to other communication cultures. Their inclusion in meetings and their substitution for less structured forms of presentation (as by overheads) meant that they were no longer only used in those organizations for which they were designed and that were acquainted with presentations and the forms of visualization that included Powerpoint presentation that had been newly introduced in organizations and settings in which no similar forms had been used before: as the interviews conducted with representatives of the most varied types of organizations show, fire brigades, window cleaning groups, and even families started to use powerpoint presentations.

This development offers one important reason for the moral condemnation of PowerPoint. As the criticism emerged in principle only during its rapid structural diffusion into various institutional spheres of society beyond those in which (and for which) it had been designed, critics seemed to react to this expansion of a genre into communicative cultures that had not been accustomed either to informational structures or to the forms of "knowledge" communication represented by PowerPoint. The moral arguments against this development, however, hardly address this issue. Pias (2009) has shown that this critique often resonated with arguments that had earlier been raised against other new technologies of communication, for example, with overhead slides. Critics have adopted classical topoi against the use of visual media, such as the suggestion that visualizations are superficial as compared to language, particularly written language (and manuscripts read by presenters),[3] while, in addition, the argument that projections appeal to "emotions" was presented in many of the critiques. Although the resentment against PowerPoint and the hegemony of Microsoft to which it contributes can be sensed in the arguments against powerpoint presentations, the extent of this discourse can be seen as an expression of the diffusion of powerpoint into the communicative culture of almost every institutional sphere in contemporary society.

## 2. Contextualization and Mediatization

The emerging generic structure of powerpoint is also reflected in the increasing standardization of powerpoint presentations. As Knape (2007: 56 trans. HK), for example, complains, the generic form "provided by PowerPoint templates is a communicative crutch for those who have ambitions but lack knowledge and proficiency." Although Knape, like many other authors, reduces his criticism to presentations as documents and, thus, underestimates the situational character of the presentation as event and the creativity of presenters' performances, his observation underlines the importance of the standardizing effects of the software provided by the technology. Powerpoint presentations build on, depend on, and exploit a complex infrastructure of technologies and their standards that is not reduced to the situation but embedded in a worldwide network. It may be at this point that the hegemonic role of one software product, Microsoft's PowerPoint, supported the standardization of the technological aspects of the presentations. Even if one concedes that software types differ in grades (and that some are possibly "better" than others in "designing information"), they all support the standardization of "information" or the "document" by means of technology and, thereby, contribute strongly to the stabilization of the communicative genre.

If one recalls the assumptions made by information theorists and if one accounts for the immense investments in "information" and information infrastructure (i.e., "documents," "technology," "society"), one may ask, as Brooks (2004: 171) does, "If people use technology for communicating over distance of time and space, why do they go out of their way to gather in co-presence?"[4] Given the fact that powerpoint presentations spread at the same time as the globalization of computers, digital documents, and the Internet, the existence of presentations as events and their neglect by the information designers lead to the following questions: Why do people still need to gather face to face in meetings in order to give presentations? Why do millions of people have to travel to meet face to face if there are technologically mediated forms of communication between them accessible and available? Or, in a more general way, why does "information" not suffice? Why does it need to be communicated by real people, by bodies, and in localized situations?

One answer to this "macrostructural" question is to be found in the basic hybridity of the genre, the "presentation as event" and the "presentation as document." Since both aspects of the presentation feature in the situation of the presentation, the analysis of the presentation can shed some light on the question of why "information" must be "presented." The results of these analyses confirm that, as opposed to the view that the "information" to be communicated is encoded in the slides, that is, their "cognitive style," their meaning is instead a situative result of their "interplay" of speech, bodily conduct, and the technology in the performance of communicative action. The "interplay" has been analyzed in terms of synchronization, coordination, and orchestration, and I have identified deixis, paralleling, pointing, body formation, projecting, and so on, in order to define the form of communication empirically. In addition to the presenter's linking words and slides, situated speech, and the encoded information, the production of meaning extends to a triangular structure of slides, including presenter, technology, and audience. In recognizing the importance of interaction, body, and space, the presentation has been shown to be an artful orchestration of meaning that is constructed creatively within the situation.

In linking the communicative action of giving a presentation to the organizational and informational infrastructure, the situative features of powerpoint presentations (as event) can be said to "add" to the presentation as document. Indeed, one may say that they complement and compensate for what the "presentation as document" is shown to be lacking by its critics. They do so in a way I want to describe as reparation, healing, or, by a more general and less normative notion introduced earlier, contextualization. Assuming the deficiencies of powerpoint slides as documents, the presentation as event allows one to "repair" it within the situation. Even if one does not agree with the harsh critique of presentations as documents (and if one would assume that a "better" software would require a situated and embodied performance, too), one can assume that it is their standardized character (including the standardized forms of visualizations, such as diagrams and icons) that needs to be "repaired." By contextualizing "information" in a situation, the performance can be seen to repair the indexicality of standardized "presentations as documents," that is, text mediated via information technologies, by means of the setting. In this way, the presentations as events perform a similar function to face-to-face interaction in other high technology settings. As analyses in computer supported collaborative work shows, the coordination of actors by means of computer mediated communication requires additional coordination and interaction between the actors and situated actions (Heath, Luff, and Knoblauch 2000).[5] Therefore, contextualization is the answer to the question of why "presentations as documents" have to be presented in events.

In the empirical analyses earlier I have amply demonstrated what I mean by contextualization: in addition to the situative indication of the social relevance of what is happening and its framing (Gumperz 1992), contextualization here also means not only the importing of but also the situative use of objects and technologies in situations of interaction. It is by means of these objects and technologies that the situation is mediated to other situations. Thus, as mentioned, it is an essential feature of powerpoint presentations that presentations as documents are imported into the situation and contextualized by a performance. The coordination and synchronization of text, slide, and speech, the orchestration of the triadic structure, are examples of the manifold practices by which the presentation as document is contextualized. Contextualization is accomplished by the various aspects of performance, such as the synchronization and coordination of presenter and slide and its orchestration with the audience, including the forms of deixis, paralleling, ratification, and the body formation. Contextualization is not just the situative realization of whatever is fixed as "information." On the contrary, the strong tendency of information technologies toward standardization, that is, standardized textual and visual (formats, templates, diagram types with marginal differences), makes it necessary to readjust them to specific situations, specific audiences, specific individual presenters, their courses of action, their intentions, and their specific claim on "knowledge."

By the notion of healing I am alluding to Garfinkel's (1967) idea that actors need methods to "heal" the indexicalities of situations, that is, the impossibility of defining the situative aspects of actions in a way that would apply across situations. Heath and Knoblauch (1999) have already applied this idea to technologically mediated communication. With respect to powerpoint, this idea is also supported by Kaplan (2010), who stresses that communicative practices of knowledge production allow the negotiation of meaning in an uncertain environment by providing spaces for discussion, recombinations, and creative transformation.

Against this background, namely, the standardization by information and the necessity to produce "knowledge," one may say that contextualization performs the function of "healing" and "repairing." It is in order to avoid this functionalist terminology, I prefer to use the notion of contextualization. The emphasis on contextualization should not be misunderstood as meaning that powerpoint presentations as a communicative genre are only a form of situated interaction. In that contextualization depends on the objects and technologies that are contextualized, it exhibits the same duality as the communicative genre: the "presentation as document" forms part of and is embedded in the situation of the presentation as event. Simultaneously the objects and technologies are transcending the local situation by the organized work of preparations, by the organization of the event and the audience, and by the provision of technical infrastructure and events.

The way that the transcendence of the situation is achieved has been referred to as mediatization. Technology, objects, and organizations mediate between situations and between people, or, to be more exact, their communicative actions. Mediatization refers to the fact that communicative actions are mediated by and performed through objects and technologies. While communicative action may be said already to be mediatized by the body's faculties of expression, mediatization refers to the mediation of embodied performance of communicative action and genre that links situations in time and space by means of technologies and action and by virtue of their objectified forms.

Mediatization allows for contextualization in that these objectivations, that is, technologies, objects, and materials can be used in situations. In order to produce a presentation, work invested in the visual design of the slides and work invested in producing a coherent text as objectified in the "presentation as document" take place in situations – be they situations of solitary work or situations of cooperative work (or again mediated, for example, by e-mails written or read). In the sense that this work also takes place in situations, one can say that the "presentation as document" mediates between situations. Therefore, one could compare the powerpoint presentation to the "mediated performance" analyzed by Auslander (1999). Whereas mediated performances, however, refer to events that are transmitted as a whole and constitute the major focus of attention recorded, such as television shows or soccer games, powerpoint presentations are mostly characterized by a different kind of mediatization: typically, it is not the event itself that is transmitted;[6] rather, it is the presentation as document that is prepared for, embedded in, and later disentangled from presentation as situative event.

Mediatization is quite obvious with respect to the chain of technology,, that is, computer, projector, and software, which sometimes palpably transcends the situation (e.g., when including Skype conferences in presentations, when using the Internet, or simply when starting with downloading one's presentation by USB stick). The mediated structure of the event itself exhibits the ways that the situation and the situated are related. For quite obviously, it is by means of technology that the software, the template, and the standardized structure of the slide and deck are "imported" into the situation, and it is by means of an organization that presenters and audiences can assemble. Since the software is linked with other software, since it allows users to insert data from other programs (texts, diagrams, photographs, videos, etc.), and since it is related to the various technical networks (intranet, Internet), it acts as an intermediary to what has been subsumed under the notion of the information society. Furthermore, since presenters, audiences, and spaces are linked to informational networks, organizational fields, and their resources, they act as an intermediary to the recent organizational structure and changes indicated above.

Before I elaborate on this point in the final part, we have to focus on another crucial issue: knowledge. In fact, both types of mediations are nicely expressed in the role of "knowledge" or "information" to refer to what is seen as the product, result, or goal of the presentation, the former rather stressing the accomplishment of the performers, the latter the "cognitive" load of the producers and the slide. The difference between "information" and "knowledge" also parallels the difference between the presentation as document and the presentation as event. Although both are interrelated in the situation of the presentation, the presentation as document forms part and is a product of the preparation or the postprocessing of presentation. Information, thus, is taken to be objectified on the slide as the "cognition" inscribed by the authors, encoded by the signs, and stored in the information systems. Since information seems not to suffice, the aspect complementing it is covered by the notion of "knowledge." Since "knowledge" is also constitutive of the knowledge society discussed in the Introduction, we should clarify how it figures in the powerpoint presentation.

## 3. Communicative Things and the Subjectivation of Knowledge

If we do not reduce "knowledge" to the somewhat deficient "informa-tion" encoded on the slides or to the "cognition" as the information the producer of the slides wants to encode, we must consider "knowledge" as meaning that is communicated in the course and by means of the presenta-tion. Although "knowledge" is constructed in and by the performance, it should not be belittled as a mere "simulation" lacking any basis in the real-ity of those actors constructing it, as Pece (2005), referring to a concept by Baudrillard, seems to suggest. Also the notion of "infotainment" seems to be misleading since it depreciates the use of visualizations as "entertaining" and less "serious" than use of words (Postman 1993). "Knowledge" here is seen as the result of a series of that which have been identified in the preceding analysis.

First, on the internal level, various visual forms of slides are conspicu-ous objectivations of knowledge. These objectivations are not reduced to the visualization of an "empirical reality," as in some forms of visualization in the sciences (Amann and Knorr Cetina 1988; Lynch and Woolgar 1990). As we have seen, the powerpoint slide is only sometimes used as a proof *ad oculos*, and then often only in passing. Even as one may identify some aspects of a visual code built on the visual elements (including words), it is exactly the visual code that is linked to, and repaired by other modes of communication and, thus, contextualized. Second, next to the visual forms of objectivations, texts and manuscripts figure prominently as a mode of objectivation. Third, synchronization, coordination, and orchestration exhibit various strategies for the construction of knowledge, such as dupli-cation, paralleling, and pointing, that is, objectivation. They are based on the triangular structure that institutionalizes the gesture of pointing so that everything said can be, in principle, understood in relation to what is shown (or not). By these means, the presentation contributes, fourth, to the con-struction of the objectivation I called communicative things: what is shown and what is talked about turn into something much more conspicuous than plain words in a speech or text or items on slides. Communicative things are what the presentation is about, what is represented by information (as representants), and what is known by the actor. They are, therefore, not dependent on the kind of objectivity that has been established in science, its distance from bodily sensory perception, and its practices of visualizing (Daston and Galison 2007). Although building on these visualization prac-tices, they only depend on the common strategies of objectivation typical of powerpoint. As we have seen, even scientific presentations are subject to these strategies, which range from parallelisms to embodied orchestration. (One may venture to argue that this is linked to the increased orientation of science toward the public and its "popularization" – yet this suspicion refers to specific developments in science and cannot be pursued here any further.)

In addition to the technological chain, the triangular structure entails the presenter and the audience. This is particularly evident in the case of pointing, which draws on the technological institution of "pointing," the presenter's body (or its extension by, e.g., a laser pointer), and the audience to which pointing is addressed. The triadic structure and its enactment as production format allow, fifth, for the spatialization of knowledge, for its temporalization, and, thus, for the objectivation as communicative thing: what is shown and what is talked about turn into something much more conspicuous than plain words in a speech or text or items on slides. As the creative use of pointing demonstrates, "knowledge" presented must not be represented on the slide or in the words; it is, in a way, produced in and by the dynamics of the triangle: it builds on the presentation as document projected on the slide; it depends on the perception and understanding of the audience, and, finally, on the speech and performance of the presenter. In this triangle, the presenter plays, of course, a most prominent role. The meaning of a presentation is considered the "presenter's knowledge." Although the meaning has been shown to result from the interplay of the triangle, we have to explain why "knowledge," a communicative thing, is ascribed to the presenter. In order to answer this question, let me briefly sketch the ways that the meaning of the presentation is constructed as the presenter's knowledge and as strategies of subjectivation.[7]

A first and obvious way in which the presenter is made the author of the presentation consists clearly in the presentation's constitutive asymmetry. It is the presenter who holds the "monopoly" of speech; the presenter also determines which slides are shown as well as when they are shown . Moreover, it is the presenter who enacts the performance by moving his or her body at the center of attention. The body is essentially involved so that the presenter is not just the "author of the text" that is spoken but is the embodiment of the presentation.

As we have seen, the asymmetry is not total. On the contrary, the slides, the projection, and the technical chain play an important role in the performance of the presentation. I have considered this role as constitutive for the genre since there is no powerpoint presentation without this technology. Its relevance becomes visible in that it may appear like a second "stage" beside the performer, who can be decentered by light, voice, or enormous projection sizes. As important, however, as the technology and as decentered as the presenter always are, the role of technology is downplayed in the performance. As a second way of ascribing "knowledge" to presenters, we can identify a strategy of subjectivation. This strategy is best expressed in the cases of failure in which the technology is foregrounded. Although technology, then, moves to the center of attention, the audience's attention typically loses focus as the technical problem lingers on, before the attention ultimately dissolves. Downplaying technology and asymmetry is, moreover, expressed in the phenomenon of embarrassment. Embarrassment by the presenters (following the reframing of the genre) implies that technologies are controlled by presenters and are part of their action plans. On these grounds, what is communicated in the performance is considered to be related to the presenter. We cannot explain the embarrassment at technological failure if it is not ascribed (and often somewhat *contra factum*) to the presenter, who is seen to be in charge of the presentation.

The asymmetry and with it, the subjectivation of the presentation, is, third, also accomplished by the audience. As we have shown, the audience is expected to be quite actively monitoring the slides and presenter in order to "know" what is being presented. Because the slides allow both presenter and audience to locate where one is in a presentation, they (as opposed to common lore) even facilitate the audience's participation. Yet, whereas interactive episodes may be part of the presentational "aggregate" of various forms, the normal expectation of audiences, particularly in formal settings, is to refrain from intervening in the acoustic focus or entering the visual stage.

The asymmetrical situation is highlighted by the fact that most presentations allow audience activity before and after the event: Audiences may, for example, clap (the applause being treated by the presenter as related to what is being presented rather than to his or her person). Despite the focus on the presentation, the "knowledge" presented must not claim uncontested authority and the presenter is not cast in the role of an almost dictatorial primary speaker who is supported by a software enforcing this "cognitive style." The audience's "voice" is routinely being heard in the parts of the events after the presentation: after the presenter closes, questions, discussions, or comments are voiced by the audience, which is allowed to "question" what has been presented as "knowledge." Also on the level of the actors, "knowledge," therefore, is not uncontested but is part of institutionalized forms that, in principle, allow for a "critique" of what is being said – even if the forms of critique vary, depending on the kind of meetings and their purposes. Although the discussions and other kinds of "institutions of critique" following and based on the presentations would deserve a study on their own,[8] they lie outside our focus on presentations. For my argument it is important to note that their very existence presupposes that the "knowledge" presented is being ascribed to the presenter. (In addition, they often presuppose a distinction between the presenter's intentions, as expressed in his or her reactions to comments, and the "knowledge" presented.)

As the asymmetry of the presentation is produced within the situation and by the interplay of presenter, audience, and technology, there are further methods of subjectivation. These are linked to the production format. Thus, the slides as documents are, fourth, typically prepared in advance by the presenter, who, therefore, functions as "author." Mostly this authorship is accounted for by the deck's being ascribed to the author. His or her name and affiliation appear at the top of the first and sometimes on all slides. Being the author, the presenter may also use the slides as a mnenotechnical device so that, in fresh talk, their content also helps to recall the "knowledge" indicated by the slides. With respect to powerpoint presentations, the authorship of presentations is an essential feature, for it is the technology that allows one to produce slides for presentations and, thus, made graphic design companies redundant. Slides, in this sense, are subjectivated in an economic sense because presenters do the work specialists did before.

The effect of subjectivation, the ascription of the knowledge to the presenter, may be quite direct, as an advice book indicates: "When you make powerful presentations, you'll make yourself invaluable to your company" (Hendricks et al. 1996: i). Powerpoint presentations, thus, are not only performances in the dramaturgic sense. The presenter is also presenting himself or herself as someone who knows how to do a presentation, or, to be more exact, how to present his or her knowledge. If I may state it in a formula, the presenter needs to know how to show what to know. By providing the subjects with a form for communicating what is to be seen as their "knowledge," the presentation can be said to contribute to an increasing form of professionalism independent of any specific profession.[9]

At this point one should stress that neither professionalism nor "subjectivation" is restricted to individuals. As the presentation may be performed by more than one presenter simultaneously, the presenter sometimes also represents a group or an organization that figures as author or principal (and is often graphically represented on the first slide). Because of their visuality, powerpoint slides provide an exceptional means of constructing collective actors, such as logos, emblems, corporate designs, or even identical slides for members of an organization. In this case, the presenter performs what is considered to be the group's or organization's knowledge.

## 4. Powerpoint Presentation in the Communicative Culture of the Knowledge Society

Given that the subject and the object of knowledge are constructed by means of the presentation itself, "knowledge" is what is communicated by the performance. *"Knowledge" is, in principle, constructed by the communicative genre itself*, or, to say it in other words, the communicative genre powerpoint presentation is a frame that indicates "knowledge." The quotation marks should make it clear that "knowledge" here does not refer to objective facts about the world. It is not even the "statements" about the world, but is, far more, about the various forms of communication by which we can claim to know something about the world. As the forms of change, powerpoint presentations are one of the ways to frame what counts as "knowledge" in the kind of society we call the knowledge society.[10] As far as the structure of diffusion of powerpoint presentations is concerned, this is not a society in which science dominates; it is instead a society in which certain communicative forms – such as powerpoint presentations – and the "communicative things" produced by them (such as presentations as documents) count as "knowledge."

Even if the performance of presentation is dominated by a presenter, and even if it includes the activities of technologies, objects, and audiences, one can distinguish different grades of asymmetry within the triadic structure. Given the empirical observation that powerpoint presentations are biased toward the presenter, the asymmetrical structure could, in principle, change. This change would lead to different notions of "knowledge." Whereas the asymmetry toward the presenter ascribes "knowledge" to the presenter's knowledge and product, the asymmetry toward the technology emphasizes the "informational," "objectivated" character of knowledge encoded in the "cognitive style" of the slides. If the presentation were based on the audience, its perspective would prevail, so that "knowledge" would be an understanding by the audience of what had been communicated.

The observation that it is the presentation as event and, thus, "knowledge," rather than the presentation as document and "information," results from the observation that presentations need to be performed – healed, repaired, and contextualized. The very diffusion of powerpoint presentations as events thus demonstrates the asymmetry toward "knowledge" rather than "information." Although the performance is characterized by the triadic structure including information technology, we find a strong bias toward the presenter, to whom "knowledge" (presented and documented) is ascribed. As the case of social media shows, this asymmetry, however, can easily be reversed in reality: powerpoint presentations can be inserted into information communication systems such as the social media. As soon as the interaction itself becomes part of the document itself, for example, in social media, presenters as well as "knowledge" become defined by systems designers. Often, systems designers claim to "model" the situative interaction or even "genres," this way turning the actor's potential to contextualize information performatively into a much more rigid informational structure built into a special software ("meeting" software, or "presentation genre" software). As a consequence, human actors may only "introduce themselves" within formats of self-presentations ("broadcast yourself," as YouTube suggests), their actions are reduced to certain moves programmed by systems designers. The recent increase of social media within the meeting industry indicates that the first attempts of integrating presentations into social media can also lead in the opposite direction and reverse the asymmetry, reducing the chance of contextualizing knowledge and thus resulting in the increasingly global standardization of "knowledge."

As long as presentations as events in their current form are asymmetrical with respect to the presenter and, thus, subjectivize knowledge, they can be compared to a discursive practice that has been analyzed by Foucault (1995). According to Foucault, discursive practices are forms that construct knowledge and subjectivity. Thus, the "examination" is a "discursive practice" that, on the one hand, defines the roles of actors with respect to knowledge, and, on the other hand, defines what is to be considered as knowledge. As convincing as this model may be, powerpoint presentations differ from it inasmuch as they transfer the control to the presenting subjects themselves, thus contributing to the subjectivation mentioned previously.[11] Given the potential creativity of the presenter within the situative context, it would be inadequate to consider the presenters as only "constructed" by the discourse, as Foucault suggests, but rather, I want to suggest, as acting in the forms of materialized communication. It is these subjects, then, in pursuing their goals in a rhetorical preparation of their presentation, who are seen as responsible for their performance, and who are embarrassed if they fail, and who are finally required to show their "competence" and professionalism.[12] Consequently, powerpoint presentations as a communicative genre are a socially acknowledged and legitimated form of subjectivized knowledge and objectivated information. This form allows both performing knowledge and storing, remembering, and reproducing knowledge as information (i.e., as slides). It even applies to the most informal presentations that, on the surface, seem not to transmit any relevant knowledge. In this sense, powerpoint is part and parcel of the knowledge society since it is an element of it and, at the same time, contributes to its construction. As Knorr Cetina (1999: 7f.) rightly stresses, "A knowledge society is not simply a society of more experts, more technological gadgets, more specialist interpretations. It is a society permeated with knowledge cultures, the whole set of structures and mechanisms that serve knowledge and unfold with its articulation." While knowledge seems everywhere, knowledge societies need to define what is (socially, economically, politically, etc.) relevant "knowledge. The definition of "knowledge," however, occurs in communicative actions and takes specific communicative forms that are recognizable as knowledge – from numbers and equations to definitions, reports or powerpoint presentations. Knowledge societies, therefore, are constructed by communicative forms constituting a specific communication culture. Powerpoint is one of the communicative genres that, therefore, constitute the communicative culture of the knowledge society.

The importance of powerpoint presentations for the contemporary knowledge society can be detected from their ubiquity. As we have seen, that ubiquity is explained, first, by the diffusion of the information technologies, that is, the information society, which provides for the standardization required by the format. Second, the ubiquity is explained by the institutionalization of the meeting and, as part of the meeting, the presentation. Their coincidence gives rise to the powerpoint presentation as a communicative genre. Third, the relevance of this communicative genre is explained by its potential to construct "knowledge" that seems so essential for contemporary society in a way that accounts for the information society, that is, the digital document, as well as for the knowledge society, that is, knowledge and its importance for organizations and cooperation (in meetings). As a result of institutionalization and diffusion as a technically mediated standardized form, the genre became stabilized very quickly on a global level.

It is certainly true that the standardized qualities of the genre resemble, as Schnettler (2007) claims, a "lingua franca" or a "basic idiom" of knowledge society. Powerpoint presentations are a form of communication that only varies slightly across the most diverse institutional spheres of society and maintains common standards even across the globe. They thus form part of a "world culture," a ubiquitous and universally standardized form of culture (Lechner and Boli 2005). The generic features are not only an effect of the standardization of technologies and the isomorphy of institutions. Instead, as a "communicative invention" that is itself structuring the communicative processes by which it is multiplied, the powerpoint presentation is part of the communicative culture of the knowledge society.

By communicative culture, I understand much more than a mere "cognitive" framework (Lechner and Boli 2005: 15) for action. Communicative culture also extends far beyond a notion of culture as a system of values or symbols. Although it shares "the value of communication," it is also more than what Castells (2009: 38) calls "the common culture of the global network society" as a "culture of protocols of communication enabling communication." Communicative culture is, as it were, signs, symbols, values, and protocols "in action," that is, communicative action. Communicative action is embodied (mediated) performance in situated time and space. Note that communicative actions must not necessarily take the institutionalized pattern of genres (Luckmann 1985). As opposed to the structure of the event, for example, though formalized in many ways, powerpoint presentation as communicative event does not seem to follow a standardized generic pattern. Powerpoint presentations are embedded in the most varied events – while maintaining their generic features. Communicative genres are courses of communicative actions that exhibit certain patterns actors expect and reproduce by means of their bodies as well as by means of objects and technologies involved in the actions' performance. This holds for a prayer, a political speech, a television show, a job interview, a sales talk, an e-mail exchange in informational networks, and, as I have tried to show, it holds for powerpoint presentations as a communicative genre of knowledge society.

The knowledge society is not only one of the reasons for the ubiquity of powerpoint presentations; it is also built on powerpoint presentations. As "knowledge" is performed in the shape of communication, they form, in a manner of speaking, one of the pillars of its architecture. The knowledge society owes its existence not only to the penetration of contemporary society by the ubiquitous powerpoint presentations. It is characterized by the ever increasing ubiquity of many forms of the communication of "knowledge" and by their growing relevance or legitimation. Their relevance and legitimation are expressed again in communication, such as the situated and mediated forms of knowledge communication that give access to certificates, to professional positions, and directly to economic resources (job interviews, examinations, presentations for competitive bids, etc.). Though only a few of these forms of knowledge communication have been studied, we can identify a number of specific communicative genres of the knowledge society: audits (Power 1999), for example; interviews (Atkinson and Silverman 1997); consultancies and coaching (Traue 2010); "small conferences" and seminars (Mead and Byres (1968)) – be they "face-to-face" or mediated by various technologies (telephone hookups, video conferences, Skype). All these forms are devoted to the communication of knowledge, as are "conversational teachings" (Luckmann and Keppler 1991), seminar discussions, lectures (reading written texts) and talks, or, to mention a recent innovation, "science slams."

Next to "representing knowledge," it is one of the features of the "knowledge society" that these communicative forms originated in and emanated from schools and universities. As the example of powerpoint presentations shows, the transfer from science into society is not the only way of achieving the social construction of the knowledge society, while "knowledge" cannot just be reduced to "scientific knowledge." It was one of the goals of this study to show that the "knowledge society" is not only, and probably not even predominantly, coined by scientific forms of communication. Rather, forms of participative primary education, of popular entertainment, and, as powerpoint has demonstrated, of business genres have been integrated into the knowledge society (and, thus, also into science).

The focus on powerpoint and the communicative construction of knowledge should not be understood as an uncontested process. Already the critique of powerpoint shows the growing opposition to a notion of knowledge that is slowly being detached from the textual and scriptural paradigm common in the humanities. In addition, there are myriad other communicative forms and genres existing and evolving that are not marked as performing knowledge: powerpoint karaoke, which plays on the lack of relevant "knowledge," serves mainly as entertainment, as do comedy shows, musical performances, or conversational encounters between friends and families. All of these forms of communication entail, of course, some knowledge (of jokes, of topics, of persons, of aesthetic styles, etc.), but they must pass as "knowledge" unless they are framed in order to pass as "socially acknowledged" legitimate knowledge, that is, in tests, contests, or professional contexts (therapies, evaluations, etc.). The communicative culture of our society is anything but uniform. There are, however, certain forms that are of such importance to society that they penetrate the most diverse range of areas of the communicative culture. Powerpoint presentation are among them.

# Appendixes

## Appendix I

### *Video and the Analysis of Communicative Action*

The most important and most specific kind of data presented in this book is based on video recordings of powerpoint presentations in various institutional settings as part of videography. By videography I mean creating video recordings in settings in which actors perform their routine duties and their recorded activities are then analyzed by the researchers who have acquired knowledge about their field of action (Knoblauch and Tuma 2011). In our study, powerpoint and other presentations have been recorded in natural settings, that is, as they occurred in the social scene. Recordings have been made by one, some by two or three cameras, covering the presenter, the screen, and the audience (from behind). Some of the recordings also cover the audience from the front. These data of video recordings (cf. Appendix II) have then been registered, cataloged, and subjected to various processes of coding (genre analytical coding, grounded theory coding) by the research team. By coding we do not mean the application of certain fixed, theoretically deduced categories of analysis to the video data, as is done in standardized video analysis. Rather, initial codes are developed from the "bottom up" (as suggested by grounded theory).[1] These codes are entered into a content log or an index describing the temporal unfolding of the interaction by reference to the video time code, so that the video fragments referred to might be found easily.[2]

The most intricate and time-consuming part has been the fine-grained analysis, which is quite commonly referred to as "sequential" or "video analysis." It is in the fine-grained analysis that the categories suggested in the empirical chapters on video have been found and formulated. The procedure for doing this kind of analysis has been described in some detail already by various authors, including Knoblauch (2006) and Heath, Hindmarsh, and Luff (2010). The analysis of the video data followed the principles formulated in these texts. It seems, therefore, legitimate to refer the reader who needs more information on the method to these texts since they further explicate the methodological premises as well as the practicalities of the research process.

The data represented in this book have been selected using a systematic kind of sampling within the video data collected, while the ethnographic collection of the data has been informed by both the analysis of the video data and theoretically informed ethnographic work.

The sampling procedure has been elaborated in Knoblauch and Tuma (2011). It is an iterative process. This iterative character of the research process also holds for the codes and the log book, which are continuously changed and corrected in the light of sequential analyses and ethnographic fieldwork. As soon as initial ethnographic understanding of the situation has been achieved, and as soon as some types of interactions have been established by fine-grained sequential analysis, codes are corroborated, and researchers select relevant situations for further scrutiny, that is, continue internal or ethnographic sampling.

One should also add that all results of fine-grained analyses have been subjected to data sessions in which a group of researchers regularly participate. Instead of repeating the procedure for analyzing video data elaborated elsewhere, I want instead to discuss shortly how this kind of video analysis is related to the general subject matter in question, that is, communicative actions.

If one looks at video analysis in the social sciences, one finds two major streams of research. One stream has tried to approach video from a hypothetical-deductive perspective (albeit the methodology is not always made clear in these studies and hypotheses are rarely formulated explicitly). That is to say, categories are deduced that have been applied as "codes" to the visual data, tested by intercoder reliability, and, sometimes, inscribed into computer programs. On the other hand, we find a stream of interpretive methods, mostly informed by hermeneutics and conversation analysis, applying the sequential analysis known from audiotapes to the audiovisual data. This second stream was almost exclusively concerned with the process of social interaction in the most diverse settings: interaction between doctors and patients, between salespersons and clients, between children playing, or in highly complex organizations where persons interact with one another by means of technology (Heath, Hindmarsh, and Luff 2010).

The use of video or, for that matter, its technical predecessor (particularly film) forms, is in fact, an essential part of the history of studying social interaction. As Heath, Hindmarsh, and Luff (2010) and Erickson (2011) have shown, the pioneers of the field had already been experimenting with audiovisual data, and some of the early applications of audiovisual data in the social sciences focused on interactions.

As there is clearly a focus on interaction within many social scientific uses of video data, the notion of interaction needs to be qualified. In many cases, videographic data collections focus particularly on what Goffman (1963) has called "focused interaction." Human actors orient themselves toward one another in a way that may be more (as in a face-to-face inter-action) or less (as in the mutual monitoring of anonymous persons in an elevator or a public place) focused. Thence, video recordings focus on what human actors focus on in acting and interacting. Powerpoint presentations are, as any other staged event, a good example for a focused interaction. In analyzing these interactions recorded by video, it has turned out eminently useful to consider in particular the temporal coordination of actors, a pro-cedure that has been termed "sequential analysis" in conversation analysis (Sacks, Schegloff, and Jefferson 1974; Schegloff 1968). Sequential analysis is based on the temporality of action and interaction and on the fact that this temporality is maintained if not intensified by the technological medium of video recordings. Like film, video is defined by the temporal sequence of frames (pictures). As a result of their temporality, pictures are watched in sequence, and sequentiality is therefore characteristic of video analysis. It is the feature of sequentiality that is the reason for the peculiar focus of many video analyses – actions, reactions, and interactions – since this medium preserves the time structure of these processes in a way unprecedented by earlier media (except film).

Sequential analysis focuses on the order of actions in interactions. It assumes that this order serves as a means of coordinating the conduct of participants and, simultaneously, as a resource for the synchronization of the meaning of interactions. In addition, the sequences can be used as a resource for the interpretation by third party observers – a feature I have exploited in the analysis of the powerpoint performances. At certain points that seem to be relevant socially, distinct structures of sequences are fixed and thus stabilized – a phenomenon that constitutes the basis for commu-nicative genres.

However, as analyses of actors working with computers and other com-munication technologies show, interaction need not necessarily be local but can be spatially distributed and coordinated by means of technologies and media. Addressees of actions may be in other places, as when addressed by mobile phone, or they may be addressed at a later time (as when they are addressed by answering machine or e-mail). This kind of mediated inter-action has proven to be of the utmost importance in powerpoint presen-tations, which turned out to be both focused interactions and mediated interactions at the same time. The case of mediated interaction throws light on a feature that is often ignored when talking about interaction in general: interactions depend basically on some form of objectivations. The e-mail sent, the voice on the answering machine, and the voice heard on the mobile phone are objectivations, as are the sounds voiced by one's own mouth, the movement of the hand while shaking, or the finger pointing to the screen. Classically, these phenomena have been called symbols; instead, I suggest referring to them as communication. As opposed to symbols (or signs), the notion of communication and, as will soon become clear, communicative action, accounts for the temporality by the production of objectivations, and communication accounts for the fact that symbols are built into a complex of objectivations, as, for example, the combination of mobile and voice, the finger and the screen (and computers and audiences, etc.).

Seen from this perspective, video analysis of interaction is necessar-ily video analysis of communication. To be more exact, video captures only two modalities of communication, that is, the visual and the acous-tic modalities, leaving out other important "social senses" (as Simmel calls them) and, correspondingly, modalities of communication. Nevertheless, video is a powerful tool for addressing exactly these two senses and captur-ing the visual and acoustic objectivations in the course of their process-ing. As the notion of communication imparts temporal processes as well as the complex interplay of materiality, the focus on human communica-tion implies a focus on human bodies and their objectivations as visual and acoustic conduct. This focus neither excludes the objects that form part of and are related to this conduct nor excludes the technologies that mediate the conduct. If we assume that any scientific analysis should reflect on its very presuppositions, we must be aware that, in interpreting audiovisual conduct, we usually refer to our subjective knowledge on the meaning of this conduct (and we use sequential and comparative empirical warrants to support interpretations). Subjectivity not only enters at the observer's end of the interpretation. At any point in the interpretation, we also refer to the actors whose conduct is interpreted. Both reasons require the acknowledg-ment of the relevance of subjectivity in the communication analyzed. It is this subjectivity of action presupposed by the observer and interpreter that is accounted for by preferring the term "communicative action" to "communication." The relevance of talking about communicative action is even more important since the person communicating can be his or her own addressee – as, for example, in leaving notes to oneself, writing a diary, or using computers without communicating with others.

Although we are only interested in the typical meaning of their actions in the situation (and not the particular meaning of an individual), we assume that actors are oriented by meaning (e.g., of turns, of body movements). There is no doubt that the most convincing results of the analysis relate to the habitualized "practices" (from pointing to the very performance of presentations). As ethnographic work shows in particular, actors also apply very specific knowledge in these situations, such as design techniques for powerpoint, language skills, or gestures learned in rhetoric classes, special knowledge acquired from books, or examples derived from one's own experience. It is this knowledge that turns the "agent" from an executor of practices or structures into an actor; it is this knowledge that has to be reconstructed ethnographically (at least in its typical content and structure), and it is this knowledge that refers through processes of communicative action to something else – the social world and our knowledge of it.

## Appendix II

### *Data*

The data used in this book have been collected in a research project supported by the Deutsche Forschungsgemeinschaft and conducted by Bernt Schnettler and me.[3] The data consist of field records, interviews, and, particularly, video-recorded records of presentations, focusing on presenters, slides, and audiences. (In many cases we also received digital copies of the slides.) The presentations have been recorded in "natural situations," that is, as part of their performance by the actors. The organizations in which we have conducted field research range from universities and research organizations (of different disciplines, such as law, social sciences, natural sciences, medicine) to administrations, private businesses, churches.. Moreover, occasions vary, such as seminars, meetings, workshops, conferences, both national and international. In addition, we have collected data from presentations using different technologies, such as software supported presentations using beamers, overhead presentations, flip-chart presentations, as well as seminars using blackboards.

The primary corpus consists of *video* data from 271 lectures and presentations. Most of the data are 196 presentations with PowerPoint software or software similar to it by video, each lasting between 2 minutes and 186 minutes. In total, these are 6,047 minutes, which is an average 31 minutes per presentation. Sixty-two presentations could be recorded with two and more cameras, including the audience and the presenter. Most data have been collected between autumn 2004 and spring 2006. In addition, there are fourteen presentations with overheads, four with flip chart, one with audio data, and one with a blackboard. Fifty-five4 cases of lectures are without any current technological aids. The video data have been recorded by the project research team participating at all events. Field protocols complemented the data collection as well as a short questionnaire for information on presenters, the event, and the legal issues of data use. Where possible, we also collected files of the slides.

In addition, I have drawn on the analysis of *slides* by Pötzsch (2007), who bases his analysis on a sample of fifty-eight presentations that have really been performed. The decks of these presentations include 653 slides. The presentations and slides selected stem from all institutional contexts accessible to the research project, ranging from science and education via administration to business.

Some thirty encyclopedias and dictionaries have been studied systematically by Mackert and Degenhardt (2007) and by me. Together we took a close look at more than fifty presentation advice books. Finally, the book is based on a series of ten interviews with representatives from various organizations. Most of the data were collected between 2004 and 2008 so that some aspects of the presentations studied may be subject to change, for, as seems clear, mediated online presentations will increase in numbers and improve in quality, thus posing a new problem. Whereas here the presentation is a face-to-face situation, these newer forms are mediated and therefore may not only cause more problems but even find more generic solutions. The study also has a regional bias since most of the presentations have been recorded in the Berlin area and in other German cities. Presenters recorded are from twenty different European nations as well as from Australia, Japan, Korea, Singapore, South Africa, and the United States. Finally, the author has to apologize for not having addressed gender issues in the data. In general it was considered that gender was not as decisive to the genre of the presentation as other aspects of the presentation. Since the subjects of the empirical presentations were also mixed, the text uses both gender pronouns interchangeably.

## Appendix III

### *Transcription Conventions*

The following transcription conventions are used to represent special features of speech; they are based on Jefferson (1984).

### Transcription conventions

| | |
|---|---|
| , ? | slightly/ strongly rising intonation |
| : . | slightly / strongly falling intonation |
| / / | simultaneity or overlapping of turns or moves (start/end) |
| [ | overlapping turn begins |
| ] | overlapping turn ends |
| (.) | short pause |
| (5.0) | long pause (in seconds) |
| dam- | unfinished utterance |
| = | quick link |
| ne::: | extended |
| * | stressed |
| ° | calm |
| LOUD | loud |
| (when) | uncertain transcription |
| ( ) | not identified utterance |
| (( | )) commentary by the transcriber/description |
| <u>Double</u> | accompanied by pointing gestures |
| <u>single</u> | accompanied by discursive gestures |
| couple | text translated into English |
| *Paar* | text spoken in original language |

## List of Diagrams, Photographs, and Stills and Sources

### *(a) Diagrams*

### Diagram 1: Levels of Genre Analysis, Data Sort, and Analytical Categories
### Diagram 2: Types of Slides
*Source*: Pötzsch, Frederik (2007) "Der Vollzug der Evidenz. Zur Ikonographie und Pragmatik von Powerpoint-Folien" in B. Schnettler

and H. Knoblauch (eds) *Powerpoint-Präsentationen. Neue Formen der gesell-schaftlichen Kommunikation von Wissen*, Konstanz: UVK.

**Diagram 3: Text on Slide and in Speech**
*Source*: Knoblauch, Hubert (2007) "Die Performanz des Wissens: Zeigen und Wissen in Power Point-Präsentationen" in *Power Point Präsentationen: Neue Formen der gesellschaftlichen Kommunikation von Wissen* Hg. Bernt Schnettler, Hubert Knoblauch, Konstanz: UVK Verlagsgesellschaft mbH, S. 125.

**Diagram 4: Sequential Reconstruction of Laser Pointer Movements: Magnifying Glass (top), Micrometer Screw (bottom). Reproduced with permission from Zoll, German Customs Chemist Conference 2004, Dr. Uwe Schlick, ZPLA Berlin**

**Diagram 5: Sequential Reconstruction of Laser Pointer Movements: "initial contact," "roling movements," "migrates," "interaction": Reproduced with permission from Zoll, German Customs Chemist Conference 2004, Dr. Uwe Schlick, ZPLA Berlin**

**Diagram 6: Presenter/Audience/Technical Chain Triangle**

**Diagram 7: Bifocal Presentation Setting**

**Diagram 8: Conference Type Setting**

**Diagram 9: Meeting Type of Setting**

**Diagram 10: Sales of Projectors in Africa, Europe, and the Middle East**

**Diagram 11: Relation between powerpoint and the dynamics of the societal structure**

*(b) Slides*

**Slide 1: Ornamental Slide**

**Slide 2: Representative Illustrative Type. Reproduced with permission from Bio-future presentation, Frau Prof. Frauke Melchior**

**Slide 3: Diagram Type. Reproduced with permission from Zoll, German Customs Chemist Conference 2004, Dr. Uwe Schlick, ZPLA Berlin**

**Slide 4: Collage of Visual Elements. Reproduced with permission from Bio-future presentation, Frau Prof. Frauke Melchior**

**Slide 5: Chapel**

**Slide 6: Statue**

**Slide 7: "Broken Rice." Reproduced with permission from Zoll, German Customs Chemist Conference 2004, Dr. Uwe Schlick, ZPLA Berlin**

**Slide 8: Paths of Development. Reproduced with permission from Overmeyer, IRS Erkner**

Slide 9: Objectives. Reproduced with permission from Zoll, German Customs Chemist Conference 2004, Dr. Dirk Meyer, ZPLA Berlin

Slide 10: Introductory Slide. Reproduced with permission from ICC KK Kappauf

Slide 11: Second Slide: Monoclonal Proliferation. Reproduced with permission from ICC KK Kappauf

Slide 12: Third Slide: The Quote. Reproduced with permission from ICC KK Kappauf

Slide 13: Fourth Slide: Evidence. Reproduced with permission from ICC KK Kappauf

Slide 14: Title and Name. Reproduced with permission from ICC KK Kappauf

Slide 15: Thank You for Listening


*(c) Stills*

Stills 1–3: Pointing Gestures. Reproduced with permission from Aktien richtig handeln, Tobias Tenner

Still 4: Pointing and Postural Change

Still 5: The Middle Position

Still 6: Face Formation

Still 7 a, b, c: Presenter Leaves

Still 8: Slide Upside Down

Stills 9 and 10: Audience Members Volunteering for Technical Support. Reproduced with permission from DPMA_Pisatzky

Still 11: Technical Failure: No Slide on the Screen. Reproduced with permission from BMBF-Forum, Prof.Stock

Still 12: Technical Disaster

Still 13: Text and Sound (Rat Tat Tat). Reproduced with permission from Zoll, German Customs Chemist Conference 2004, Dr. Dirk Meyer, ZPLA Berlin

Stills 14 and 15: Audience of Two Formal Presentations

Stills 16 and 17: Two Rather Informal Presentational Settings. Reproduced with permission from Wieder Tobias Tenner, Aktien richtig handeln

# Notes

## 1. Introduction

1. That is an argument put forward by the "Actor Network Theory." The simplification is due to a reduced notion of actor, or better, of action, which seems not to be aware of the rich Weberian tradition in sociology. It is for this reason that the notion of communicative action shall be elaborated in the framework of this analysis.
2. This is linked to a methodology that is aware of the hermeneutic problems involved. This methodology has already been sketched by Schutz; its specific application to video data on communicative action analyzed here is explicated in Appendix I.
3. For the range of data used here, particularly in the analysis of video, slides, and normative preconceptions about powerpoint, see Appendix II.
4. Cf. Schiller (1989); or, as an overview, Webster (1995).
5. Even the information scientist Fox (1983: 37) admits that "information science is in the rather embarrassing position of lacking any clear understanding of its central notion."
6. As an example, UNESCO (2005: 47) defines "information" as "raw data, the basic material for generating knowledge" (UNESCO 2005: 47).
7. In the context of knowledge management, knowledge "means the embeddment of information in patterns of experiences and expectations" (Wilke 2001: 383, trans. HK).

## 2. On the History of PowerPoint

1. The development of PowerPoint has been described in various "short" histories, yet a comprehensive reconstruction is still missing, so that I have had to base my account on other sources and some interview material.
2. From the perspective of workplace studies that I share, it would also be necessary to study the activities by which the slides are being produced before and by which they are processed after the presentation. I have not covered these questions by means of video data, yet there are various other data in this study that help at least to address these questions indirectly, as, for example, the

analysis of advice books in Chapter 4 and the treatment of what happens after the presentation in Chapter 7.

3. The U.S. Naval Air Warfare Center Training Systems Division claimed to have used overhead already during the Second World War and even to have adopted it for public education, "including the overhead projector, which was originally developed for navigation training" (Pias 2009: 21, trans. HK).

4. The organizational unit of PowerPoint had already been reorganized in 1994, having grown from two developers in 1987 to nine in 1990 and twenty-one in 1995.

5. As stated in an interview with me. Cf. "Data" in "Appendix II."

6. He suggested that in 1984 in about 14% of computers presentation graphics had been installed, a number that he expected to increase to more than 50% in 1989.

7. Already in 1968, Joseph Licklider, one of the leading figures of ARPANET, tested a "project meeting held through a computer" in which "you can dump through the speaker's primary data without interrupting him to substantiate or explain" (Licklider and Taylor 1968: 25).

8. The fact that the presentation is simultaneously a demonstration of the software is, by no means, exceptional. Also in our data we encounter presentations in which software programs are introduced to the audience. In these cases, the demonstration is one of the various purposes of presentations that shall be elaborated in the discussion of the external level.

9. "Dilbert" comic strips on PowerPoint started in 1996, but only in 2000 was the first PowerPoint shown as part of a presentation illustrating the "effects" of powerpoint, "PowerPoint Poisoning."

10. The report which followed the accident suggests another reason for this failure. Apparently, the relevant units in charge of security gave the presentation as event no attention and failed to join it.

11. As for the relations between cognition and (instructional) design since the 1980s cf. Reiser (2001).

12. As an ironic footnote one may mention that the notion has been coined (among others) by Alfred Schutz – who is quite far from a cognitivist paradigm.

13. There are also design oriented surveys, such as the study by Dave Paradi (from the "PowerPoint Lifeguard," who set the task of safeguarding people from "death by PowerPoint"). His 688 unspecified subjects criticized that "the speaker read the slides to us" (62%), the "text so small that I couldn't read" (46.9%) and the "slides hard to see because of color choice" (Paradi 2005).

14. Although most of these studies used the spelling "PowerPoint," the preference for the spelling "powerpoint" is quite adequate since hardly any of these studies positively checked that the software used was, indeed, PowerPoint.

15. Austin et al. (1986: 12f.) quote a study by the University of Pennsylvania, "Effects of the Use of Overhead Transparencies on Business Meetings," supporting the view that visuals (overheads) are part of the presentation, for presenters using overheads were perceived as significantly better prepared, winning approval twice as often as speakers without visuals, generating 33% more on the spot decisions, and reducing meeting length.

16. This development has been studied by Yates (1993).

### 3. Communicative Action, Culture, and the Analysis of Communicative Genres

1. It is quite significant that the criteria Yates and Orlikowski suggest for analyzing "genres" overlap with what Hymes (1974) proposes to define as the event, of which he sees the genre to be one element.
2. Readers interested in the empirical analysis may skip this part, which is elaborated in Knoblauch (1995).
3. For more detailed information on the method and data, see the Appendixes.
4. In earlier texts, this level was termed "situational realization." a notion that is obviously not able to indicate the importance of the temporal, spatial, and bodily aspects of its performance. Cf. Knoblauch and Luckmann (2004).
5. This notion of performance draws more on Goffman (1980/1959) and Hymes (1974) than on the various later "performative turns."
6. With respect to powerpoint presentations, Atkinson (2007) assumes that they exhibit a ritual pattern of crisis, climax, solution, and catharsis – an assumption we could not verify in our data.
7. For an overview of the huge range of studies conducted in this field cf. Bauman and Briggs (1990).

### 4. The Internal Level: Slides, Speech, and Synchronization

1. In speech act theory, felicity conditions are those conditions that guarantee that a special act fulfills its intended purpose, that is, that a promise is a promise. For a critique cf. Goffman (1981a).
2. http://www.managementconsultingnews.com/interviews/weissman_interview.php.
3. Fischer-Lichte, cited in Lobin (2009: 72) (my translation).
4. Presentationzen.com; Infosthetics.com; Duarte (2008); Reynolds (2008).
5. The rule of three refers to the form of three part lists suggested by classical rhetoric; the rule of seven (never use more than about seven items/bullets) has the same origin but is, however, legitimated by reference to the information psychologist Miller and his paper "Magical Number Seven," which became a topos in the study of cognition since Miller (1956).
6. Pötzsch's analysis follows the suggestion made by Twyman (1979), who proposes a schema that classifies pages according to twenty-eight categories of visual composition, ending up with mainly verbal, numerical, pictorial, and schematic elements dominating. For an overview of slide designs, cf. "The Periodic Table of Visualization": http://www.visual-literacy.org/periodic_table/periodic_table.html.
7. The table is adapted from Pötzsch (2006, 2007), who stressed that he does not account for the iconographic features of the slides.
8. This part of the analysis is based on Pötzsch (2006, 2007), on whose work Diagram 1 draws.
9. The notion of synchronization goes back to Alfred Schutz and his theory of intersubjectivity. Cf. Schutz (1974).

10. More recent PowerPoint versions allow for the option of adding speaker notes to the slides on the screen or even splitting the screen so that manuscripts can be read, yet in our data we have not witnessed any case in which this function was used.

11. In the words of Hanks (1990: 5), "the term deictic in traditional grammar designates (roughly) linguistic elements which specify the identity or placement in space or time of individuated objects relative to the participants in a verbal interaction. English 'this', for instance, in one of its central uses, identifies a specific object given in the immediate spatial proximity of the speaker who utters the form."

12. For this case and its analysis cf. Brinkschulte (2008). The conventions for the transcription of spoken text are represented in Appendix III.

13. In this sense, the technical chain can be seen as a kind of institutionalization of pointing, in the social constructivist sense of technology's being a form of institution, as Rammert (2006) and Pinch (2008) argue.

14. Lists are not a peculiar feature of presentations; they are also found in rhetorical speeches and in everyday conversation (Jefferson 1990).

15. The name of the organization has been replaced by XXX for reasons of anonymity.

16. The notion of simple forms refers to Jolles's (1982) notion of *einfache Formen*, minor genres

17. Other formats, such as Pecha Kucha developed in Japan, are defined by the 20 × 20 rule, that is, that every self-selected speaker has twenty slides to show and must restrict the projection event of any slide to 20 seconds (6 minutes 40 seconds in total), so that the seriality and temporality define this form.

18. Misspellings are part of the original slides.

## 5. The Intermediate Level: Pointing, the Body Formation, and the Triadic Structure of Powerpoint Presentations

1. As Hindmarsh and Heath (2000) show, interaction is the prerequisite in order to make that at which one points to a relevant object.

2. In one of the most encompassing studies of pointing, Kendon (2004: 199–224) distinguishes different forms of pointing by identifying various positions of the hand: in its most common form, pointing may be done by the extended index finger. Pointing may also be done by using the open hand. The hand may be opened in an upward direction or in a downward direction; palms may be turned to the pointing subject; in rare cases, pointing may also be done with the thumb. Kendon argues that the different forms of pointing are related directly to their different functions and meanings. Thus pointing with the open hand would occur when the actor attempted to comment on an object. Pointing with the hand turned outside would be used when the object related to was being highlighted. Other forms of pointing, he suggests, are also related to certain "semantic themes."

3. Discursive gestures are defined as accompanying the text in, for example, marking the rhythmic structure. Cf. Müller (1998).

4. According to Ekman and Friesen (1969), emblems are gestural signs with a culturally fixed meaning.
5. As Giedion (1987: 131) claims, the arrow consisting of a triangle and a rectangle was invented by artists like Klee, e.g., in his drawing *Gestaltung des schwarzen Pfeiles*.
6. The variety of forms for pointing, such as arrows, for printed texts is described by Storrer and Wyss (2003).
7. Also paralleling can be performed in a creative way. A speaker may refer to the last item on a slide first without, as mentioned, even explicitly accounting for the change of order through words or pointing in paralleling the words. Presenters may also simply not relate to anything that is mentioned on the slides, or they may show general parallels as in the example just shown. Such creative paralleling may also be conducted across a series of slides.
8. The creative use by means of iconic gestures, words, and visuals can also be found without powerpoint. Thus, we find data in which speakers create an imaginary space by means of the words (imagine someone standing at the door) and then point at the imaginary person on the scene so that some people may even look in that direction.
9. For this reason, the more presenters are seen to monitor the audience and switch positions, the more these movements are seen as relevant indications by the audience.
10. I am grateful to Bruno Michon, Christoph Nagel, and Georg Krajewsky for helping me to reproduce this picture, which builds on an older photograph from Kendon (1990).
11. With respect to whiteboards, Suchman also (1990: 315) observed that they not only provide a "second interactional floor" but that this is also "sequentially interleaved with that of talk."
12. With respect to the basic triangle, there is no essential difference between neophytes and experienced users. Although the former may be detected by the lack of smoothness in their movements, particularly expressed in extended attentiveness to the technical items instead of the slide, their papers, or the audience, the basic triadic relationship is a pattern also found among neophytes (who can exploit its similarity to the body formation of regular interactions). Similarly, the variants of presentations (such as lectures and shows) are also found among experienced users.
13. In their analysis of pointing at pictures, Pozzer-Ardenghi and Roth (2005: 277) remark, "that gestures and body orientation constitute important resources for establishing coherence during lectures that allow audiences to appropriately connect photographs and speech."
14. Lobin (2009) has suggested distinguishing different types that are less related to the performance: visualization or documentation designates those presentations in which slides refer to speech, visualization and orientation to those in which speech refers to slides, and finally association and description to those without any reference. As the role of synchronization has shown, all forms can occur quite frequently in any presentation: speech may relate to the slides at one point and be unrelated to it at the next point, with the relation produced by means of deixis, recognition markers, and duplication, as well as by

paralleling. Only some of the talks and speeches appear to be "clear cases" with respect to the relation of speech and slides.

15. As a variant of this type there is also a technical option for the "kiosk" presentation format in which the presentation is shown automatically by the computer.

16. As Goffman (1981b: 5ff.) has shown, the presequence is a ritual act accounting for the fact that the primary speaker rule may be broken and thus the face of the speaker or of the audience member may be threatened.

17. As Goffman (1981b: 3) stresses, the participation status is the status of actors relative to the utterance or, in our case, communicative action.

18. This part draws on an analysis carried out by Schnettler (2006) and Schnettler and Tuma (2007).

19. In conversation analysis, the transition relevance place is the point where the turn of a speaker is perceptibly designed to end so that the next speaker may take the floor. Cf. Sacks, Schegloff, Jefferson (1974).

20. By collective communicative action I refer descriptively to those phenomena in which the acts of single individuals cannot be identified any more clearly either by the video analyst or by the participants. Often, these collective actions take on an emergent meaning, so that one is seduced to say that the audience laughs, the audience stands up, etc.

21. This analysis builds on Schnettler and Tuma (2007) and Schnettler (2006), where the cases can be found analyzed in more detail.

22. There might be didactic or aesthetic reasons, as some artists, like Baselitz, paint pictures upside down.

23. In our data, presenters prepared for such situations by producing overhead foils in addition to powerpoint. This habit seems to have changed since – indicating again the end of the transition from overhead to powerpoint presentations. Note that there are certainly other technologies that can be used in order to produce a presentation, such as flip charts or blackboards. Under other circumstances, even the lack of laser pointers or microphones would be discerned as a technical problem affecting the very performance of the presentation.

24. Since all actors tend to support the smooth flow of interactions, embarrassing situations frequently depend on "tact," i.e., rituals by which the coactors try to save face.

25. Therefore, the genre varies with the technology, and different technologies form its boundaries, as the use of paper slides earlier demonstrates. Whether the use of mediated forms of communication, e.g., with video conferencing systems connecting participants at remote locations so that the participants as well as the presentations are mutually represented on the screen, makes an essential difference needs to be clarified.

26. Presentations with material objects tend to be called "demonstrations" or "demos" (Brooks 2004: 36). As in Tupper Ware parties analyzed by us and opposed to objects used to illustrate "knowledge," demonstrations allow for the bodily access to them that transforms the monological structure of the presentations into dialogical formats. An important and significative

exception are presentations of digital objects, such as software and visual-izations – the very format out of which the powerpoint presentation grew historically.

### 6. The External Level: Settings, Meetings, and the Ubiquity of Powerpoint

1. The greater importance of the slides than of the talk that defines the presen-tation becomes very clear in cases when the talk is shorter than commentaries or questions at other meetings. Thus, at certain large conference meetings supposed to "connect" persons and parties (i.e., researchers and financial sup-porters), presentations may be as short as "one minute one slide."
2. "Structure" here is to be understood as an abstraction from the forms of com-munication by means of data that are "abstract" or only indirectly indicate what is under study; the same holds, of course, for the diffusion process.
3. Of course, these objects "are subject" to rhetorical considerations. Thus, already in classical oratory questions were asked concerning the location of speaker and audience in space, the size of the audience, or its composition, and advisory books for PowerPoint presentation suggest considering the question of where to place the laptop or when and how to use a microphone.
4. Yates (1993) reports that early in the twentieth century, DuPont had built a special room in which visual charts were stored and could be presented to an audience. Another impressive example can be seen in the Churchill War Rooms in London's Imperial War Museum.
5. Sometimes the audience or presenters ask for the dimming or darkening of the room. The reasons they give refer to the weakness of the projector's bulbs, sunlight, the importance of the visual features of the slides, yet there are no constant "real" reasons: "real" weak projectors do not always trigger the demand for darkening, and broad daylight does not typically offend speakers or audiences.
6. According to Atkinson (1982) formality is here understood as an accomplish-ment produced by the actors and the objects in the settings.
7. The "Convention Liaison Council Manual" (1994) is used for organization of conferences in conference hotels; it also lays out the various setups and require-ments mentioned (explicitly calling the meeting type the "school room"); only one general type is missing, the banquet type. Guide books to presentations also typically distinguish among various space types in order to recommend where to stand, where to put the screen, etc. Cf. Hendricks et al. (1996: 93ff.).
8. Bifocality can also be produced situationally, e.g., when presenters walk into the auditorium, continuing their presentation, so that they can only be heard by parts of the audience. There can also be, of course, a basic reframing of the situation, e.g., if the presenter withdraws and leaves the focus to a media presentation, such as films or pictures, thus transforming a presentation into a film or slide show. This transformation, however, is dependent on the trans-formation of the basic triangular structure. Any additional objects and spatial

orders do not affect the genre but the style of the presentation, which exhibits a continuum between formal and informal.

9. For the relation between the notion of transcendence and the notion of signs, cf. Luckmann (1972), Schutz/Luckmann (1989), and Knoblauch (2001). I refer here to the "little transcendences" of space and time as well as to the "middle transcendences" of other subjects.

10. As for the role of materialities, cf. Pinch (2008).

11. The path of institutionalization may even allow one to trace the reason for the two types of settings back to the time of their invention. The overhead projector the inventors of PowerPoint tried to substitute was used in light rooms where the "human presenter is visible" (Austin, Rudkin, and Gaskins 1986: 18), the 35-mm slide, from which the "slide" inherited its name, in dark rooms with invisible presenters. Overheads, they observed, would be better for addressing small meetings, slides for larger meetings in projector rooms. The computer presentations they envisaged "should give rise to an entirely new phenomenon – presentations with the informality of overhead transparencies, delivered in lighted business meetings, but using video generated directly from diskettes instead of actual overhead foils" (Austin, Rudkin, and Gaskins 1986: 22). This structure is, of course, in flux, considering recent trends toward "nomadic" offices, open spaces, and nodal points of encounter. Cf. Myerson and Ross (2003).

12. I would guess that the (Habermasian) belief in the symmetry of communication that is shared by many knowledge workers also contributes to the maintenance of the meeting type.

13. As Katz (1999: 37) rightly notes, the body itself is a means for transcending the situation, too. "Bodies make us mortal in the long run, but until they do they are vehicles of situational immortality, constantly conferring the gift, unwanted or not, of signifying life beyond the deaths of the localized interactions that constitute our mundane social lives."

14. Thus in an analysis of the e-mails of a group of computer language designers Orlikowski and Yates (1994) found memos, dialogues, ballots, and proposals, yet they also noted a lack of reports and presentational activities.

15. As one of the few studies, Pfadenhauer (2008) has analyzed the processes by which events are organized in a systematic way. Hitzler and Betz (2011) have also contributed to this topic in their study on the organization of the Catholic World Youth Day.

16. Powerpoint also forms part of "science slams" in which speakers present their project in an entertaining style to a largely nonexpert audience; often the entertaining part extends the design of the slides by using comic strips and animated movies and objects. Speakers may wear costumes, and amusement is one of the major goals of the presentation.

17. The karaoke case would deserve an analysis in itself, since the comic effects not only derive from the strange mismatches between the slide and the speech but also from the changing production format of the presenter, who either makes up the speech well (and this is what causes amusement) or does not (which obviously has a less amusing effect on the audience).

18. Cf. Stark and Paravel (2008). The notion of demonstration is not being defined and is not in accordance with the notion proposed here.

19. Systematic management received much less attention than the scientific management by Frederick W. Taylor. Whereas this mainly concerned the factory floor, Taylor's was part of a larger movement, that of systematic management, which was built on the assumption that individuals were less important than the systems in which they functioned (Yates 1989: 10). It was to integrate the horizontal flows and solve the problem of vertical coordination by transcending the individual memory by depersonalizing written forms (since the telephone failed to replace the internal forms), such as "shop papers," inhouse magazines, manuals, reports, and memos (Yates and Orlikowski 1992).

20. One indication is from time budget studies, which indicate that by the 1960s managers spent about 7% of their time in meetings (whereas informal discussions consumed almost half of their working hours (Stewart 1967: 44f.). This does not support the assumption by Bolte et al. (2008) that informal communication is less hierarchical than committees.

21. Other evidence would include time budget studies, which, with a few exceptions, however, hardly cover meetings. Only the Japanese study by Suzuki, Hashimoto and Ishii (1997) asked for time spent at conferences and lectures in Japan. The 1073 persons interviewed spent an average 0.182 hours per day "attending conferences and meetings" plus 0.222 "attending lectures plus classes" (which is more than the time they use the PC). 58.25% of those who attended conferences and meetings considered this as part of the basic activity of "work" and 13.82% as part of "study" whereas 83.44% would join lectures as part of their basic activity of "study", and for 10.19% lectures form part of their work.

22. "When meetings are combined with expositions, the event is called a convention" (Montgomery and Strick 1994: 13).

23. Rogers (1995: 11) relates the concept of diffusion to a variety of different kinds of innovations. An "innovation is an idea, practice, or object that is perceived as new by an individual or other unit of adoption." Communication is, to him, a means of diffusion and not an "object," "idea," or "practice."

24. Cf. Mattelart (2003); Schiller (1989); or, as an overview, Webster (1995).

25. http://www.itu.int/ITU-D/ict/statistics/at_glance/KeyTelecom99.html.

26. The data are from Ebrain Market Research (2002: 80f.).

27. From my interview with Richard Bretschneider, on June 6, 2010.

28. In the sciences, projections have been used in lectures for centuries. Thus, already after the publication of Athanasius Kirchner's description of the *laterna magica* in 1671, Johannes Zahn suggested using it in order to project small anatomical pictures onto the white wall. For quite some time, the *laterna magica* maintained a somewhat spiritualist image in being related to necromancy and apparitions; cf. Peters (2007). Already the popularization of science in the nineteenth century relied on innumerable scientific lectures, which, in their need for illustrations, used various methods of projection. By the turn of the twentieth century, presentations evolved from instruments of "professors of magic" into an indispensable companion of traveling scientific lecturers, as the German physicist Reinhard stated in 1904 (Peters 2007). Projections had become an important means of presenting visual evidence. Louis Pasteur, for example, projected yeast cultures in order to demonstrate the subject matter of his talk.

29. The data were accessible in 2010 on http://ieexplore.ieee.
30. Schultz already studied the use of powerpoint among students in business classes in the mid-1990s and found strong acceptance (Schultz 1996/1997: 160); there are good indications that librarians seem to have used PowerPoint already in the mid-1990s.
31. For more detailed analysis of the use of powerpoint in schools, cf. Lorenzen (2010).
32. Susan Hedahl and Lucy Hogan from Wesley Theological Seminary in Washington, D.C., reported by e-mail on an interview study they conducted in the United States but have not yet published. They found that PowerPoint is used quite differently. In some congregations, for example, PowerPoint is used to project announcements or the words to hymns and scripture readings, but the preacher does not use it in the sermon. If PowerPoint is used, it demonstrates an overwhelming preference for photographic images of nature scenes – flowers, clouds, running streams. They might project an image of a burning candle but stop short of projecting paintings or print art. In the preaching of a sermon, they suggest drawing a distinction between projecting text, primarily an outline of the sermon, and using images and film clips to supplement the sermon, functioning as illustrations and examples. A popular trend involves preachers' projecting a sentence with a missing word. Then, as the sermon unfolds, the preacher answers the question, which enables the listener to supply the missing word – which is then projected on the screen, completing the sentence.
33. These data were accessible in 2010 on http://ieexplore.ieee.
34. Interview with R. Bretschneider in 2010. The lack of interest in organizations outside business is seen in the fact that they are late adopters. "Schools are usually 2, 3 versions back. They are not quick adopters. They are not going to see the fruits of that for another 10 years."
35. I have complemented this examination by adding a series of English dictionaries, which are being quoted here.
36. The *American Heritage Dictionary* of 1993 (1982) defines a presentation as "a speech that is set forth for an audience." In 1999, the *Oxford American Dictionary of Current English* (199: 623) mentions as one aspect of "presentation," "a demonstration or display of materials, information, etc.; a lecture."
37. I am alluding here to the distinction between "general" and "special" knowledge by Berger and Luckmann (1966). Of course, the "everyone" reading encyclopedias is the "well informed citizen" (Schutz 1964). Note at this point that also in this case "knowledge" (about the "presentation") refers to communicative knowledge (i.e., the word and its semantic aspects).
38. Although many might contend that the genre was common in academia very early on, I could not find strong indications of it in the encyclopedias.
39. While the sciences are one source for the development of the visually supported speech events that came to be called presentations, similar forms also evolved in business. Thus, Yates (1989) found the use of slides for business reports in the early decades of the twentieth century. "For such reports, either lanterns used with slides or reflecting lanterns (which did not require specially prepared slides but could project an image from cards, papers, or books) could

be used to display graphs or tables" (Yates 1989: 99). At the American chemical company DuPont, one of the trailblazers of presentations, in 1904 meetings in which graphs were used were already occurring. Starting with a few, their number increased to an average of twenty after 1911. This "uniquely DuPont" use of graphs became more widespread, so that it was the norm by the second half of the twentieth century.

40. Already at this point the authors advised against the overuse of visual aids, which "must be chosen with care" (Adler and Elmhorst 1996: 359f.).

## 7. Conclusion: The Ubiquity of Powerpoint and the Communicative Culture of the Knowledge Society

1. Hans-Dieter Hellige, quoted by Pias (2009: 30).
2. Mead and Byers designated the small conference a "communicative innovation," "a group small enough to sit around one large table, called together for a specific purpose, at a specific place, for a limited time ... to consider new aspects of a specified topic" (1968: 5).
3. Ruchatz (2010) demonstrates nicely how already in the early twentieth century slides were used as "popular" forms of knowledge transmission, e.g., by the German Society for People's Education. Wilson (1870) complains: "A small picture, seen by passing it from hand to hand, seems comparatively tame; but when represented to all eyes at once, enlarged in life size and to life-like appearance, it is viewed with cumulative enthusiasm."
4. This question has also been raised in various forms by other researchers. With respect to academic presentations Lobin (2009: 72), for example, asks, why, "despite a large industry of scientific publications, conferences are still held."
5. The notion of "healing" or "repair" could also be replaced by "interpretation." Following Pinch and Bijker (1987) that technologies have an interpretive flexibility that allows different social actors to use them in different ways, the event can be seen as such an interpretation of the technology. Instead of interpretation, however, I have proposed the notion of contextualization, which stresses its situative character.
6. There is no doubt that in the future mediation can be elaborated so that, for example, presentations can be imparted in video conferences. As it happened with the transformation from overhead to powerpoint presentation, this transformation can even lead to changes and changing roles of the presentation technology.
7. Subjectivation does not mean that subjects are constructed by communication, as some discourse theories have it, but rather that knowledge is ascribed to subjects. I have elaborated this notion in Knoblauch (2009).
8. The powerpoint presentation could, thus, be studied as a form of "public discourse" in Habermas's (1981) sense.
9. Following DiMaggio and Powell (1983: 152), one could therefore consider professionalization as one reason for the success of powerpoint presentations.
10. This does not mean that there may be no "false knowledge," yet the determination of what is false would be dependent on what is lacking in the form of

communication. Thus, a good powerpoint presentation is good in that what it presents follows the generic pattern.

11. The analogy can be extended since one could argue that the process of subjectivation is produced by the communicative form more than by the presenter, who is only cast in the role of the subject by the presentation's inbuilt asymmetry.

12. As its inventor, Robert Gaskin (2009: 6) already assumed that the success of this software depended on the increasing importance of the "knowledge worker" in companies, i.e., people such as "the analysts, engineers, and the like (who) spend a large amount of time on presentations to share information and to gain consensus."

## Appendixes

1. Cf. the methodology of the refined version of grounded theory (cf. Glaser and Strauss 1967; Strauss and Corbin 1990).

2. Sophisticated software (such as Dartfish) increasingly allows one to create visual code books with video samples and simply to insert drawings and highlight relevant movements directly in the video. NVivo, ATLAS.ti, HyperRESEARCH, and Transana allow one to code video "on the fly."

3. This overview on the data is based on Petschke (2007).

# References

1962 *Oxford Illustrated Dictionary*, Oxford: Oxford at Clarendon.

1995 *Cambridge International Dictionary of English*, Cambridge: Cambridge University Press.

Adams, S. 1994 *Always Postpone Meetings with Time-Wasting Morons*, Kansas City, MO: Andrews & Mcmeel.

Adler, R. B. and Elmhorst, J. M. 1996 *Communicating at Work: Principles and Practices for Business and the Professions* 5th ed., New York: McGraw-Hill.

Ahmed, C. 1998 "Powerpoint versus Traditional Overheads: Which Is More Effective for Learning?" Available at: http://www.eric.ed.gov/ERICWebPortal/ contentdelivery/servlet/ERICServlet?accno=ED429037 (Accessed March 21, 2011).

Amann, K. and Knorr Cetina, K. D. 1988 "The Fixation of Visual Evidence," *Human Studies* 11: 133–69.

Antunes, P., Costa, C. J., and Pino, J. A. 2006 "The Use of Genre Analysis in the Design of Electronic Meeting Systems," *Information Research* 11: 3.

Atkinson, C. 2007 *Beyond Bullet Points: Using Microsoft® Office PowerPoint® 2007 to Create Presentations That Inform, Motivate, and Inspire*, Redmond, WA: Microsoft Press.

Atkinson, M. 1982 "Understanding Formality." *British Journal of Sociology*, 33: 322–45.

1984 *Our Masters' Voices*, London: Methuen.

Atkinson, P. and Silverman, D. 1997 "Kundera's Immortality: The Interview Society and the Invention of the Self," *Qualitative Inquiry* 3(3): 304–25.

Auslander, P. 1999 *Liveness: Performance in a Mediatized Culture*, London: Routledge & Kegan Paul.

Austin, D., Rudkin, T. and Gaskins, R. 1986 "Presenter Specification," *Forethought Inc.*

Bajaj, G. 2008 "An Interview with Richard Bretschneider." Available at: www. indezine.com (Accessed June 15, 2010).

Bartsch, R. A. and Cobern, Kristi M. (2003) "Effectiveness of PowerPoint Presentations in Lectures," *Computers & Education* 41(1): 77–86.

Bateman, J. A. 2008 *Multimodality and Genre: A Foundation for the Systematic Analysis of Multimodal Documents*, London: Houndmills.

Baumann, R. and Briggs, C. L. 1990 "Poetics and Performance as Critical Perspectives in Language and Social Life," *Annual Review of Anthropology* 19: 59–88.

Bazerman, C. 1995 "Systems of Genres and Enactment of Social Intentions" in A. Freedman and P. Medway (eds) *Genre and New Rhetoric*, London: Taylor and Francis.

Bellamy, K. and Mclean, D. 2003 "The Mechanics of PowerPoint," *Journal of Audiovisual Media in Medicine* 26(2): 47–78.

Berger, P. L. and Luckmann, T. 1966 *The Social Construction of Reality: A Treatise in the Sociology of Knowledge* 1st ed., New York: Doubleday.

Betz, G. and Hitzler, R. 2011 "Steuerung komplexser Projekte. Zur Institutionellen Einbindung urbaner Mega-Event-Organisationen" in G. Betz, R. Hitzler, and Michaela Pfadenhauer (eds) *Urbane Events*, Wiesbaden: Verlag für Sozialwissenschaften.

Biber, D., Finegan, E., Biber, D. and Finegan, E. 1994 "Introduction" in *Sociolinguistic Perspectives on Registers*, Oxford: Oxford University Press.

Bijker, W. E. 1995 *Of Bicycles, Bakelites, and Bulbs: Toward a Theory of Sociotechnical Change*, Cambridge, MA: MIT Press.

Blokzijl, W. and Andeweg, B. 2005 "The Effects of Text Slide Format and Presentational Quality on Learning in College Lectures." Available at: http://doi.ieeecomputersociety.org/10.1109/IPCC.2005.1494188 (Accessed June 20, 2010).

Blokzijl, W. and Naeff, R. 2004 "The Instructor as Stagehand: Dutch Student Responses to PowerPoint," *Business Communication Quarterly* 67(1): 70–7.

Boltanski, L. and Chiapello, È. 1999 *Le nouvel esprit du capitalisme*, Paris: Gallimard.

Bolte, A., Neumer, J. and Porschen, S. 2008 *Die alltägliche Last der Kooperation: Abstimmung als Arbeit und das Ende der Meeting-Euphorie*, Berlin: Edition Sigma.

Brenden, A. and Goodhue, J. 2005 *The Lawyer's Guide to Creating Persuasive Computer Presentations*, Chicago: American Bar Association.

Brinkschulte, M. 2008 "Bericht zum funktionalen Folieneinsatz beim Argumentieren in Powerpoint-Präsentationen," Manuscript Berlin, Technical University.
2007 "Lokaldeiktische Prozeduren als Mittler zwischen Rede und Powerpoint-Präsentation in Vorlesungen" in B. Schnettler, H. Knoblauch (eds.) *Powerpoint-Präsentationen: Neue Formen der gesellschaftlichen Kommunikation von Wissen*, Konstanz: UVK.

Brooks, J. 2004 *Presentations as Rites: Co-Presence and Visible Images for Organization Memory Collectivity*, Ann Arbor: University of Michigan.

Bühler, K. 1982 *Sprachtheorie202F: Die Darstellungsfunktion der Sprache* Ungekürzter Neudr. d. Ausg. Jena, Fischer, 1934, Stuttgart, New York: Fischer.

Bumiller, E. 2010 "We Have Met the Enemy and He Is PowerPoint," *New York Times*, April 24, 2010.

Burchfield, R. W. (ed.) 1982 *A Supplement to the Oxford English Dictionary*, Oxford: Clarendon Press.

Byrne, D. 2003 *Imagining Emotional Epistemological Information*, New York: Todomundo.

Carney, B. and Feigenson, N. 2004 "Visual Persuasion in the Michael Skakel Trial: Enhancing Advocacy through Interactive Media Presentations," *Criminal Justice* 19(1): 22–35.

Castells, M. 2009 *Communication Power*, Oxford and New York: Oxford University Press.

1996 *The Information Age: Economy, Society and Culture: The Rise of the Network Society*, Oxford: Wiley Blackwell.

Couldry, N. 2008 "Mediatization or Mediation? Alternative Understandings of the Emergent Space of Digital Storytelling," *New Media and Society* 10(3): 372–93.

Crane, D. 1992 *The Production of Culture: Media and Urban Arts*, Newbury Park, CA: Sage.

Daston, L. and Galison, P. 2007 *Objectivity*, New York: Zone Books.

DiMaggio, P. and Powell, W. W. 1983 "The Iron Cage Revisited: Institutional Isomorphism and Collective Rationality Inorganizational Fields," *American Sociological Review* 48: 147–60.

Dordick, H. S. and Wang, G. 1993 *The Information Society: A Retrospective View*, Newbury Park, CA: Sage.

Dreyer, K. J. 2001 "Special Report. Using Microsoft PowerPoint for Electronic Presentations," *Radiographics: The Journal of Continuing Medical Education in Radiology* 21(5): 1318–21.

Duarte, N. 2008 *Slide:ology: The Art and Science of Presentation Design*, Cambridge: O'Reilly.

Ebrain Market Research 2002 *Electronic Market Data Book*, Arlington, VA: Consumer Electronics Association.

Ekman, P. and Friesen, W. V. 1969 "The repertoire of nonverbal behavior," *Semiotica* 1: 63–8.

Engleberg, I. N. and Daly, J. A. 2005 *Presentations in Everyday Life: Strategies for Effective Speaking*, Boston, New York: Houghton Mifflin.

Erickson, F. 2011 "Uses of Video in Social Research. A Brief History," *International Journal of Social Research Methodology* 14(3): 179–89.

Essex-Lopresti, M. 2003 "Using PowerPoint," *Journal of Audiovisual Media in Medicine* 26(2): 79.

Farkas, D. K. 2006 "Toward a Better Understanding of Powerpoint Deck Design," *Information Design Journal/Dokument Design* 14(2): 161–71.

Feldman, T. 2002 "The Intersection of Powerpoint and Interventional Cardiology," *Catheterization and Cardiovascular Diagnosis* 57(3): 412.

Fenich, G. 2008 *Meetings, Expositions, Events, and Conventions: An Introduction to the Industry*, Upper Saddle River, NJ: Pearson/Prentice Hall.

Fischer, J. and Delitz (eds) 2009 *Die Architektur der Gesellschaft*, Bielefeld: transcript.

Foucault, M. 1995 *Diszipline and Punishment: The Birth of the Prison*, New York: Vintage.

Fox, C. J. 1983 *Information and Misinformation: An Investigation of the Notions of Information, Misinformation, Informing, and Misinforming*, London: Greenwood.

Friedhoff, R. M. 1991 *The Second Computer Revolution: Visualization*, New York: Free Press.

Gabriel, Y. 2008 "Against the Tyranny of PowerPoint: Technology-in-Use and Technology Abuse," *Organization Studies* 29(2): 255–76.

Garfinkel, H. 1967 *Studies in Ethnomethodology*, Englewood Cliffs, NJ: Prentice Hall.

Gaskins, R. 2009 "Homepage of Robert Gaskin." Available at: www.robertgaskin. com (Accessed January 20, 2010).

Giddens, A. 1984 *The Constitution of Society: Outline of the Theory of Structuration*, Berkeley: University of California Press.

Giedeon, S. 1987 *Die Herrschaft der Mechanisierung*, Frankfurt: Athenäum.

Glaser, B. and Strauss, A. 1967 *The Discovery of Grounded Theory*, Chicago: Aldine.

Goffman, E. 1963 *Behavior in Public Places: Notes in the Social Organization of Gatherings*, New York: Free Press.

    1967 "Embarrassment and Social Organization" in E. Goffman (ed.) *Interaction Ritual: Essays on Face-to-Face Behavior*, Garden City, NY: Anchor Books.

    1981a *Forms of Talk*, London: Blackwell.

    1974 *Frame Analysis: An Essay on the Organization of Experience*, New York: Harper & Row.

    1981b "The Interaction Order," *American Sociological Review* 48: 1–17.

    1980 *The Presentation of Self in Everyday Life*, Harmondsworth: Penguin.

Goodwin, C. 1986 "Audience Diversity, Participation and Interpretation," *Text* 6(3): 283–316.

Grady, J. 2006 "Edward Tufte and the Promise of Visual Social Science" in L. Pauwels (ed.) *Visual Cultures of Science: Rethinking Representational Practices in Knowledge Building and Science Communication*, Lebanon, NH: Darthmouth University Press.

Griffin, R. E. 1995 "Electronic Presentations in the Corporation: How Are They Being Used?" Available at: http://www.eric.ed.gov/ERICWebPortal/content-delivery/servlet/ERICServlet?accno=ED391523 (Accessed April 14, 2011).

Gumperz, J. 1992 "Contextualization Revisited" in A. di Luzio and P. Auer (eds) *The Contextualization of Language*, Amsterdam and Philadelphia: Benjamins.

    1981 *Discourse Strategies*, Cambridge: Cambridge University Press.

Günthner, S. and Knoblauch, H. 1995 "Culturally Patterned Speaking Practices – the Analysis of Communicative Genres," *Pragmatics* 5: 1–32.

Habermas, J. 1981 *Theorie des kommunikativen Handelns*, Frankfurt/Main: Suhrkamp.

Halazonetis, D. J. 2000 "Advanced Powerpoint Animation Techniques: Part I," *American Journal of Orthodontics and Dentofacial Orthopedics* 117(6): 737–40.

Hanke, J. 1998 "Survey Offers Glimpse of the Average Presenter," *Presentations* 13: 6.

Hanks, W. F. 1990 *Referential Practice: Language and Lived Space among the Maya*, Chicago: Chicago University Press.

Haviland, J. B. 1993 "Anchoring, Iconicity, and Orientation in Guugu Yimithirr Pointing Gestures," *Journal of Linguistic Anthropology* 3(1): 3–45.

Heath, C. 1986 *Body Movement and Speech in Medical Interaction*, Cambridge: Cambridge University Press.

Heath, C., Hindmarsh, J. and Luff, P. 2010 *Video in Qualitative Research*, London: Sage.

Heath, C. and Knoblauch, H. 1999 "Technologie, Interaktion und Organisation: Die Workplace Studies," *Schweizerische Zeitschrift für Soziologie* 25(2): 163–81.

Heath, C. and Luff, P. 2000 *Technology in Action*, Cambridge: Cambridge University Press.

Heath, C., Luff, P. and Knoblauch, H. 2000 "Technology and Social Interaction: The Emergence of 'Workplace Studies,'" *British Journal of Sociology* 51(2): 299–320.

Hendricks, W., Holliday, M., Mobley, R. and Steinbrecher, K. 1996 *Secrets of Power Presentations*, Franklin Lakes, NJ: Career Press.

Hensel, M. 1990 *Die Informationsgesellschaft: Neuere Ansätze zur Analyse eines Schlagwortes*, München: Fischer.

Heritage, J. and Watson, R. 1979 "Formulations as Conversational Objects" in G. Psathas (ed.) *Everyday Language: Ethnomethodological Approaches*, New York: Free Press.

Hindmarsh, J. and Heath, C. 2000 "Embodied Reference: A Study of Deixis in Workplace Interaction," *Journal of Pragmatics* 32: 1855–78.

Holland, W. P. 1921 *Business Statistics: Their Preparation, Compilation and Presentation*, London, New York: Pitman.

Hornidge, A.-K. 2007 *Knowledge Society: Vision and Social Construction of Reality in Germany and Singapore*, Berlin: LIT.

Howell, W. S. and Bormann, E. G. 1988 *The Process of Presentational Speaking* 2nd ed., New York: Harper & Row.

Hughes, S. 1980 *Professional Presentations: Practical Guide to the Preparation and Performance of Successful Business Presentations*, Sydney: McGraw-Hill.

HVS 2007 *Convention, Sports & Entertainment Facilities Consulting*, Chicago: Tinley Park Convention Market Study. Available at: http://www.tinleypark.org/documents (Accessed May 12, 2010).

Hymes, D. 1974 *Foundations in Sociolinguistics: An Ethnographic Perspective*, Philadelphia: University of Philadelphia Press.

ICCC 2002 *The International Meetings Association: The International Meetings Market 1994–2003*, Amsterdam: ICCA.

International Telecommunications Union 2009 *Measuring the Information Society: ICT Development Index*, Geneva: ITU.

Isaacs, W. 1993 "Taking Flight: Dialogue, Collective Thinking, and Organizational Learning," *Organizational Dynamics* 1: 61–83.

Jefferson, G. 1973 "A Case of Precision Timing in Ordinary Conversation: Overlapped Tag-Position Address Terms in Closing Sequences," *Semiotica* IX: 47–96.

— 1990 "List Construction as a Task and Interactional Resource" in G. Psathas and R. Frankel (eds) *Interactional Competence*, New York: Irvington.

— 1972 "Side Sequences," in D. Sudnow (ed.) *Studies in Social Interaction*, New York: Free Press.

— 1979 "A Technique for Inviting Laughter and Its Subsequent Acceptance Declination" in *Everyday Language: Studies in Ethnomethodology*, New York: Irvington.

1984 "Transcription Notation" in J. M. Atkinson and J. Heritage (eds) *Structures of Social Action*, Cambridge: Cambridge University Press.

Joffe, J. 2007 "An die Wand geworfen," *Die Zeit* 31: 42.

Jolles, A. 1982 *Einfache Formen*, Tübingen: Niemeyer.

Kaplan, S. 2010 "Strategy and Powerpoint: An Inquiry into the Epistemic Culture and Machinery of Strategy Making." Available at: http://ssrn.com/abstract=1569762. (Accessed June 12, 2010).

Katz, J. 1999 *How Emotions Work*, Chicago: University of Chicago Press.

Keller, J. 2003 "Is PowerPoint the Devil?" *Chicago Tribune*, 5.

Kellner, D. 2006 "Media Culture and the Triumph of the Spectacle," *Fast Capitalism* 1.1(15). Available at: http://fastcapitalism.com. (Accessed June 12, 2010).

Kendon, A. 2004 *Gesture: Visible Action as Utterance*, Cambridge: Cambridge University Press.

1990 "Spatial Organization in Social Encounters: The F-Formation System," *Conducting Interaction: Patterns of Behavior in Focused Encounters*: 209–38.

Keppler, A. 1985 *Präsentation und Information" Zur politischen Berichterstattung im Fernsehen*, Tübingen: Narr.

Keyton, J. 2005 *Communication and Organizational Culture*, Thousand Oaks, CA: Sage.

Kim, D. 1993 "The Link between Individual and Organizational Learning," *Sloan Management Review* 1993: 37–50.

Kjeldsen, J. E. 2006 "The Rhetoric of PowerPoint," *Seminar-Net – International Journal of Media, Technology and Lifelong Learning* 2: 1–17.

Knape, J. 2007 "Powerpoint in rhetoriktheoretischer Sicht" in H. Knoblauch and B. Schnettler (eds) *Powerpoint-Präsentationen. Neue Formen der gesellschaftlichen Kommunikation von Wissen*, Konstanz: UVK.

Knoblauch, H. 2001 "Communication, Contexts and Culture: A Communicative Constructivist Approach to Intercultural Communication" in A. d. Luzio, S. Günthner, and F. Orletti (eds) *Culture in Communication: Analyses of Intercultural Situations*, Amsterdam, Philadelphia: John Benjamins.

1995 *Kommunikationskultur: Die kommunikative Konstruktion kultureller Kontexte*, Berlin, New York: De Gruyter.

1987 "'Lacht euch gesund, bei mir ist lustige Werbung': Die Rhetorik von Werbeveranstaltungen bei Kaffeefahrten," *Zeitschrift für Soziologie* 16(2): 127–44.

2008 "The Performance of Knowledge: Pointing and Knowledge in Powerpoint Presentations," *Cultural Sociology* 2(1): 75–97.

2009 *Populäre Religion*, Frankfurt/Main: Campus.

1990 "The Taming of Foes: Informal Discussions in Family Talk" in I. Markova and K. Foppa (eds) *Asymmetries in Dialogue*, New York: Harvester Wheatsheaf.

2006 "Videography: Focused Ethnography and Video-Analysis" in H. Knoblauch, B. Schnettler, J. Raab, and H.-G. Soeffner (eds) *Video Analysis – Methodology and Methods: Qualitative Audiovisual Data Analysis in Sociology*, Frankfurt/Main, New York: Lang.

2005 *Wissenssoziologie* 2. rev. ed., Konstanz: UVK.

Knoblauch, H. and Luckmann, T. 2004 "Genre Analysis" in U. Flick, E. v. Kardoff, and I. Steinke (eds) *A Companion to Qualitative Research*, London: Sage.

Knoblauch, H. and Tuma, R. 2011 "Videography: An Interpretive Approach to Video-Recorded Micro-Social Interaction" in E. Margolis and L. Pauwels (eds) *The Sage Handbook of Visual Methods*, Los Angeles: Sage.

Knorr Cetina, K. D. 1999 *Epistemic Cultures: How the Sciences Make Knowledge*, Cambridge, MA: Harvard University Press.

2001 "Postsocial Relations: Theorizing Sociality in a Postsocial Environment" in G. Ritzer and B. Smart (eds) *Handbook of Social Theory*, London: Sage.

Knorr Cetina, K. D. and Cicourel, A. V. (eds) 1981 "Advances in Social Theory and Methodology" in *Advances in Social Theory and Methodology: Toward an Integration of Micro and Macro Sociology*, London: Routledge & Kegan Paul.

Kress, G. 2003 *Literacy in the New Media Age*, London: Routledge & Kegan Paul.

2010 *Multimodalit: A Social Semiotic Approach to Contemporary Communication*, London, New York: Routledge & Kegan Paul.

Kress, G. and Leeuwen, T. 1996 *Reading Images. The Grammar of Visual Design*, London, New York: Routledge & Kegan Paul.

Krotz, F. 2001 *Die Mediatisierung kommunikativen Handelns*, Wiesbaden: Westdeutscher Verlag.

Kuhlen, R. 1995 *Informationsmarkt: Chancen und Risiken der Kommerzialisierung des Wissens*, Konstanz: UVK.

Ladkin, A. and Spiller, J. 2000 *The Meetings, Incentives, Conferences and Exhibitions Industry*, London: Travel & Tourist Intelligence.

Lang, A. 2000 "A Limited Capacity Model of Mediated Message Processing," *Journal of Communication* 50: 46–70.

Lange, V. 2004 *Meeting Madness*, Darmstadt: Steinkopff.

LaPorte, R. E., Linkov, F., Villasenor, T., Sauer, F., Gamboa, C., Lovelekar, M., Shubnikov, E. and Sekikwa, A. 2002 "Papyrus to Powerpoint: Metamorphosis of Scientific Communication," *British Medical Journal* 325: 1478–81.

Latour, B. 1994 "On Technical Mediation – Philosophy, Sociology, Genealogy," *Common Knowledge* 3(2): 29–64.

2008 *Re-Assembling the Social: An Introduction to Actor-Network Theory*, Oxford: Oxford University Press.

1993 *We Have Never Been Modern*, New York: Prentice Hall.

Lechner, F. and Boli, J. 2005 *World Culture: Origins and Consequences*, Malden, MA: Blackwell.

Lencioni, P. 2004 *Death by Meeting – a Leadership Fable about Solving the Most Painful Problem in Business*, San Francisco: Jossey-Bass.

Levasseur, D. and Sawyer, K. 2006 "Pedagogy Meets Powerpoint: A Research Review of the Effects of Computer-Generated Slides in the Classroom," *Review of Communication* 6(1–2): 101–23.

Licklider, J. C. R. and Taylor, R. W. 1968 "The Computer as a Communication Device," *Science and Technology* 76: 21–31.

Liebert, W.-A. 2005 "Präsentationsrhetorik," in *Historisches Wörterbuch der Rhetorik*, vol. 7. Tubingen: Max Niemeyer, 32–9.

Lobin, H. 2009 *Inszeniertes Reden auf der Medienbühne: Zur Linguistik und Rhetorik der wissenschaftlichen Präsentation*, Frankfurt/Main: Campus.

Lofland, J. 1971 *Analyzing Social Settings: A Guide to Qualitative Observation and Analysis*, Belmond, CA: Wadsworth.

Lorenzen, J. 2010 *Powerpoint-Präsentationen in der Schule: Eine gattungsanalytische Fallstudie zur neuen Kommunikationsform der Wissensgesellschaft.* Diploma Thesis. Berlin: Technical University.

Lorenzen, J. and Degenhardt, F. 2008 "Bericht zur Publikumsgruppe, AG Interaktionen," Berlin: Technical University (Manuscript).

Lowry, R. B. 1999 "Electronic Presentation of Lecture – Effect upon Student Performance," *University Chemistry Education* 3(1): 18–21.

Luckmann, T. 1985 "The Analysis of Communicative Genres" in B. F. Nell, R. Singh, and V. M. Venter (eds) *Focus on Quality: Selected Proceedings of a Conference on Qualitative Research Methodology in the Social Sciences,* Durban: Institute for Social and Economic Research.

1972 "Die Konstitution der Sprache in der Welt des Alltags" in B. Badura and K. Gloy (eds) *Soziologie der Kommunikation,* Stuttgart, Bad Cannstadt: Fromann Holzboog.

2003 "Moralizing Sermons, Then and Now" in R. Fenn (ed.) *The Blackwell Companion: The Sociology of Religion,* New York: Blackwell.

Luckmann, T. and Keppler, A. 1991 "'Teaching': Conversational Transmission of Knowledge" in I. Markova and K. Foppa (eds) *Asymmetries in Dialogue,* New York: Harvester Wheatsheaf.

Luhmann, N. 1984 *Soziale Systeme,* Frankfurt/Main: Suhrkamp.

Lundby, K. 2009 *Mediatization: Concept, Changes, Consequences,* New York: Lang.

Lynch, M. and Woolgar, S. 1990 *Representation in Scientific Practice,* Cambridge: Kluwer.

Machlup, F. 1962 *The Production and Distribution of Knowledge in the United States,* Princeton, NJ: Princeton University Press.

Mackert, M. and Degenhardt, F. 2007 "Ein Bild sagt mehr als tausend Worte: Die Präsentation als kommunikative Gattung" in B. Schnettler and H. Knoblauch (eds) *Powerpoint-Präsentationen: Neue Formen der gesellschaftlichen Kommunikation von Wissen,* Konstanz: UVK.

Mantei, E. J. 2000 "Using Internet Class Notes and PowerPoint in the Physical Geology Lecture," *Journal of College Science Teaching* 29(5): 301–5.

Mattelart, M. 2003 *An Introduction to Information Society,* London: Sage.

Mead, M. and Byres, P. 1968 *The Small Conference: An Innovation in Communication,* Paris, The Hague: Mouton.

Microsoft Memo 1988 "Microsoft Memo August 8." Available at: http://robert-gaskin.com (Accessed February 6, 2009).

Mieckowski, Z. 1990 *World Trends in Tourism and Recreation,* New York: Lang.

Miller, C. R. 1984 "Genre as Social Action," *Quarterly Journal of Speech* 70: 151–67.

Miller, G. A. 1956 "The Magical Number Seven: Some Limits on Our Capacity for Processing Information," *Psychological Review* 63: 81–97.

Montgomery, R. J. and Strick, S. K. 1994 *Meetings, Conventions, and Expositions: An Introduction to the Industry,* New York: Wiley & Sons.

Morse, S. 1980 *The Practical Approach to Business Presentations,* London: Management Update.

Müller, C. 1998 *Redebegleitende Gesten. Kulturgeschichte – Theorie – Sprachvergleich,* Berlin: Arno Spitz.

Myerson, J. and Ross, P. 2003 *The 21st Century Office,* New York: Rizzoli.

Nass, C. I. 1988 "Work, Information, and Information Work" in R. L. Simpson and I. H. Simpson (eds) *Research in the Sociology of Work: A Research Annual*, Greenwich, CT: Jai.

Nora, S. and Minc, A. 1981 *The Computerization of Society*, Boston: MIT Press.

Nunberg, G. 1999 "The Trouble with Powerpoint – the Slide Presentation Is Costing Us Some Useful Communication Tools, like Verbs," *Fortune* 140: 330–3.

Orlikowski, W. J. and Yates, J. 1994 "Genre Repertoires: The Structuring of Communicative Practices in Organizations," *Administrative Science Quarterly* 39(4): 541–75.

Paradi, D. 2005 "What Annoys Audiences about Powerpoint Presentations." Available at http://ezinearticles.com/?What-Annoys-Audiences-About-Power Point-Presentations?&id=236985

Parker, I. 2001 "Absolute Powerpoint – the Software That Tells You What to Think," *New Yorker*, May 28, 2001: 76–87.

Parslow, G. R. 2003 "Multimedia in Biochemistry and Molecular Biology Education: Commentary: PowerPoint: An Obligatory Change," *Biochemical Education* 31(1): 62–3.

Parsons, T. 1964 *The Social System* 2nd ed., Glencoe, IL: Free Press.

Pavio, A. 1990 *Mental Representations: A Dual Coding Approach*, New York: Oxford University Press.

PC Magazine 2007 "Innovators: Robert Gaskin," *PC Magazine*, February 14, 2007.

Pece, G. S. 2005 *The PowerPoint Society: The Influence of PowerPoint in the U.S. Government and Bureaucracy*. PhD thesis. Blacksbury: Virginia State University.

Pellmann, F. 2002 "PowerPoint-Präsentationen im Geschichtsunterricht," *Geschichte lernen* 15(89): 62–5.

Peters, S. 2007 "Projizierte Erkenntnis: Lichtbilder im Szenario des wissenschaftlichen Vortrags" in G. Boehm, G. Brandstetter, and A. Müller (eds) *Figurationen: Transdisziplinäre Bildforschung*, München: Fink.

Petschke, S. 2007 "Der Datenkorpus des DFG-Projektes' 'Die Performanz visuell unterstützter mündlicher Präsentationen'" in B. Schnettler and H. Knoblauch (eds) *Powerpoint-Präsentationen: Neue Formen der gesellschaftlichen Kommunikation von Wissen*, Konstanz: UVK.

Pfadenhauer, M. 2008 *Organisieren: Fallstudien zum Erhandeln von Events*, Wiesbaden: VS.

Pias, C. 2009 "'Electronic Overheads': Elemente Einer Vorgeschichte Von Powerpoint" in W. Coy and C. Pias (eds) *PowerPoint: Macht und Einfluss eines Präsentationsprogrammes*, Frankfurt/Main: Fischer.

Pinch, T. 2008 "Technology and Institutions: Living in a Material World," *Theory and Society* 37: 461–83.

Pinch, T. and Bijker, W. E. 1987 "The Social Construction of Facts and Artifacts: Or How the Sociology of Science and the Sociology of Technology Might Benefit Each Other" in W. E. Bijker, T. P. Hughes, and T. Pinch (eds) *The Social Construction of Technological Systems*, Cambridge: Cambridge University Press.

Porat, M. 1977 *The Information Economy: Definition and Measurement*, Washington, DC: OECD.

Postman, N. 1993 *Technopoly: The Surrender of Culture to Technology*, New York: Vintage.

Pötzsch, F. S. 2007 "Der Vollzug der Evidenz: Zur Ikonographie und Pragmatik von Powerpoint-Folien" in B. Schnettler and H. Knoblauch (eds) *Powerpoint-Präsentationen: Neue Formen der gesellschaftlichen Kommunikation von Wissen*, Konstanz: UVK.

2006 "Formen visuellen Wissens: Die Klassifikation und Typen der PowerPointFolie. Manuscript, Technical University of Berlin.

Power, M. 1999 *The Audit Society: Rituals of Verification*, Oxford: Oxford University Press.

Pozzer-Ardenghi, L. and Wolff-Michael, R. 2005 "Photographs in Lectures: Gestures as Meaning-Making Resources," *Linguistics and Education* 15: 275–93.

Rammert, W. 2006 "Die technische Konstruktion als Teil der gesellschaftlichen Konstruktion der Wirklichkeit" in D. Tänzler, H. Knoblauch, and H.-G. Soeffner (eds) *Zur Kritik der Wissensgesellschaft*, Konstanz: UVK.

Rammert, W. and Schulz-Schaeffer, I. 2002 "Technik und Handeln: Wenn soziales Handeln sich auf menschliches Verhalten und technische Abläufe verteilt" in W. Rammert and I. Schulz-Schaeffer (eds) *Können Maschinen denken? Soziologische Beiträge zum Verhältnis von Mensch und Technik*, Frankfurt/Main: Campus.

Rankin, E. L. and Hoaas, D. J. 2001 "The Use of PowerPoint and Student Performance," *Atlantic Economic Journal* 29(1): 113.

Rapoport, A. 1994 "Spatial Organization and the Built Environment" in T. Ingold (ed.) *Companion Encyclopedia of Anthropology*, London, New York: Routledge & Kegan Paul.

Reiser, R. A. 2001 "A History of Instructional Design and Technology. Part I: A History of Instructional Media," *Educational Technology, Research and Development* 49: 53–64.

Rendle-Short, J. 2006 *The Academic Presentation: Situated Talk in Action*, Aldershot: Ashgate.

Reynolds, G. 2008 *Presentation Zen: Simple Ideas on Presentation Design and Delivery*, Berkeley, CA: New Riders.

Rheinsberger, H.-J. 1997 *Toward a History of Epistemic Things*, Stanford, CA: Stanford University Press.

Rogers, E. M. 1995 *Diffusion of Innovation* 4th ed., New York: Free Press.

Ruchatz, J. 2010. "Vorträgesind Silber, Dias sind Gold" in P. Boden and D. Müller (eds), *Populäres Wissen im medialen Wandel seit 1850*. Berlin: Kadmos.

Sacks, H., Schegloff, E. and Jefferson, G. 1974 "A Simplest Systematics for the Organization of Turn-Taking in Conversation" in J. Schenkein (ed.) *Studies in the Organization of Conversational Interaction*, New York: Academic Press.

Saunders, A. G. and Anderson, C. R. 1929 *Business Reports: Investigation and Presentation*, New York: McGraw-Hill.

Schegloff, E. 1968 "Sequencing in Conversational Openings," *American Anthropologist* 70: 1075–95.

Schiller, H. 1989 *Culture Inc.: The Corporate Takeover of Public Expression*, New York: Oxford University Press.

Schnettler, B. 2006 "Orchestrating Bullet Lists and Commentaries: A Video Performance Analysis of Computer Supported Presentations" in H. Knoblauch, B. Schnettler, J. Raab, and H.-G. Soeffner (eds) *Video Analysis – Methodology and Methods: Qualitative Audiovisual Data Analysis in Sociology*, Frankfurt/Main, New York: Lang.

2007 "Präsentationspannen: Risiken ritualisierter Wissenspräsentation" in R. Schlesier and U. Zellmann (eds) *Ritual als provoziertes Risiko*, Würzburg: Königshausen & Neumann.

Schnettler, B. and Knoblauch, H. 2007 *Powerpoint-Präsentationen: Neue Formen der gesellschaftlichen Kommunikation von Wissen*, Konstanz: UVK.

Schnettler, B. and Tuma, R. 2007 "Pannen – Powerpoint – Performanz: Technik als, handelndes Drittes' in visuell unterstützten mündlichen Präsentationen" in B. Schnettler and H. Knoblauch (eds) *Powerpoint-Präsentationen: Neue Formen der gesellschaftlichen Kommunikation von Wissen*, Konstanz: UVK.

Schoeneborn, D. 2008 *Alternatives Considered but Not Disclosed: The Ambiguous Role of PowerPoint in Cross-Project Learning*, Wiesbaden: VS.

Schultz, W. C. 1996 "Animation with PowerPoint: A Fog Cutter," *Journal of Educational Technology Systems* 25(2): 141–60.

Schulz-Zaner, R. and Riegas-Staackmann, A. 2004 "Neue Medien im Unterricht: Eine Zwischenbilanz" in *Jahrbuch der Schulentwicklung: Daten, Beispiele, Perspektiven*, Weinheim, Munich: Juventa.

Schutz, A. 1962 "Common Sense and Scientific Interpretation of Human Action" in *Collected Papers I*, The Hague: Nijhoff.

1974 *The Phenomenology of the Social World*, Evanston, IL: Northwestern University Press.

1964 "The Well-Informed Citizen" in *Collected Papers. Vol. II: Studies in Social Theory*, The Hague: Martinus Nijhoff.

Schutz, A. and Luckmann, T. 1994 *Structures of the Life World II*, Evanston, IL: Northwestern University Press.

1989 *The Structures of the Life-World*, Evanston, IL: Northwestern University Press.

Schwartzman, H. B. 1989 *The Meeting: Gatherings in Organizations and Communities*, New York, London: Sage.

Simons, T. 2005 "Does Powerpoint Make You Stupid?" *Presentations* 18: 3.

2000 "Multimedia or Bust?" *Presentations* 7 (March *2000*): 48–50.

Smart, L. E. and Arnold, S. 1947 *Practical Rules for Graphic Presentation of Business Statistics*, Columbus: Ohio State University Press.

Soeffner, H. G. 1997 *The Order of Rituals: The Interpretation of Everyday Life*, Translated by Mara Luckmann, New Brunswick, NJ: Transaction.

Sproull, L. and Kiesler, S. 1995 *Connections: New Ways of Working in the Networked Organization*, Cambridge, MA: MIT Press.

Stark, D. and Paravel, V. 2008 "Powerpoint in Public: Digital Technologies and the New Morphology of Demonstration," *Theory, Culture & Society* 25(5): 30–55.

Stehr, N. 1994 *Knowledge Societies*, London: Sage.

Stewart, R. 1967 *Managers and Their Jobs*, Basingstoke: Macmillan.

242

References

Stoner, M. 2007 "PowerPoint in a New Key," *Communication Education* 56(3): 354–81.
Storrer, A. and Wyss, E. L. 2003 "Pfeilzeichen: Formen und Funktionen in alten und neuen Medien" in U. Schmitz and U. Wenzel (eds) *Wissen und neue Medien: Bilder und Zeichen von 800 bis 2000*, Berlin: Erich Schmidt.
Strauss, A. and Corbin, J. 1990 *Basics of Qualitative Research*, New York: Sage.
Streeck, J. 1994 "Gestures As Communication. II: The Audience As Co-Author," *Research in Language and Social Interaction* 27: 239–67.
Suchman, L. 1987 *Plans and Situated Actions: The Problem of Human Machine Communication*, Cambridge: Cambridge University Press.
1990 "A Representing Practice in Cognitive Science" in M. Lynch and S. Woolgar (eds) *Representation in Scientific Practice*, Cambridge: Cambridge University Press.
Suzuki, H., Yoshiaki, H. and Ishii, K. 1997 "Measuring Information Behavior: A Time Budget Survey of Japan," *Social Indicators Research* 42: 151–69.
Szabo, A. and Hastings, N. 2000 "Using IT in the Undergraduate Classroom: Should We Replace the Blackboard with Powerpoint?" *Computers & Education* 35: 175–87.
Tannen, D., Wallat, C., Jaworski, A. and Coupland, N. 1987 "Interactive Frames and Knowledge Schemas in Interaction: Examples from a Medical Examination/ Interview" in *The Discourse Reader*, London, New York: Routledge & Kegan Paul.
Techmeier, B. 1998 "Der Kongressvortrag" in L. Hoffmann, H. Kalverkämüer, and H. E. Wiegand (eds) *Fachsprachen/Languages for Special Purposes*, Fachtextsorten der Wissenschaftssprachen, Berlin, New York: De Gruyter.
Ten Have, P. 1989 "The Consultation as a Genre" in B. Torode (ed.) *Text and Talk as Social Practice: Discourse Difference and Division in Speech and Writing*, Dordrecht: Foris.
Tomasello, M. 2008 *The Origins of Human Communication*, Cambridge, MA: MIT Press.
Traue, B. 2010 *Das Subjekt der Beratung*, Bielefeld: transcript.
Tufte, E. R. 2006 *Beautiful Evidence*, Cheshire: Graphics Press.
2003 *The Cognitive Style of PowerPoint*, Cheshire: Graphics Press.
Twyman, M. 1979 "A Schema for the Study of Graphic Language" in P. A. Kolers, M. E. Wrolstad, and H. Bouma (eds) *Processing of Visible Language*, New York, London: L Plenum.
Ulmer, B. 1988 "Konversionserzählungen als rekonstruktive Gattung: Erzählerische Mittel und Strategien bei der Rekonstruktion eines Bekehrungserlebnisses," *Zeitschrift für Soziologie* 17: 19–33.
UNESCO (ed.) 2005 *Towards Knowledge Societies*, Paris: United Nations Educational.
Van Dijk, T. 1980 *Macrostructures: An Interdisciplinary Study of Global Structures in Discourse, Interaction, and Cognition*, Hillsdale, NJ: Erlbaum.
Walker, J. A. and Chaplin, S. 1997 *Visual Culture*, Manchester: Manchester University Press.
Weber, K. and Ladkin, A. 2004 "Trends Affecting the Convention Industry in the 21st Century," *Journal of Convention & Event Industry* 6(4): 47–63.

Weber, M. 1980 *Wirtschaft und Gesellschaft*, Tübingen: Niemeyer.

Webster, F. 1995 *Theories of the Information Society*, London: Blackwell.

Weiner, B. and Alkin, M. 1992 "Motivation," in M. Alkin (ed.): *Encyclopedia of Educational Research*. New York: MacMillan (6th edition), 860–5.

Wilke, H. 2001 "Wissensgesellschaft" in G. Kneer, A. Nassehi, and M. Schroer (eds) *Klassische Gesellschaftsbegriffe*, München: Fink.

Wilson, E. L. 1870 "The Magic Lantern in Its Relation to Photography," *Photographic Mosaic*, 118–19.

Winn, J. 2003 "Avoiding Death by PowerPoint," *Journal of Professional Issues in Engineering, Education and Practice* 129(3): 115–18.

World Tourism Organization 2006 *Measuring the Economic Importance of the Meetings Industry – Developing a Future Satellite Account Extension*, Madrid: WTO.

Yates, J. 1993 *Control through Communication: The Rise of System in American Management*, Baltimore: Johns Hopkins University Press.

1989 *The Rise of System in American Management*, Baltimore: Johns Hopkins University Press.

Yates, J. and Orlikowski, W. J. 1992 "Genres of Organizational Communication: A Structurational Approach to Studying Communication and Media," *Academy of Management Review* 17(2): 299–326.

2008 "The PowerPoint Presentation and Its Corollaries: How Genres Shape Communicative Action in Organizations" in M. Zachary and C. Thralls (eds) *The Cultural Turn: Communicative Practices in Workplaces and the Professions*, Amityville, NY: Baywood.

# Index

advice book, 60, 67, 68, 69, 70, 71, 100, 133, 156, 184, 185, 203, 214, 220
aggregates, 97
  aggregate character, 97
Aldus Persuasion, 32
apostrophe, 110
Apple Laser Printer, 32
arts, 83, 178, 181
asymmetry, 126, 144, 151, 164, 191, 201, 202, 203, 204, 230
  asymmetrical, 12, 122, 163, 164, 202, 204, 205
  asymmetry of the presentation, 203
audience, 4, 8, 19, 20, 24, 25, 28, 35, 36, 38, 39, 41, 42, 44, 45, 47, 51, 58, 62, 63, 65, 67, 69, 70, 76, 79, 81, 85, 86, 89, 91, 93, 98, 99, 103, 107, 110, 113, 115, 116, 117, 118, 119, 120, 121, 122, 123, 124, 125, 126, 127, 128, 129, 130, 131, 133, 134, 135, 138, 140, 141, 142, 143, 144, 145, 147, 148, 149, 150, 152, 154, 156, 157, 159, 161, 163, 164, 167, 168, 169, 170, 171, 172, 173, 176, 181, 184, 185, 187, 189, 196, 197, 198, 199, 201, 202, 203, 204, 209, 212, 213, 214, 220, 223, 224, 225, 226, 228
  audience interaction, 78, 125, 126, 134, 152
  audience reaction, 126, 131, 164
  disengagement from the audience, 116
  size of the audience, 158, 159, 225
author of the presentation, 201
author of the text, 201
AutoContent Wizard, 33, 100, 101

backstage, 116
Bell Northern Research, 29, 30, 31

bifocality, 148, 149, 225
black boxing, 57
blackboard, 56, 149, 154, 156, 157, 185, 213, 214
body, xv, 24, 47, 51, 53, 54, 55, 61, 62, 66, 72, 83, 97, 103, 106, 107, 112, 114, 115, 116, 117, 118, 119, 120, 121, 122, 123, 124, 129, 130, 131, 133, 134, 135, 143, 150, 152, 153, 155, 157, 161, 163, 164, 196, 197, 198, 201, 207, 212, 213, 223, 226
  bodily interaction, 55
  body formation, 24, 66, 114
    body formation projecting, 196
  body movements, 107, 114, 115
bullet lists, 73, 74, 86, 97, 99, 187
*bullet points*, 1, 41, 73, 90, 101
business, 7, 16, 28, 29, 30, 33, 34, 35, 38, 39, 45, 47, 48, 57, 72, 79, 100, 101, 157, 159, 160, 163, 165, 173, 174, 176, 178, 179, 181, 182, 183, 184, 185, 186, 187, 192, 193, 194, 208, 213, 214, 226, 228
  business reports, 184, 228

cartoon, 97, 133
chain of technology, 135, 149, 152, 156, 199
chronologies, 75
clip, 33, 74, 228
cognition, 4, 5, 9, 14, 18, 38, 41, 42, 43, 44, 46, 199, 200, 220, 221
cognitive style, 41, 42, 43, 196, 202, 204
coherence, 80, 89, 90, 93, 94, 97, 98, 99, 223
**collage of visual elements**, 77, 216
*colloquial formality*, 81
communication culture, 4, 23, 58, 64, 194, 206

245

*Embodied Interaction: Language and Body in the Material World*
Jürgen Streeck, Charles Goodwin, and Curtis LeBaron, Editors

*Cultural Development of Mathematical Ideas: Papua New Guinea Studies*
Geoffrey Saxe

*Constructing the Self in a Digital World*
Cynthia Carter Ching and Brian Foley, Editors

*Video Games, Learning, and Society*
Constance Steinkeuhler, Kurt Squire, and Sasha Barab, Editors

*The Learning in Doing series was founded in 1987 by Roy Pea and John Seely Brown.*